A HUNGER FOR
HEALING

Also by J. Keith Miller

A Hunger for Healing Workbook

The Taste of New Wine

A Second Touch

Habitation of Dragons

The Becomers

The Edge of Adventure (with Bruce Larson)

Living the Adventure (with Bruce Larson)

The Passionate People (with Bruce Larson)

Please Love Me

The Single Experience (with Andrea Wells Miller)

The Scent of Love

The Dream

Hope in the Fast Lane (previously published as *Sin*)

Facing Codependence
(with Pia Mellody and Andrea Wells Miller)

And of related interest:

Breaking Free: A Recovery Workbook for Facing Codependence
by Pia Mellody and Andrea Wells Miller

J. Keith Miller

A HUNGER FOR HEALING

The Twelve Steps as a Classic Model for Christian Spiritual Growth

HarperSanFrancisco

A Division of HarperCollinsPublishers

A complete program to support group use of this book has been developed by NAVPRESS. It includes a series of video tapes and a leader's guide. For information about a video based version of *A Hunger for Healing,* call 1–800–366–7788, or write NAVPRESS, P. O. Box 35001, Colorado Springs, CO 80935.

To contact J. Keith Miller about speaking engagements, write or call Michael McKinney, McKinney Associates, Inc., P.O. Box 5162, Louisville, KY 40205, or call 1(800)955-4746.

Unless otherwise indicated, scripture quotations contained herein are from the Revised Standard Version of the Bible, copyrighted 1946, 1952, 1971 by the Division of Christian Education of the National Council of the Churches of Christ in the U.S.A.

FIRST HARPERCOLLINS PAPERBACK EDITION PUBLISHED IN 1992

Library of Congress Cataloging-in-Publication Data

Miller, Keith.
    A hunger for healing: the Twelve Steps as a classic model for Christian spiritual growth / J. Keith Miller.—1st ed.
      p.   cm.
    Includes bibliographic references.
    1. Twelve-step programs—Religious aspects—Christianity.
    2. Spiritual life—Anglican authors. 3. Miller, Keith. I. Title.
BV4409.2.M54   1991
248.8′6—dc20   90–55295
    ISBN 0–06–065716–2 (cloth)   CIP
    ISBN 0–06–065767–7 (pbk)

96 97 98 99 RRD 20 19 18 17 16 15 14 13 12

*It is the pain of living that creates
a hunger for healing that only
God can satisfy*

CONTENTS

CONTENTS

PREFACE

Why would a seriously committed Christian write a book about the Twelve Steps of Alcoholics Anonymous as a means of spiritual growth for Christians?

To answer this I must tell you a little of my own personal story. When I was a very small boy I didn't think my father loved me—at least he could not love me in a way I was able to understand. He was a good man, but he loved my only brother, Earle, five years older than I. Earle was named after my father and went on hunting and fishing trips with him. But I was too little to go along. I would stand at the door and cry when they left. My father evidently didn't like me around, although I wanted very much for him to love me and play with me. My mother said my time would come, so I waited. But when I was older and my brother began spending time with his friends, my father was going through a difficult period financially and lost interest in hunting and fishing. He traveled for weeks at a stretch. When he got home he was often tired and discouraged and didn't have time for me. I felt very lonely, and I thought there must be something wrong with me.

Unable to get love from this distant man, I turned to achievement at a very early age. When I would do well in sports, he would mumble, "Good boy." I don't know how many young men in this country have substituted achievement for love in this way, but I am one. I went out to win the world through hard work—compulsive work as it turned out. I now know that I worked so hard for recognition because underneath I was terrified of being rejected by others, as I felt I had been by my father.

Things went very well for me in the world of school. But beginning the summer I graduated from high school a series of tragedies hit our family. My brother was killed in a plane crash in 1945; my father developed serious heart disease in 1949 and died in 1950; and my mother was diagnosed with cancer in 1950.

In 1956, while nursing my mother through the final stage of her illness, I was at a very low point.

By this time I had been through college and was in the oil exploration business in Tyler, Texas. I was twenty-eight years old, married, and had two beautiful little girls. And my mother was dying of cancer. I had been feeling great anxiety and fear about my own future for years; finally, on a roadside in the tall pine woods country in east Texas, between Tyler and Longview, I turned to God in a desperate moment and offered him my life. As soon as I did, I was relieved of my sense of shame, fear, and failure and was given new meaning in my life: to tell people that there is hope if one will surrender to God as revealed in Jesus Christ. For the next few years I knew some peace and a strong sense of direction. Before long I started to speak, to witness to what I was discovering in trying to live for God.

I kept looking for books to give people that described my new experience of faith. Most of the contemporary books I found at that time said, in effect, "If you commit your life to Jesus Christ, your problems will disappear." But my experience was that I got a whole new set of problems. Things that hadn't been issues at all before had to be considered now.

In 1962 I was asked to be the first director of a conference center for laypeople, Laity Lodge in the Texas hill country. As the center grew, the need increased for a book to hand people, a book about the actual problems of living a life committed to Christ. Finally I produced a manuscript made up of talks I was giving at conferences in the lodge: *The Taste of New Wine*.

This book was one of the first two published by Word Books in Waco, Texas. It sold hundreds of thousands of copies overnight (over two million ultimately). Suddenly I was thrown into the spotlight. I became a "Christian star." In the next few years I was asked to speak all over the world. I was available to people night and day. My old work addiction kicked back in, only now it was a *Christian* work addiction. I thought I was doing all that work for God, but to do it I neglected my family—just as my father had neglected me. Because I was doing it for Jesus, it was hard to criticize.

After several more successful books and much traveling and speaking, I began secretly to suspect that I was a special and gifted person. And because I was consciously so sincere and committed to Christ, I couldn't understand why all those around me weren't thrilled with all that was happening. But of course some of them were not happy with my almost total absorption with my work. At some level I knew I wasn't handling my relationships very well, but I couldn't *see* my compulsive behavior. I was filled with resentment, frustration, and rebellion. Finally, in 1976, my wife and I were divorced.

Overnight a large part of the church said, "Bye, bye," and disappeared from my life. The thing I had feared most since I was a little boy had finally happened. I'd been rejected. Bruce and Hazel Larson and some friends in a Christian small group held me while I wept and tried to sort out my life. I was filled with shame and a sense of failure and didn't want to see anyone in the Church.

But then I got angry. I heard that someone had written a book with a title like *The Church Is the Only Army That Shoots Its Wounded!* And I shouted, "Yes!" and shook my fist at the Church.

But one morning during that time, when I was praying, a quiet voice said inside me, "Keith, quit blaming the Church for your sins. *You're* the one who behaved sinfully and got the divorce. You deal with your own sin, and I'll take care of my Church!"

And so I did. I eventually confessed and made what amends I could. I read the Bible again to see what sin and salvation were all about. I realized that I was like many people who have been converted or healed by Christ, like the man Jesus spoke of who was healed of a demon and had a spiritual "clean house." Because the man didn't put a healing program in place of the demon, it came back and brought seven more demons, and the man was in worse condition than he had been before Jesus touched him (see Luke 11:24–26).

My spiritual search, as well as my deteriorating personal relationships and some frightening stress-related heart symptoms, led me to a treatment center for my compulsive and addictive behavior, and there I was advised to get into a Twelve-Step program. As the acid of my pain began to eat through the wall of my denial, I started to perceive my dishonesty with myself, my incredible self-centeredness and need for attention, and my grandiosity.

As I was reading the Bible and working the Twelve Steps, I began to see that here in this "secular" program, a bunch of former drunks had taken some biblical principles, many of which the Church has largely neglected or eliminated, and had formed a spiritual "way." This path has not only brought me into a deeper and more realistic relationship with Christ than I had ever known but has also turned out to be a way of calming and healing the driven compulsive life of intensity and fear that (after the first exciting "honeymoon" years) my Christian faith had not been able to touch.

I have been in a Twelve-Step program for over five years now, and some of us have started a Twelve-Step group for Christians in our church to work on our blocks to loving God, other people, and ourselves.[1] My experience in Twelve-Step groups has convinced me that God has provided a way of spiritual healing and growth that may well be the most important spiritual model of any age for contemporary Christians. I wrote this book because I have found more self-worth in God, more serenity than I have ever known, and a way to deal specifically with the personal problems that have kept me anxious and afraid all my life. I sense that there are many other Christians who know their lives and relationships are in trouble but don't know how to change.

A Spiritual Revolution

Richard Grant, a friend who is an astute psychologist and theologian, wrote recently,

> We are in the midst of an "anonymous" spiritual revolution. The American experiment in democracy has finally produced a spirituality that matches its experience: the Twelve Steps. Recovery communities are spreading like a grass-fire across the United States, dealing with a seemingly endless variety of compulsive disorders: alcoholism, drug addiction, overeating, codependence, compulsive spending, etc. . . .

> The Twelve Steps connect with the people of the United States because the Steps are democratic, have a profound respect for the experience and rights of the individual, and do not permit theological ideas to impede spiritual growth. In fact, it seems that the Twelve Steps relegate definitions and ideas to a secondary position. Teachers in the Twelve-Step communities have authority based on personal experience of their own recovery, not based on formal education or credentials. . . .

> In the Twelve Steps, one's *idea* of God is entirely subordinate to the *experience* of a Higher Power as real in one's life.[2]

What About Jesus and the Higher Power?

The freedom to choose one's view of God is sometimes frightening to institution-oriented Christians, but it is only a raw expression of the freedom all Christian denominations faced at their inception. The striking thing about the Twelve-Step pilgrim's movement through the program is that after a few months or years the personality of God that comes into focus is so often that revealed through the life, death, and resurrection of Jesus of Nazareth. My own faith is unashamedly Christian, but this program is also for those who start with no faith, only pain and frustration.

Most religious bodies want prospective members to conform to certain specific beliefs before they are allowed in the group. There is no question that *what* you believe about God is very important over the long haul. For instance, if God is loving, supportive, and moral, as he is in Christianity and the Twelve Steps, a believer has a different experience of spiritual growth than if God is demanding, capricious, selfish, and immoral. But the primary difference between the Twelve Steps and most Christian approaches lies in *how one gets to know* what kind of God one is dealing with.

In Christianity the tests of belief are mostly written and cognitive (Credo, faith statements, and the Bible). In the Twelve Steps one finds out what God is like by entering a community of people who have made a radical commitment of their lives to God. As newcomers see God working in the lives of people in that community, they learn about his nature and how he operates. As they work the Steps and put their own lives in the hands of this God (whatever they call God at first) they discover firsthand the loving, redeeming, supporting, moral, and confronting nature of God. Later many of them see that this is in fact the same God that Christians believe in, and numbers of them join the Church.

There they discover what has been written in the Bible about this God they have come to love and depend on. They may be thrilled to find out about eternal life, which seems like a bonus to them because they came to believe and committed their lives to God on the basis of what God does in the here-and-now world of sin and addiction. It is interesting to note that this getting to know the living God through the community of believers instead of through an acceptance of the authoritative New Testament was the experience of the early church for over three hundred years, because the New Testament wasn't completely put together and accepted by the Church until A.D. 393.

The experience of the Twelve Steps, like that of the Christian church, is based on the assumption that God is in fact real, "alive," and capable of revealing himself as he truly is through a personal relationship with people in a community of faith. As a Christian, I am very grateful that I have both the Christian church with its Bible and liturgy and the Twelve Steps as aids to authentic spiritual growth.

The people whom God uses to teach a new spiritual way often are not recognized religious leaders but those who appear to be ordinary men and women, carpenters like Jesus, tent-makers like Paul, teachers of rhetoric like Augustine, soldiers like Ignatius Loyola, or students of literature like Thomas Merton. Their methods have the smell of earth and the sights and sounds of real life about them.

The founders of Alcoholics Anonymous who developed the Twelve Steps of A.A. were such a group. They were experiencing the pain of an apparently incurable spiritual and emotional illness, alcohol addiction, that was destroying their minds, their bodies, and their ability to make a contribution to society. Their "disease" had driven God out of their lives; they and their compulsions had replaced him as the center of their motivations and relationships. Medical science and even the Church had virtually given up trying to treat these lost people; their addiction had withstood all known medical and spiritual approaches.

Then, in the experience of their own powerlessness, admitting the bankruptcy of their self-centeredness and the insanity of their self-destructive addictive behavior, these spiritually crippled men and women turned to God and each other as their only hope. As they gave up on their own power and their own agendas and turned their lives and their wills over to God, they rediscovered some amazing secrets that many parts of the Church had lost along the way. They developed a hunger for healing and a hunger for God. They discovered a more simple way to live, trying to find and do God's will amid the noise and shattering vibrations of contemporary life. In becoming "weller than well" many of these men and women have found healing in their primary relationships, the peace of surrender, the humility and self-acceptance that follow confession and making amends, and the joy and sense of purpose in doing God's will and sharing the hope and healing they are finding.

The Twelve Steps have been used to deal with addictions to alcohol, food, recreational and prescription drugs, sex, gambling, and spending, and addictions to different kinds of unhealthy relationships that people form to try to alleviate or erase their pain. Separate movements have been established to deal with each of these addictions.[3] The simple yet profoundly powerful spiritual model that is hidden within the Twelve Steps has caused these groups collectively to become perhaps the fastest-growing spiritual movement in America today.

This growth is remarkable, because Twelve-Step groups are all "anonymous"; that is, no one is to tell who belongs, unless telling will help a sufferer. The groups have no professional or designated leaders. They have no financial "pledges" and won't accept large sums of money, own no real estate, and have no evangelism campaigns; most significantly, *no one wants to join!* (Most of these characteristics are amazingly similar to those of the early Christian church.) Moreover, their remarkable growth has taken place as many Christian churches are declining in membership.

I believe this growth is occurring because the Twelve Steps bring biblical principles of faith to bear on the pain of contemporary people in a way that leads sufferers into a close living relationship with God and frees them to live a meaningful life seeking God's will. For me, having studied the Bible for years, there is no question that the "Higher Power" of the Twelve Steps is the same God revealed in the life, death, and resurrection of Jesus Christ.

In this book I have tried to take the reader inside the spiritual process of each of the Twelve Steps to taste the healing, growing experience that is this way of surrendering ourselves to a Higher Power—to us Christians, the God of Jesus Christ. Here I have found a way to follow Christ that is leading me beyond myself into trying to do the will of God in his world.

ACKNOWLEDGMENTS

Writing adequate acknowledgments for the help I received while writing this book is not possible. I have learned and absorbed so much from members of the Twelve-Step community during the past five years that my head was swimming with insights gained from meetings, sponsors, friends, and all kinds of Twelve-Step literature as I sat down to write the talks that are the basis of this book.* The books listed under Selected Reading and their authors have been particularly and specifically helpful. As I read and reread some of the books, I began to get a broader and deeper picture of the spiritual growth that can come through working the Twelve Steps with a group of recovering people. Where I quoted directly from any book I have given specific credit, but I know that there were times while writing that ideas "came to me," the sources of which were these books—which I recommend to anyone wishing to go deeper into the origins and practices of this amazing program.

Nowhere is the above more true than with reference to *Alcoholics Anonymous* (the "Big Book") and the *Twelve Steps and Twelve Traditions* (the "Twelve and Twelve"). My debt to the authors of these two volumes, which are the authoritative books for all Twelve-Step programs, is incalculable, and I particularly recommend these two volumes to the

---

* These talks were taped on twelve audiocassettes and can be ordered from Villa Publishing Company, 6105 Mountain Villa Circle, Austin, TX 78731.

reader with additional questions about the Twelve Steps. I have read and reread these books many times during the past five years, and I have studied the books in the Selected Reading list in trying to grow in my own recovery.

The Twelve-Step program, like the New Testament church, is a community affair. Most of what is written in the pages to follow has come to me through the caring help I have received from God's wonderful people, in and outside Twelve-Step programs.

My special thanks to the following friends who read all or parts of this book in manuscript form, specifically encouraged me along the way, or looked up a reference and called me: Bob and Pauline Bartosch, Pat Boone, Bill Carter, Brooks Goldsmith, Richard Grant, Charles and Carolyn Huffman, David Nelson, and Rick and Vicki Spencer. Their help made this a much better book than it would have been, but because I did not follow every suggestion, I cannot blame them for the faults still here, which are my responsibility.

Thanks to Ann Tucker for her tenacity, patience, and ability in keeping on at the word processor as we were getting the manuscript ready to go. And I want to thank my wife, Andrea, especially, not only for her patience and love but also for her invaluable help with editorial suggestions, structure, and cutting as I tried to "put eighty pounds of sand in a forty-pound bag."

For me, writing a book is a joint venture, and the older I get the more I realize that any book I write is almost totally made up of bits and pieces handed to me by others who have walked ahead on the path. I am grateful to those who are named here and many other spiritual pilgrims, including the members of an adult class at St. Matthew's Episcopal Church who let me read the rough ideas to them and then shared their experience, strength, hope, and counsel with me as the translation into a book developed.

A HUNGER FOR
HEALING

Chapter 1

THE TWELVE STEPS AS A MEANS OF "GETTING WELL SPIRITUALLY" AND DOING GOD'S WILL

How can the Twelve Steps be of any use to committed Christians already seeking to be God's people and do God's will? Especially how can the program be of use to Christians who are not alcoholics, overeaters, drug addicts, compulsive gamblers, or sex addicts and do not have family members involved in such addictions? And even if we agreed that these steps would bring one closer to God and to doing his will, how would a Christian take the steps without a specific addiction to focus them on?[1]

It is true that a Christian with no clearly definable addiction finds it more difficult to recognize the need for and then to partake of the benefits of this Twelve-Step way of life. But it is also true that without a strong motivation, usually involving pain, it is difficult for a Christian to pay the price to master *any* of the classic Christian spiritual ways. An alcoholic who has lost family, job, and health and is facing loss of freedom in court has some very concrete evidence that he or she needs help. But Christians who have not faced these particular difficulties do not see that *they* are powerless and need help too. Yet many of these same Christians have become aware of feeling spiritual and emotional pain, anxiety, and confusion within themselves. I believe that these symptoms are indications of the same spiritual disease that underlies alcoholism and other addictions.

The similarities to the underlying spiritual disease addressed by the Twelve Steps strongly suggested to me a connection between the way of life prescribed by those steps and a committed Christian's spiritual growth. This book describes how certain Christians, even without a specific substance addiction, can apply the Twelve Steps as a powerful model and "medicine" in their lives for alleviating emotional pain and stress and for practical spiritual development in Christ.

Which "Certain" Christians Can Receive This Help?

The method of spiritual growth described here is for Christians whose spiritual practices are not working—even though they believe in God and want to trust him with their whole lives. If they are honest, these

Christians know they are not happy, and certainly not serene. Their personal lives are troubled; their intimate relationships are clouded by conflict and confusion; and they find that significant people in their lives can't understand them or love them as they feel they should be loved. These people's resentment, anger, fear, shame, guilt, loneliness, feelings of low self-worth, and pain about their relationships and about living generally often feels "larger than life."

They may have tried many times to change their behavior or the behavior of the people around them. They may even have called God (Father, Son, and Spirit) in on the struggle to change those close to them or to change themselves. Yet when those whom these frustrated Christians try to "help" don't cooperate, the Christian helpers become angry and hurt, thinking, "Why do they resent me? They'd be so much happier if they'd just do what I say. I'm only trying to help them, after all!"

But in our clearer moments some of us Christian helpers have realized that we can't fix even our own pain—not even with our prayers for God's help. We have seen that this secret pain of life does not respond to our manipulations and our prayers to make it go away. Increasing numbers of good Christian people are in pain, and they are realizing that they may not have the power or the spiritual resources to overcome this pain by themselves.

The Source of This Pain

Traditionally we Christians have been told that Jesus Christ came "to save us from Sin." But who has heard a good sermon on Sin lately? Many of us have pretty well forgotten what Sin is all about. In the Church we have practically eliminated dealing with Sin as a central agenda for Christians. This is a little strange, because virtually all Christian bodies consider the atonement for or the overcoming of Sin as the central message of the New Testament.

At an existential, everyday level of thinking, *sin* is thought to refer to "bad things one does" such as theft, adultery, murder, gossiping, judging, and so forth. But as William Temple pointed out, these things are only symptoms of a deeper disease. He says there is only one Sin (with a capital *S*), and that is putting ourselves in the center of our lives and other people's lives where only God should be.[2] Sins with a small *s* are those specific things we do as a result of putting ourselves in the center (like stealing, adultery, and trying to control people).

There is a difference between "Hebrew Sin" and "Greek Sin." Hebrew Sin involves conscious violation of God's commandments. Greek Sin (illustrated in Greek tragedies) involves a kind of willful unconsciousness, unwillingness to recognize a tragic flaw that in the end brings about the destruction of oneself and others. Both conscious and unconscious aspects are involved in the Christian view of Sin.

The idea of referring to Sin as a "disease" troubles some people, who think I am saying that one is not responsible for one's sinful behavior. In other words, if Sin is a disease and I can't help myself, why not go on and sin? I am not saying that at all, but merely stating what biblical theologians have always known: Sin is a pernicious condition that all have (1 John 1:9) and that we can't defeat on our own. Otherwise why would Christ have to "come and save us from sin"? Sin is like compulsive or addictive habits that seem to control our actions even when we don't want them to and after we swear we will "never do it again." Paradoxically, even though we are powerless to defeat Sin on our own, we *are* responsible for our Sin and for seeking help to stop sinning, a seeking that leads us to God.

Putting myself in the center gives me the idea that I'm a little better, a little more important, than my wife, my children, and other people, so that it seems to me that my ways are the better ways, the right ways. Consequently I tend to try to impose my will on the people around me. I am not aware of this, because I don't dwell on my specialness consciously. In fact, the primary symptom of the Sin-disease is "denial": *I can't see* Sin's grandiose controlling symptoms in my own actions—although I can clearly see this kind of controlling operating in others' behavior.

When I operate out of this central position, I try to control people, places, and circumstances around me, and I have the sense that I know what is best for everyone close to me. This can be true for ministers and church leaders as well as ordinary "sinners." Eventually, when the pain of rejection by and conflict with those we attempt to control gets unbearable, we come face-to-face with our own powerlessness—our inability to fix other people or change our own lives.[3] To alleviate the pain and fear of our bruised relationships and our powerlessness, we often engage in compulsive behaviors. We may wind up working addictively (even as ministers) or eating too much or drinking too much. This is what addictive behavior is about—covering our intense pain so we don't have to feel it.

It was *very* difficult for me to admit my own powerlessness as a Christian. After all, I "had Christ," and I had many Christian friends who had some power and could help me. But I finally realized that nobody could help me with my Sin, my control disease, and the fear and pain it was causing me. The source of this pain was *inside myself* in my invisible and "benevolent," but self-centered and myopic, "conductor of the local world" attitude.

Because I was a Christian I knew there was a Higher Power. For me, his name was Jesus Christ. But I had never fully faced the nature of my inability to overcome my own Sin and had no idea that recognition of my powerlessness was the doorway to spiritual growth and a whole new relationship with God.

Beyond Reason and "Religion" into the Spiritual Realm

In our humanity we often want a "spiritual program" that is logical, one we can add up like a column of figures and get a sum. But the Twelve-Step program is a lot more like making pickles than it is like doing sums. You cannot analyze cucumbers or even sprinkle them with salt to make pickles. You have to *soak* them in the salt water. And to get into recovery through the Twelve Steps one must "soak" in the process and meetings of the Twelve-Step program. Over the months you begin to absorb things you are unaware you are absorbing, and one day you become conscious that you are "a pickle," a different kind of person permeated with a new sort of serenity and love, a different kind of humility, and a different kind of openness.

I was told that once you face your own pain and your powerlessness over it, the surprises come. God seems to have made us in his image and put in us legitimate personal power. It's as if our personal power, folded carefully down inside us, begins to unfold, to blossom spiritually within us, releasing energy to live creatively and lovingly. Many of us are so inhibited by our past that we are afraid to use our legitimate power for fear we will hurt somebody's feelings, or for fear we will fail. But as we enter the Twelve Steps, we find ourselves in the midst of an exciting spiritual discipline that frees us from the crippling restraints of our past and gives us serenity and purpose at the same time. Only God's power can defeat our Sin, but part of what God's power does is release the personal power he has given each of us as creatures in his image.

As we begin to access God's power to defeat the Sin-disease and discover and use our own legitimate power to live, we step into the spiritual world, where God shares the keys to life and reality. In fact I soon learned that in Twelve-Step programs the word *spiritual* is quite different from the word *religious.* Spirituality has more to do with how much one is in touch with reality—one's own reality and feelings, the reality of other people, and ultimate reality, which is God and his will.

The Reason for Spiritual Discipline in the Christian Life

Our task with spiritual growth is not merely to get "holy," not merely to think holy thoughts so that we can experience the presence of the Holy Spirit, but to "exercise ourselves into godliness." Our task is to remove the self-imposed blocks or character defects that stand between God and us. We do this so we can be awakened, meet God personally with our own true selves, and do his will. To wake up and get at this task was also the purpose of the saints in their spiritual disciplines. As William Law put it, "For God has made no promises of mercy to the slothful and negligent. His mercy is only offered to our frail and imperfect, but best endeavors, to practice all manner of righteousness."[4] Spiritual discipline was not about reaching some higher state, "getting spiritual." It was (and is) about getting ready to know God. Archbishop William Temple said that "the heart of religion is not an opinion about God, such as Philosophy might reach as the conclusion of its argument; it is a personal relationship with God."[5]

The Twelve Steps reveal that spiritual disciplines or exercises are primarily ways to discover our own blocks to truth and right living; we can't see them because of our Sin and denial. Spiritual growth through discipline is a way to face, discover, and let God remove the character defects that distort our perception of reality and of God and ruin our lives and relationships.

A Spiritual Discipline for Today Is Hard to Find

I have talked to very few people outside Twelve-Step groups who have found a spiritual discipline that is suitable for the issues that cripple many people today. Although there is a rich heritage of Christian disciplines in the history of the Church, some of these disciplines, effective in themselves, are embedded in a context very foreign to contemporary living. Men and women who do practice spiritual disciplines today have had to translate them across many centuries and across cultural oceans.

Some other Christians conceive of God as a sweet Being who never asks them to do anything to change their behavior. The only discipline that might be required of them is attendance at church, and that's not even mandatory. Beyond attendance, no spiritual disciplines are required or even suggested by many churches today, no concrete ways to remove blocks and the pain they cause and to get close to God and other people again. Many Christians are just not motivated to grow and change spiritually. In *The Road Less Traveled*, the psychiatrist Scott Peck writes,

> There are many people I know who possess a vision of (personal) evolution yet seem to lack the will for it. They want, and believe it is possible, to skip over the discipline, to find an easy shortcut to sainthood. Often they attempt to attain it by simply imitating the superficialities of saints, retiring to the desert or taking up carpentry. Some even believe that by such imitation they have really become saints and prophets, and are unable to acknowledge that they are still children and face the painful fact that they must start at the beginning and go through the middle.[6]

I believe the Twelve Steps offer a discipline that is thoroughly of and for today. Millions of people find that working these steps frees them from compulsion and creates serenity, peace, joy, and healthier relationships with God and others. And, significantly, the program produces people who reach out to others in pain.

Biblical Roots Found in the Twelve Steps

The spiritual direction of the Twelve Steps came out of the Christian biblical tradition. In choosing the first alcoholics to transform into the great healers of our time, God did the same thing Paul reports God's doing in the first century: "God chose what is foolish in the world to shame the wise, God chose what is weak in the world to shame the strong" (1 Cor. 1:27). In forming Alcoholics Anonymous, God took a drunk stockbroker and a drunk doctor, both of whom seemed hopeless cases, and gathered around them a collection of apparently incurable alcoholics whose lives and relationships were in ruins. Out of this group he created a sensitive, caring, healing spiritual community.[7] People coming into Alcoholics

Anonymous, for instance, find a forgiving, redeeming, rigorously honest, moral, and loving Higher Power who is amazingly like Jesus Christ, as the person of God. Those of us in Twelve-Step programs know that, for us, doing these steps is the only form of spiritual discipline we've found for maintaining sanity, sobriety, clarity, serenity, and spiritual growth under the conditions of contemporary life.

Those who do not understand alcoholism may think that alcohol is the only issue in Alcoholics Anonymous. But alcohol is only the toxic symptom, the occasion for taking a look at the deep self-centered spiritual disease that I have been describing. As *Alcoholics Anonymous* (the Big Book) puts it, "Selfishness—self-centeredness: that, we think, is the root of our troubles." And to get well, "First of all we had to quit playing God" (p. 62).

Spiritual Growth Just Happens

The Twelve-Step process is an experience of *being changed* by a loving, supportive God who knows what we need and helps us through our pain to see and give up our own selfish agendas and surrender to his. We are not in control of the outcome of this process. At times we are excited and delighted witnesses to our own self-transformation. At other times we are immersed in pain and discouragement at the slow pace of change, but with less and less fear of such pain and more and more confidence that we will emerge on the other side of it in a better place, closer to God.

As you will see, the experience of Twelve-Step people is that the steps are most effective when taken in the context of doing certain things:

1. Attending Twelve-Step meetings
2. Reading certain material
3. Praying and meditating
4. Accepting guidance from a sponsor through the process of "working the steps"
5. Giving away what one is finding

In the chapters to come, we will look at each one of the Twelve Steps. At the end of each chapter there are some exercises to guide those who would like to begin taking the steps. I want to state very clearly that there is not a prescribed "correct" way to take the Twelve Steps. Each pilgrim must make many decisions about the best way for him or her. The material in this book came from many sources and was filtered through my own life and experience while working the steps and working with others in the program (see Selected Reading).

Welcome to an amazing spiritual adventure!

Chapter 2

STEP ONE

We Admitted We Were Powerless over Our Sin—That Our Lives Had Become Unmanageable*

A biblical experience of Step One:

I do not understand my own actions. For I do not do what I want, but I do the very thing I hate. . . . I can will what is right, but I cannot do it. For I do not do the good I want, but the evil I do not want is what I do. Now if I do what I do not want, it is no longer I that do it, but sin which dwells within me. Romans 7:15–20

---

* The Twelve Steps have been adapted in this book to relate to Sin with permission of Alcoholics Anonymous World Services, Inc. For the Twelve Steps as they appear in the Big Book, and in their adapted form, and for the Twelve Traditions of A.A., see appendix C.

When I was a young boy they told me that the bumblebee shouldn't be able to fly, that aerodynamically the bee's body wouldn't stay airborne with its short wings. The Twelve-Step program is a little like that. Through it several millions of people whom medical science and psychology had given up on as hopeless have been healed and have stepped into a new dimension of spiritual living. This is a program of spiritual flying, of overcoming life's "impossible" obstacles and allowing God to touch us, to heal us, and to draw us to himself and into a new life.

This is a program of getting off the ground emotionally and spiritually for people who have been grounded, blocked, depressed, and stymied by the pain of bruised relationships and broken dreams because of the Sin-disease and the character defects and addictions it triggers.

(I am aware that for people raised in a highly moralistic Christianity or an atheistic "medical model" world the idea of combining "sin" and "disease" may be mind-boggling. But when one sees "Sin" as that tenacious but denied tendency to "put oneself in the center and take control," when one realizes the addictive, disease-producing nature of that tendency in spite of all kinds of devastating consequences, then the idea that Sin is the compulsive spiritual "disease" underlying all addictions does not seem so farfetched.)

In some ways this is the most difficult chapter I've ever written, because in it I'm trying to describe something that, if you are in denial, may be almost impossible for you to see: the nature of powerlessness and unmanageability in the lives of people who are apparently coping adequately. But what I am counting on is that you feel some significant personal pain, frustration, fear, resentment, shame, guilt, anger, or discouragement that persists even after you have tried everything you know to do to make things right.

The danger in trying to talk about the Twelve-Step program is to bury its lean, living strength in concepts—as we Christians often do with the gospel message. Everybody who has tried to boil it down to concepts has failed to capture the Twelve-Step experience—at least as I have known it. I'm trying not to do that. Instead, I want to present the spiritual process that is inside the Twelve Steps, and Step One in particular, so that Christians and others without a chemical addiction can see the subtle power of the Sin-disease and the impossibility of defeating its symptoms on one's own.

Step One has to do with our inherent fear of turning loose our control over ourselves, others, and our futures enough to admit our own weakness and inability to fix life and to change the people, places, and things around us. Paradoxically, it is only as we turn loose that we can get free and, like a bumblebee, airborne, in our case, with God. The following discussion deals with the nature of powerlessness and unmanageability and with taking Step One.

Admitted We Were Powerless?

Look at most of us in the United States. Powerless? It sounds ridiculous. If you are really happy at this point and are not frustrated and looking for answers for your own life and relationships, do something with your time besides reading this book, because the Twelve Steps will not be of much help to you. They are not for everybody. This way of living is for a certain group of us who have seen that our lives and relationships are in serious trouble. We have become ready to admit that our religion is not enough to handle the compulsive fear and pain we can't get rid of. We have seen that we need additional spiritual strength from a Higher Power, whom we call God, to live life with serenity and purpose. And we have become ready to look seriously at this Twelve-Step program as a way to freedom and spiritual maturity.

It seems to be a bedrock truth that you cannot get this spiritual strength until you can see your own human limitations and quit struggling to "do it yourself." Most of us in middle-class America have done fairly well materially in life. We may have a couple of cars, a house, a job. We take credit for and pride in all the good things we've done and acquired. It seems to us that we have the power; *we* did it—even though those of us who are Christians "give God the credit" when we talk about such things. Those of us in religious work pray a lot, "God give us the power to do (whatever it is we are about to try)." Then even if he does, we still think of ourselves as having done whatever we've accomplished. And in a real sense this is true. But success and getting things we want leads us to the delusion that we can *change* people and personal circumstances through our power and methods of control. We don't know that this is a delusion until people important to us begin to rebel, and our control is seen to be very limited or illusory. A child may start using drugs or run away from home—or a mate may do these things.

Our denial, which hides our controlling ways from us, leads us to blame others for our unhappiness and to criticize them. And frequently that's our escape, our way of not facing the things *inside us* that lead to our unhappiness and our way of avoiding the awareness that we may be powerless to "fix" everyone and be happy. But because we still seem to be "in control" (after all, it's their fault they left, and maybe I can still think of a way to get them to change), how can we admit that we are powerless and that our lives have become unmanageable? How can we who are holding jobs, paying bills, raising children, and looking adequate according to the standards of society honestly admit to powerlessness when we appear to be living our lives satisfactorily?

Those of us with integrity can't truthfully say we are *completely* powerless just because we're having a few problems. Doesn't everybody have a few problems? Of course. So the idea of "complete powerlessness" is really hard to see. And I believe that is largely because the Sin-disease deludes us about our power and the areas in which it is not effective. We think we are supposed to be in control and exercise our power to do what we have determined to do, when in reality we who have committed our lives to God are supposed to have surrendered our control center to his will. We say, "Thy will, not mine, be done." There is a paradox involved in using our own will and being willing to act on God's will. Both require action, and it is difficult to discern the difference: which things are within *our* power to change and which we are powerless over. I believe Step One is about such discernment, learning to tell by the results of our actions whether or not we are powerless.

When our actions (even many well-intentioned actions) continually lead to anger and resentment or rebellion from those with whom we interact, when we keep doing things we have firmly decided we *don't want to do,* and when we fail to do what we've decided is best for us, we begin to see that in fact we do not have the power to change we thought we had. Seeing that we are not able to stay on a diet or a budget or give up compulsive eating, smoking, or sexual habits, for example, is often the doorway to a new perspective on our powerlessness.

But how can we arrive at an honest awareness that we are powerless over many areas of our lives when the thought has never really occurred to us? And how can we break out of this delusion about our power?

The Message We Receive About Control

First it's helpful to look at where we got the idea that we're supposed to be in control and exercise our power. Many of us who were children before the Second World War were taught either openly or subtly to compete and to win. As I grew up and observed my parents I saw that in some very important ways life was all about being in control and not letting other people control you.

We went out into the world from our family trying to be outstanding, to get attention. As young people we were doing whatever we could to control other people's reality, their opinions about us: shouting, pushing, singing, playing basketball, acting, "getting elected," being a cheerleader, making good grades, writing poetry, or just trying to look pretty or handsome to get recognition, to gain the approval we needed in order to show how important and special we were. Or if we couldn't compete in these ways we may have tried to be the toughest or the sexiest or the party animal or the one with the largest capacity for alcohol.

As we got past our teenage years some of us learned to be quieter. On the surface we tried to look cool and relaxed, but inside, where it didn't show (sometimes even to us), we were acting out the childhood injunction to "be in control."

Some of us didn't respect brashness in the way other people dressed or behaved to show themselves off. We thought they were crass in the way they tried to get attention. Instead we tried more conservative, less visible ways to manipulate attention. We looked down on those obvious ones, yet we played out the same control games to a different audience, usually a smaller, more sophisticated audience.

As we move through life we begin to take pride in those things that seem to reflect our success. We say that we are "proud of" our wives or husbands, our children, our homes, our cars, our friends, our church. And we look at all these people and things and assure ourselves that we are in fact in control, that we are happy, that we have power, that we are complete. I'm not saying that it's wrong to enjoy these things or to be satisfied with them. But when we are not happy unless things are going well (meaning the way we want them to) with all these people, things, and institutions, we are using control of these outward things as evidence of our *worth as a person.* It is essential, therefore, that we *stay* in control of our lives (and the lives of others around us) in order to have a sense of value and be happy. We tend to hide any evidence of weak or selfish behavior that might reveal a lack of power or reveal that our motives for "advising the family" are in fact very self-serving.

Clues That Reveal Our Attempts to Control

Irritation and Blaming.   For many of us whom the world would say have it made, who seem to have plenty of power, certain experiences begin to belie our having everything under control. Even when we feel in control at a conscious level we keep finding ourselves irritated that things don't go exactly the way we want. We tend to blame our failure to have things under control on other people or on circumstances. "It's because of these unreasonable people around here," we say. We're resentful; we snap at our family members and try to fix them, the very people we're proud of. We start fouling our own nest, sabotaging the good life we believe we have built.

Other Disturbing Emotional Experiences.   We may begin to feel restless, angry, fearful, and ashamed. We may feel shame when we don't do things perfectly, because we're supposed to be in control. We may feel sad for no reason at all. We may feel afraid of sharing our thoughts and feelings with the people closest to us, because they might leave if they knew how mad at them we are, or disgusted, or bored, or turned off, or afraid, or whatever it is we feel. We may then fall into self-pity because they don't understand us (even though we won't tell them what we're feeling). We may feel angry because they don't guess who we are or what we want from them, because "if they really loved us," of course, they would be able to guess.

We'll Do Almost Anything to Appear to Be in Control—Even Lie

Another strange phenomenon arising out of this deep-rooted message that we must be in control is that fear of losing control makes us liars who do not know that we lie. It was quite a while before I could see that I'm a liar, because that certainly did not fit my conscious picture of myself as a good man, perfectly moral and in control.

I once read an Adult Children of Alcoholics' list of twenty characteristics. I could easily recognize nineteen of them in myself. I said to my wife, "Honey, thank goodness there's one thing I don't have that's on this list."

She said, "What's that?"

I said, "It says we lie a lot." And she just smiled. I was furious at her reaction. Two years later when my denial broke about this unconscious form of exaggeration-alibi lying, I remembered her reaction to my denial and understood it.

If we were truly in control we certainly wouldn't have to lie. The king doesn't have to lie. But for those of us who are trying to *appear* to be in control, anything that threatens to reveal our imperfection can trigger an automatic and unconscious lie. Let me give you an example of the way it starts slowly creeping in.

In the morning, my wife asks, "Keith, will you mail these letters today? It is *very* important that they go out today."

"Sure, don't worry. I'll mail them."

The next day, she asks, "Keith, did you mail those letters I gave you yesterday?"

Inside I clutch, and my mind reacts with a split-second satisfactory response. "Don't worry about those letters," I say, "they are on the way." I then go out and mail them, because I did, in fact, forget to mail them the day before after promising to. I have *lied,* rationalizing that I have not really lied, because I knew I'd go out after supper and mail them. In my mind the letters are "on the way." In recovery in a Twelve-Step program, I am learning to say, "No, I forgot. And I want to make amends to you. I'll go mail them right now."

Another example of lying is when we exaggerate stories to make sure we keep our listener's interest. If, for example, I saw a three-car wreck with two people injured, I might say, "There were several cars, and injured people were strewn all over the highway." Two injured people is plenty, but I have often exaggerated in this way.

At the same time we're lying to the people around us this way, we get resentful when they accuse us of it. Others will catch the discrepancies in what we are saying and doing and become irritated by what we're doing or by our refusal to admit it. Eventually the people around us may get sick of our pushing them around and lying to them, and they may back away or leave us. When they do, we are mystified, because we're behaving as we always have. We know something's wrong in the relationship, but we're not aware of *doing* anything to cause their reactions, especially something like lying. This is how our lives and happiness, supposedly under control, start to disintegrate.

All the While We Believe
We Can Stop or Change at Any Time

Being "in control" implies that you can stop or change what you have been doing, even if you have been doing it compulsively. But eventually some things begin to happen to us that we cannot stop or change. For instance, we may be filled with excessive and even groundless fear about finances or about our children or about our primary relationship, or we may be filled with jealousy or resentment. Although we tell ourselves there is no need to feel the way we do and we pray to God to remove these feelings, we *cannot stop*.

We may also become approval seekers or success seekers. Many of the great business tycoons in this country destroyed people in their climb to the top. But they could not stop their headlong race. Some of them later tried to compensate for their earlier greed and excess by giving libraries or making grants to various good causes or doing good public works. But none of that helped the people who did business with them along the way and lost everything because of their Sin-disease. The amazing thing is that these driven, successful people often *could not stop* their compulsive working even if they had heart attacks or other warnings, even though they kept telling themselves and their families, "I'll slow down after this deal," or, "after I make this amount of money."

Another control strategy people find they cannot change is an addiction to excitement. Some men and women are bored with normal, everyday life and must go to exciting, inspiring meetings or be with exciting people or go to exotic places. If life gets boring, they will do something to stir things up, even if the action they take is self-defeating. I have a friend whose family said that if things got boring he'd "set the house on fire" to liven things up. And he could not stop doing this until he got in a Twelve-Step program. He controlled situations by getting people's lives—including his own—in chaos. Because he knew how it happened, he *felt* in control, though his family was afraid and miserable much of the time.

Some people steal, have affairs, take terrible risks in business, or do other hazardous things just to keep the excitement going and prove to themselves, "I am still alive and in control of my happiness." Some people squeak by with success from their risky ventures; others risk and fail, suffering harmful consequences to one degree or another. But in either case, the attraction to risking is strong, and such people continue to put themselves in jeopardy "for the thrill of it" as a form of compulsive controlling.

The experience of thousands of people who have worked the Twelve Steps is that the bottom line to this business of facing our powerlessness is that we *cannot* continue to try and control our happiness and change other people's feelings and behavior and still have honest, intimate relationships with them. Moreover, many people are, indeed, powerless to control what they have assumed they do control.

Our Lives Had Become Unmanageable

The rest of Step One adds insult to injury. Not only does the first Step say we are powerless, but it goes on to say that we admitted that our "lives had become unmanageable." I really balked at that. My life was *not* unmanageable. But the truth is that just as we deny our powerlessness, we hide, even from ourselves, some of the inner signs that our lives are unmanageable. We experience exaggerated feelings that threaten to overwhelm us. But we can't own these feelings.

Loneliness. People say that power isolates. It seems to me there are at least two reasons why this is true. First, when we are concerned primarily with power, we can't reveal our true agenda, because part of that agenda involves controlling people, having power over them. If we were to tell people that, they would become angry and resentful, so we have to hide our true intentions and often withdraw from intimacy with the people around us.

The second reason power is lonely is that this Sin-disease, or control-disease, makes us think of the people around us as objects, materials for "building our kingdom." We assign to one family member the "cooking and housekeeping" departments of our personal kingdom; there's the "sharp, successful kids" department; and there's the "social acceptance" department. Of course, we don't usually consciously try to run people's lives, but we subtly try to shape their behavior to look good for us, and if they don't meet our needs, help fulfill their part of *our* program as we envision it, we can get irritated and angry with them. And we also become increasingly lonely, because it is difficult to relate to people as objects in a way that satisfies our human need for contact and intimacy.

Loss of Feelings.   The process of trying to control all these people and keep all our expectation balls in the air at once may also work like a narcotic to numb our feelings. Those of us who have plenty of material possessions often don't experience many deep feelings. We can't have joy because we can't stand pain, but pain evidently comes into the heart through the same doorway as joy. When we use something—from a vacation, to buying new clothes, to tranquilizers—to blot out the pain of life, we block out the joy as well. We are therefore often numb people, who have plenty of everything but can't feel the love for and from those people with whom God has given us to live.

Broken Relationships and Resentments.   Because the primary symptom of the Sin-disease is denial, we do not know that we are controlling, yet we can pick up the slightest hint that someone else is trying to control us. Because many of us are almost obsessed at an unconscious level with being right, being perfect, being number one, or otherwise in control, we have a kind of radar that picks up on every slight, every subtle put-down, every criticism. We can pick them up instantly, often even when they are unintended. Other people might miss these attempts to control—but not us.

When our family challenges our control, we pick up every subtle hint that it might be a criticism of us. In righteous indignation and resentment we begin to collect injustices they have perpetrated against us, injustices we can see quite clearly. We know unquestionably when *they* are wrong, even though we can't see the shortcomings of our own that may have led to their "attack" on us.

Something tells us we better not be up front and direct about their injustices, because there could be a real blowup. And besides, at some level we see that there "could be" a little truth in what they're claiming about us. But finally we collect enough of their injustices to cash in for justified rage—or even a divorce. Those who are very scrupulous and righteous have got to have good reasons to do these things. In the Sin-disease we rationalize that if all these injustices are true then any "normal person" would "have the right to" be in a rage—or get drunk, go on a spending spree, have an affair, get divorced.

Uncontrollable, Exaggerated Feelings. Automatic or compulsive behaviors and exaggerated feelings develop that we can't control. We say, "I'm getting too fussy in traffic. I'm going to relax and drive less aggressively." Then somebody cuts in front of us, and we have a rage attack, lean on the horn, shake our fists, and give them a loud, abusive lecture that they cannot even hear about their poor driving habits.

Making Rules That We Ourselves Don't Keep. We tell our family, "We are not spending any more money this month." And then we go out and buy a new dress or tennis shoes or a shotgun or whatever we want. When we are reminded that we "weren't going to spend any more money this month," we rationalize our failure to keep the rule we set down by saying something like, "Well, some good things have happened financially I didn't tell you about." But in fact we did the spending because we wanted to; our behavior was compulsive and unmanageable.

Forgetting to Do the Things That Nurture Our Relationships. We intend to write thank-you letters on time: "I've got to write Aunt Minnie. She sent that present last Christmas, and it's August!" And we don't do it. We promise we're going to come home on time; then we're late. We see the family of someone who's dying of cancer and tell them that we are going to call or write the patient, and the patient dies before we ever call.

We may start forgetting birthdays or anniversaries when it's terribly important to those around us that we remember. Or we may forget to meet someone we promised to see. In all these ways we would be able to see that our lives were unmanageable, *if* we could own our obviously unmanageable behavior. But we are in denial and can't "see" what we are doing, so we don't recognize how unmanageable our lives are.

Geographical Cures. When enough unmanageable things start happening in their lives, people often think that moving to another house, marriage, city, or job will help. In Twelve-Step language, this is called an attempt at a geographical cure. So we change jobs, or move to a new town or house or apartment, or get a new boyfriend or girlfriend, or divorce and remarry. I moved something like twenty times in twenty-three years. I was in the oil exploration business during most of those years, but some of those moves probably could have been avoided; I liked to move "to get a new start." A move does give us a short time in which we can use our old modes of operation before being discovered as not in control. But eventually issues come to the surface, and we have to face our powerlessness and the unmanageability—or move again.

I have a friend in the oil exploration business. His wife kept saying, "Our problem is that we are all cramped in this house. We've got all these kids, and I've got cabin fever. That's why you and I can't get along." They had six children about a year apart in age. As each child came along, she said, "We need more space." So they bought and sold a series of four houses. Finally, he told me, "We moved into a brand-new fifteen-room home in the nicest area in our state. The day we moved in, we had the worst argument we had ever had in our lives." And he said, "Keith, right then I knew it wasn't the house." Geographical cures seldom solve our problems. And they certainly do not get us into recovery from the Sin-disease.

Fear of Authority Figures.   Some of us who see ourselves as being powerful and in control are afraid of authority figures, men or women. Some men are giants in their business life and terrified of their wives, as they were of their mothers. And some women can run a bank, but at home they timidly say to their husbands, "I'm sorry. I don't know what I did with that five dollars." It is when they see that they can't quit deferring in an unhealthy way to authority figures that they may finally see that their lives are unmanageable.

Feeling a Confused Sense of Unreality.   After we begin seeing how powerless we are to stop some of the things we are doing, we may begin feeling a kind of confused sense of unreality. We're frantic all the time. We've got more to do than we can handle. But we're not really conscious of how hectic and confused our lives are; we think it's temporary and "normal." When it becomes clear that it isn't temporary, we become depressed about our lack of ability to "get things straightened out" (or to get some person straightened out). This frustration and confusion are common symptoms of the experience of powerlessness and unmanageability.

We may fear that we don't belong anywhere, or that we're not adequate, able to make things right. We may feel "different," not like other people, absorbed in ourselves in some unnatural way. Yet we can't stop thinking about our problems.

Unexplainable Physical Symptoms.   These depressing feelings may move into our bodies in the form of ulcers, stomach pains, intestinal dysfunction, skin disorders, headaches, nonorganic heart problems, back and muscle joint pain, or urinary problems. Not every case of such physical illnesses is caused by the Sin-disease, of course, but there are cases whose symptoms seem to be nonorganic, and doctors cannot find any physical reason for them. At their root may be the unrecognized attempts to control beneath the powerlessness and unmanageability I am describing here.[1]

A Growing Compulsion to Control, in Spite of Harmful Consequences.   We may respond to our confusion and physical disorders (due to "stress" we are told) with withdrawal or increased attempts to control. We often experience baffling rejection from our loved ones. We have hopeless feelings that we're not going to make it somehow, or that our child's not going to make it, or that we are going to fail in our primary relationship or our vocational life. We may fill our days and nights with fear as we obsessively worry about "our problem."

As our fears that we will not be able to fix things increase, we may experience an even stronger need to have people "do it our way or leave." We become dissatisfied with the things we have acquired that were supposed to make us happy. The further into this self-doubt we get, the more we need people to do things our way to verify that we are, in fact, in control. So we may become even more controlling and never see it.

At last we may say, "Enough of this confusion. I know what's best for people, and I'm furious that they're rejecting me. And I'm sick of being overcommitted and doing more things than I can handle. I am going to get this mess straightened out!"

We Try to Fix Ourselves

But rather than say, "Help! My life is not right. I can't do it myself," we mount a gigantic effort, still trying to use and enhance our own power to remedy these problems.

We may go to more conferences or read more self-help books, trying to get new information about solving our problems so we can get things under control. Many of us who have almost everything we need take time to go to conferences to find what's not working and why. We get new information on how to pray or study the Bible. We may have been praying for thirty years, but we still feel we're not doing it right somehow. We are attracted to seminars and books that tell us how to live through the various issues of our lives: how to grieve, how to play, how to relate, how to raise our children, how to make money, how to make love, how to save money and how to conserve it, how to leave money to our family—all without losing control.

Much of the information we gain may be helpful, but often it only feeds the delusion that we can find the power to overcome our Sin on our own. It leaves us smarter but lonelier and more discouraged.

Addictions.   It is when people can't get control of their lives and relationships after much trying that they block out the pain with addictive substances or behaviors (e.g., work, food, alcohol, sex, religion, relationships). Sometimes Christians frantically "work for the Lord" at this stage to try to control the pain caused by their Sin-disease. Religious work addiction is a serious symptom of the Sin-disease. Eventually, however, the pain and frustration of the addiction often become more painful than the pain the addiction started out to cover. The addict feels a growing sense of failure—failure to be perfect and failure to stay in control of his or her life and work. Note how frantic Paul is in Acts 8 and 9 before his confrontation on the road to Damascus. This sense of failure is a terrible ego insult to a proud person who has always been able to "handle things." One's whole self-esteem seems to be seriously damaged or destroyed.

The Last-Ditch Effort
to Prove We're in Control

When our self-esteem gets crushed, or it looks as though we're going to be powerless, we're like ants rebuilding an anthill. We start scrambling and piecing back together our image of being in control, building it up again so that we will look adequate, powerful. The alcoholic stops drinking altogether for thirty days, ninety days, four months, to prove there is no problem. The sex addict is faithful for a time to save his or her marriage. The work addict takes a week off to prove he or she is okay. But whereas sanity would tell us to quit self-destructive behavior altogether, the compulsive person eventually snaps back into the thick of the dysfunctional behavior after the test period is over, even more powerless to see the disease and his or her denial of it.

What is it that can finally break down the delusion of power and bring us to the point of acknowledging the powerlessness that has been there all along?

Pain, the Doorway to Recovery

I believe the delusion of control and power finally breaks down at the point where we are not able to alleviate our stress and our pain through *any* effort in our repertoire. Evidently what we all want is happiness, yet with all we have accomplished or acquired with our attempts to be in control, many of us reach a place at which we not only cannot control our happiness—even with an addictive substance or behavior—but we cannot control our pain and stress, which has reached an agonizing level. By this time the family may have left; the job may be gone; or one's health may have been destroyed.

But we don't have to go this far down. We can see the patterns of powerlessness and go for help. When we begin to realize how we act and feel when no one is around, or in our car alone in traffic, or in line in a store, or when we listen to a political commentator, or in our most intimate relationships in our homes or in our beds, we can look around in our lives and see other signs of powerlessness and unmanageability. In the end it is usually the pain of our compulsions, addictions, and denial and the resulting strained or broken relationships that drive us to the stark awareness of our powerlessness. Unfortunately it may take a tragedy or crisis to break through our delusion of power—a divorce, a family member's addiction, a runaway child, a terminal illness, a bankruptcy, a death.

Bill W., a co-founder of A.A., talks about reaching a point where nothing in his life worked. Nothing seemed to give him peace of mind and happiness. He saw that he was powerless on his own to gain happiness, and at that point he "hit bottom," as we say. To hit bottom means suddenly realizing, "I *can't* fix myself; I'm lost."

People in the Twelve-Step programs know that until you're hurting enough, the steps won't work for you. But for the fortunate sufferer, there comes a time when he or she says, "I've *got* to get well. I can't stand living like this anymore." And that is when one is ready for the miracles of the Twelve Steps.

All our training to succeed on our own makes it very difficult to come into a Twelve-Step program and admit by doing so that we are powerless to fix ourselves alone. It is not necessary to give up the life-long striving to win, to be number one in our vocations and personal relationships, to begin the Twelve-Step adventure; all that's necessary is a recognition of powerlessness. But that is plenty. To the average control-oriented American, and perhaps especially to a convinced Christian, it sounds insane to admit that we are powerless to fix our lives and that they are unmanageable.

A Program of Paradoxes

But the Twelve-Step program is paradoxical. It's sort of like swimming. I used to teach little boys how to swim at a summer camp. Many of them would start out terribly frightened of the water and cling to me. The idea of losing control and drowning terrified them. I would put my hands under them and tell them just to give themselves to the water, and it would hold them up. But they wouldn't do it. Finally when they did relax and turn loose, they were amazed to discover that the water did support them, and they were swimming within hours. In a similar way, when my own pain and stress drove me to the Twelve Steps, I was afraid that I would sink and lose what control I had if I surrendered my illusion of power and admitted that my life was unmanageable. But finally, when the pain was severe enough and I was reassured that it wouldn't kill me, I did admit my powerlessness, and I too was amazed that God through the program held me up. That was when I began to swim into the healing of the Twelve-Step process.

A Christian Step

There is something strangely familiar about this process to Christians. Jesus said, "He who loses his life for my sake will find it" (Matt. 10:39). The doorway to healing through the Twelve Steps involves this same secret Jesus talked about. We give up our delusionary control in order to gain a reality-oriented self-control. His "follow me" adventure began with a turning loose process amazingly like Step One.

Before the crisis that leads to hope, we had become fixed on unsolvable dilemmas, problems that we were powerless to solve in the ways we were trying to solve them. When we couldn't solve these problems, feelings of shame, fear, anger, resentment, guilt, self-justification, and frustration were activated or increased. All our fears, our sense of inadequacy, and our other painful feelings came out and began to dance with us in our loneliness. Because we were desperately afraid of failing and needed to come out looking cool and adequate, we expended an enormous amount of energy trying to deny our basic powerlessness, which we would eventually learn is something that *all* human beings face.

When I came to this point, I had been told for weeks that I was in denial, that I wasn't facing the fact that I was a person who *had* to be right and who tried to control the lives of other people around me— with advice about what they ought to do, with gifts, and with all kinds of subtle control devices. I was told that I was compulsive to the point of addiction about several areas of my life. I was told that I was hurting my own health as well as my relationships both by my controlling and by the addictive habits I used to try to cover up the pain and rejection my behavior was causing.

But I could *not* see it. I thought I just needed some good breaks financially and I would quit working so hard and drinking so much. I thought that people around me were being unreasonable and unfair in their judgments of me.

One night I couldn't sleep. I had been awake all night, tossing, turning, and wrestling with the notion that there really was something terribly wrong—and that it just might be about me. Then it came to me in an instant, "Maybe you *are* in denial! Maybe you *can't* see that you are controlling when you try to help people close to you!"

At that point my denial cracked open, and I saw that I am a controller, that I desperately need to be right, to control people, places, and things to get what I think is the right outcome—in my life and in the lives of people in close continuing relationships with me.

I said, "Oh no. No! *No!*" And then I turned to God and said in shame and guilt something like this: "Lord, I can see it now. I am a compulsive controller. And I have hurt the very people you have given me to love by attempting to 'fix' them and determine what's best for them. I can see that I am powerless to change this behavior. I couldn't even have seen it without you. My life is unmanageable."

I had taken Step One.

TAKING STEP ONE

Note to the reader: If you are seriously considering taking the Twelve Steps for your own recovery and spiritual growth, you may want to stop at this point and read appendix A: "Sponsorship." It is crucial to a successful Twelve-Step program to have a mentor, or "sponsor," to guide you through the process of taking the Steps. This is a New Testament principle many people are finding essential to authentic spiritual growth. Paul and Barnabas took Silas, Timothy, and Mark and were mentors to them in the faith. (See Acts 15:39–16:5.)

Step One
*We admitted we were powerless over Sin—
that our lives had become unmanageable.*

You may wish to use a separate notebook to record your responses to the questions and issues that follow the discussions of each step. Begin to examine your life as it is. Be as honest as you can about each issue listed.

Continual or Excessive Feelings over Which I Am Powerless

1. Describe, on paper, recurring fears (e.g., about finances, family members, authority figures, sex, God).

2. Describe resentments or anger (e.g., about family members, job, government, church, other institutions and people).

3. Describe guilt or shame (e.g., about specific past actions, not being perfect in some area).

4. Describe sadness or self-pity about at least three things.

5. Describe pain about three situations, people, or thoughts.

6. Describe jealousy (e.g., about material things, love relationships).

7. Describe how frantic excitability manifests itself in you.

8. Describe how loneliness feels.

9. Describe in what areas you experience numbness or lack of feelings (or confusion) and how these feel.

10. Describe distressing physical symptoms over which you are powerless (e.g., indigestion and/or upset stomach, allergies, trouble sleeping, headaches, skin disorder, muscle or bone problems, sexual dysfunction).

Behaviors Over Which I Am Powerless

1. List foods, drinks, medicines that you keep eating, drinking, or taking even though you do not want to.

2. List and describe other compulsive behaviors—things that you keep doing though you know it is not in your best interest to do so. These may include sexual behavior (e.g., excessive masturbation or use of pornography and/or sexual fantasies, having affairs, continual or excessive demands on your partner for sex), gambling or taking risks you can't afford, exaggerating stories, making excuses, lying, justifying yourself (give examples), giving advice or controlling where people don't want you to.

People Over Whom I Am Powerless

List the people (1) in your family, (2) at work, (3) at church and other places whose behavior irritates you and what it is they do that you can't get them to quit doing.

Summary Statement and Taking the Step

If after considering the issues set out in the past few pages, you can see that in fact you are powerless and that in one or more areas your life is unmanageable, then you may be ready to take Step One.

If you are ready to admit your powerlessness you can do it by writing out the following statement and/or telling it to your sponsor or the members of a Twelve-Step meeting (if you have no sponsor).

"I, _____ , admit that I am powerless and that my life has become unmanageable."

Copy the statement in your notebook either as it is or in your own words (being sure to use the words *powerless* and *unmanageable*).

You have now taken Step One. It will be helpful to you and others in the program if you will begin to share in meetings these ways in which you have discovered that you are powerless. This will help you find the reality and humility essential for progress and may help others to see their own denial and powerlessness so they too can begin this phase of their spiritual journey. If there is something that seems too "shameful" or threatening to share in a meeting, don't share it. Or you may want to talk with your sponsor before sharing it. The idea is not to become a "stripper," but to begin owning and sharing your reality as a part of the healing process.

Chapter 3

STEP TWO

*Came to Believe That a Power
Greater Than Ourselves Could
Restore Us to Sanity*

A biblical experience of the power of
coming to believe:

*And the blind man said to him, "Master, let
me receive my sight." And Jesus said to him,
"Go your way; your faith has made you
well." Mark 10:51,52*

A biblical experience of being
restored to sanity:

*And they came to Jesus and saw the demoniac
sitting there, clothed and in his right mind,
the man who had had the legion [of demons].
Mark 5:15*

In Step One, we admitted we are powerless, but that leaves us with a terrible void. Knowing our best efforts won't solve our deepest problems, what can we do? The second Step says, "There is a *Higher* Power, a power greater than you that can overcome your disease and help you envision life as it can be lived."

People with all kinds of beliefs about God walk up to this second Step. They have in common only an awareness that they are trapped by an addiction or the Sin-disease and cannot "manage" their lives. Step Two says that after admitting one's powerlessness, all that is required to begin this faith journey is a *willingness* to believe—no content, no creed, no church affiliation, no religious experience, just a willingness, a sense of openness to a "Higher Power." Hearing this is often very disturbing to Christians, who think that the spiritual life begins with a willingness to believe in Jesus Christ. But a little thought reveals that long before a person makes a specific commitment to Christ there has been some sort of awakening of the desire to believe. Authentic Christian conversion is similar to joining a Twelve-Step group, in the sense that first comes the awareness of one's powerlessness to solve the most basic problems one is facing. Then, perhaps, one meets a loving Christian, hears a speaker, reads a book, or sees a movie in which faith plays a part.

This was true of the apostle Paul. He was killing Christians when he saw and heard Stephen pray for those who were stoning him to death, saying, "Lord, do not hold this sin against them" (Acts 7:60). Seeing that kind of faith in one who was being killed must have profoundly affected Paul, because soon after comes the story of his conversion to Jesus (Acts 9:1–31). Perhaps the greatest theologian after Paul was Augustine. Augustine as a nonbeliever was evangelized by Bishop Ambrose of Milan. Although greatly impressed by Ambrose's ability as a preacher, theologian, and bishop, Augustine was so entranced with the *life* of the Christian Ambrose that he watched the bishop by the hour to absorb what it was about him that awakened such a longing for faith in Augustine. Then, when his pain was enough, Augustine opened the Bible when he was alone and believed in Jesus.[1] In fact, most Christians can point to a person whose life drew them into faith before they knew anything about theology.

This prior step of "willingness to believe" is often left out of contemporary discussions of Christian conversion, but it deserves our attention.

Some people coming to the Twelve Steps are atheists who believe they can demonstrate that God isn't.[2] There are also agnostics who are in doubt because they don't think anyone can prove that God is. Then there are former churchgoers who have lost their faith or rejected it. Many of these people were hurt, abused, or rejected by someone who claimed to be a Christian or by some religious group that they felt judged and condemned them for being powerless over an addiction. These former churchgoers often don't know what they believe, but they certainly don't want to be mistaken for Christians or even for "being religious." The founders of A.A. realized that many people who were alcoholics weren't treated very well in the Church of fifty years ago. They were considered to be moral degenerates by many Christians who did not understand the nature of addiction. Although some alcoholics carried a lot of guilt and half-believed that what Christian "moralists" said about them was true, many secretly felt that inside, behind their compulsive and inebriated behavior, they were good people caught in a powerful craving that no amount of willpower could overcome.

Also coming into the program today are thousands of committed Christians who *are* believers and whose faith in Christ is solid but for whom that faith doesn't work anymore with regard to the compulsive "need to control" and other addictive behaviors. Problems began to crop up in their lives and relationships, along with frustrations and anxieties that they didn't have when they first became Christians. I was one of these. There was little doubt in my mind ever about the existence of God and the reality of Jesus Christ. And I was consciously committed to him with my whole life (as Lord and Savior). But at a certain point all my belief and commitment weren't effective in getting control of my life because I couldn't see my basic Sin—that in my denial I had put myself in the center where only God should be.

It was in the company of all these kinds of people with painful or negative feelings about life and or the Church that I moved toward the Twelve Steps and ran into the concept of a "Higher Power."

In their genius, the founders of A.A. realized that the key to unlocking the doorway to authentic faith is a *willingness* to believe. Their experience convinced them that if they used the "key of willingness," the large doorway to a specific faith in a living God and a new life would swing open. So the literature about the Twelve Steps says that to begin you can take anything to be your Higher Power. For instance, the people in the group at a meeting can be your Higher Power. Obviously those people in the group are coping with their powerlessness and finding a new power to live, and the beginner is not. Or the Higher Power can be something in nature, anything that the new member wants to make it. You can even have "a doorknob" be your Higher Power when you first come into this program.

A doorknob? Now that *really* bothers Christians. When Christians hear this, they all of a sudden raise strong objections and walk away from the Twelve Steps. But I am convinced that the "Higher Power" concept is one of the most profound discoveries of the Twelve-Step approach in helping people *move into* the faith process so they can find an authentic faith in God and a new life.

The Faith Process

Evidently, the way belief works from the believer's perspective is that the act of faith not only gives access to a great power from outside the believer but also releases latent power from *within* him or her.

Let's say that a man admits that he is powerless and his life is unmanageable and is invited to come to a Twelve-Step program. On the inside he feels he has a mind full of confusion, of hot emotional spaghetti that's alive and over which he is powerless. He is told that the Higher Power will give him the strength and insight to unsnarl the spaghetti. This man says, "I don't know if I can believe in God." So the Twelve-Step people say, "It doesn't matter. Start with whatever you have to as a Higher Power. Try the group, a sunrise, or a doorknob."

This works as a start because the *act of believing* changes the focus of the man's life, removes it from an ever-tightening cycle of self-absorption, from attempts to control unmanageable problems alone, and from immersion in a welter of self-centered emotions like shame and fear. The simple act of believing can give him a new direction when he believes there is help beyond his own inadequate resources. As the new person focuses on working a simple, positive program, believing that it will work because of the witness of others (new Christians believe for the same reason), a different mental climate develops. The new man in our example hears that this belief in a Higher Power will heal him from the disease that has crippled his life. By attending meetings, every week he sees walking miracles of change, people who were as powerless as he receiving the power to live differently. Now he can cooperate and work the steps without sacrificing his intellectual integrity, because he has objective evidence (in their lives) that believing in a Higher Power can bring change.

It is very difficult to doubt the authenticity of what happens at most Twelve-Step meetings. When people are truly sharing their feelings and what's going on in their lives, you can smell the reality. Anyone who tries to fake it or show off lasts about five minutes. The contrast between the showoff and the honest sharing of the others usually reveals the fakery with no attack or confrontation even being necessary. New people are advised not to straighten anyone out who "doesn't sound real," because that person may be doing his or her best at that stage of recovery. The new person is advised about all sharing in groups to "take what will help you, and leave the rest." There is a very sensitive "unreality detector" in the spirit of a Twelve-Step meeting.

Through believing that a Higher Power can help, a man or a woman formerly eaten up with raging fear, anger, shame, doubt, guilt, and frustration may become calm and begin to grow spiritually by focusing on doing some simple steps, going to meetings, reading the Big Book, and talking to a sponsor. This person is not alone; there are caring brothers and sisters who really do understand because they are dealing with the same problems the newcomer has. The simple act of believing that a Higher Power can restore us to sanity leads us into a family and into a new life where we can begin to see and experience a little sanity.

There is great relief in this act of faith. We begin to absorb the concrete evidence that the crazy, dysfunctional thoughts and feelings we've had are quite similar to everybody else's. It's almost an ego insult! We thought we were unique. We talk in the program about the feeling of uniqueness that we have had and how it can be a "terminal uniqueness," because our notion that we and our problems are "different" can keep us from finding a dynamic source of help.

The Content and Process of Step Two

The creative and healing power released by the simple shift from the self-willed, self-centered "I'll do it myself, thank you" attitude of the Sin-disease to the belief that a Higher Power can give us perspective and strength to solve our problems is so great that the very act of believing often relieves the confusion and fear temporarily and moves us into the process toward healing—even if the Higher Power chosen first doesn't actually have the power to solve any problems. But this beginning leads to more, much more.

This spiritual process I am describing is not so different from the evangelism used by my friend the late Reverend Sam Shoemaker, the Episcopal clergyman in whose church Alcoholics Anonymous had its first meeting in New York City.[3] Sam suggested to people who didn't believe in God that they enter "a thirty-day prayer experiment."[4] He told them, "Don't pay any attention to whether you believe or not. Just pray every day for thirty days that God will meet you at the point of your greatest need, and see what happens to you." Literally hundreds of people have become committed Christians doing that thirty-day prayer experiment. It seems that as one becomes involved in the *action* of faith some of the objections to the *content* of a specific faith evaporate, and one is led quietly into a belief in the living God—and to seeing the face of God in Jesus Christ.

The miracle that happens for many people who first take God as a doorknob is that faith, a simple act of trust, opens the locked doorway of isolation, enabling them to step out into a new light, into a new world, a new family of faith in the living God.

The Higher Power Looks Familiar

I came into a Twelve-Step program as a Christian with a graduate degree in theology and a serious commitment of my life to Christ that I'd been trying to live for twenty-nine years. I just *knew* this Higher Power or "doorknob" approach to God was *not* the way you were supposed to do faith. I was a little horrified, in fact, and I thought to myself, "This faith in God is serious business. They're going to lead people astray and get into big trouble here." But my own pain was severe and *my* faith was not working, so I kept silent and listened and watched. The months went by, and I had a very humbling experience. As I watched the Higher Power reveal itself to various people in the group, its personality always had certain definite familiar characteristics. I knew that if everyone were "making up" their own Higher Power, this wouldn't happen. It couldn't. The personality of the Higher Power revealed in those meetings was always loving and forgiving; gave people however many new starts they needed to get into recovery and to get well; was rigorously honest, moral, courageous, and strong but never abusive; and was loyal beyond belief whether people deserved it or not. In fact, as I looked carefully at the Higher Power in the Twelve-Step program, I realized that it had a haunting family resemblance to Jesus Christ.

I learned that several of the founders of A.A. were Christians and had Episcopal and Catholic priests as friends and advisers when they hammered out the Twelve Steps and the approach to God. I remembered Christ's words when he spoke about a man who was casting out demons but was not his follower, "Do not forbid him. . . . For he that is not against us is for us" (Mark 9:39–40). Jesus knew that the God the man was referring to was the same God, even though the man healing wasn't a follower of Jesus. He knew that God was alive and could do his healing work wherever he was called on in faith.

As my own years in the Twelve-Step program have gone by, I have found that my faith in God and Jesus Christ has been strengthened and made more real through working the steps. And this has been true for many people I know. Because people coming into the program almost always develop a great hunger to know more about God, many of them go to churches and become Christians. In the past three years more than twenty Twelve-Step meetings have begun to convene every week in our church. Many people have come from these meetings into membership classes to join our congregation.

In the last analysis, Jesus seemed to feel that it is *by their fruits* that you shall know them (Matt. 7:19). "Do they just talk about God, or do they change and deal with their diseased behaviors?" is the question.[5]

Restoration to Sanity

The second half of Step Two states that we came to believe that God (a Higher Power) "could restore us to sanity." It is very difficult for a person who is coping at all to accept the notion that he or she may in some way be "insane." What many of us said when first encountering Step Two was something like, "OK, you can say I have problems and I am powerless, but I am *not* insane." I've had people coming to Step Two tell me, "This step is obviously for people who are *really* insane. But because I have never even been treated by a psychiatrist, much less been in a padded cell or a mental institution, obviously this step doesn't apply to me." Although I am smiling as I write these words, I have to say, "Yes, it's true that Step Two is for those who are insane."

My dictionary says that being sane is "to be free from hurt or disease . . . having mental faculties in such condition as to be able to anticipate and judge the effects of one's actions." Another definition is "being without delusions or prejudice: free of ignorance: logical, rational, sensible." The primary synonym for sanity was "wise."[6] We need to gain humility enough to face that it's not natural or wise or "sane" to be in emotional turmoil all the time, to be fearful, anxious, resentful, or picky. This sort of turmoil results from our compulsive need to control, our Sin-disease. Unless we recognize that continuing this behavior in our lives is insane, we can't recover; we cannot really own our powerlessness.

One of the marks of people who come into Twelve-Step programs and see their denial crack open is a new awareness of the habitual recycling of irrational behaviors in their lives, of repeating self-defeating patterns, thoughts, and actions. As we go to meetings, we begin to become aware that we have had the same recurring painful problems, bruised relationships, and exaggerated feelings year after year. In meetings and talks with other Twelve-Step members we hear people identify these same behaviors as "insane" in their lives. We hear this especially as we start working Step Two.

I began to recall many habits that hurt me and other people and that I repeated for years without even being aware I was doing so (e.g., feeling resentment and fear, procrastinating, giving advice, dumping feelings, putting myself down when I made a mistake). I recalled repeatedly experiencing the negative results of these recurring self-defeating behaviors and thought patterns and being miserable each time, but I accepted the negative response by others to my unconscious abuse as being *their* fault. This was all a part of my "being surrounded by unreasonable, controlling, or imperfect people." I tried to be more thoughtful to them so they would change, but I didn't seriously consider doing anything about *my* most controlling, self-defeating behaviors—because I couldn't even see them for what they were: *my* Sin, *my* problems. So I was living out the program's definition of "insanity" by "doing things the same way and expecting different results."

For instance, someone important to me, whether I knew him or her well or not, would hurt me or embarrass me, make fun of me in some way. I'd go about my work and try to shrug it off, but then I would find resentment coming up like an alligator out of the swamp of my unconscious. I would wallow in the resentment for hours, sometimes for days.

I'd replay the unforgivable thing the person had done to me or plan revenge or punishment; all this would be going on while I was going about the everyday duties and habits of my life and work—sometimes even while I was preparing to give talks about Jesus Christ. But I didn't know *my resentment* was a problem. I thought the problem was what the other person had done to me. In the program I was told to turn loose my resentment. But my inner response to that was that I "wasn't going to let them off that easy"—even though the person who had hurt me might be out playing golf and not even aware of my resentment. I was in denial. I was repeating this process again and again; I could not stop the resentment that was destroying my peace of mind. Repeating this pattern was, I finally saw, not sane.

In other irrational ways I sabotaged my success and ruined a good career. I remember a time when my income was much more than twice my expenses, but I would wake up every morning fearful about my finances. I couldn't tolerate failure, and I couldn't stand success. As I look back I can see clearly that such behavior and thinking was hardly "sane."

Another thing I would do was worry for days about a decision one of my grown children was going to make, even though the "child" might be thirty years old, have earned at least two degrees, and be full of wisdom. That sort of behavior on my part, I saw, was not sane either.

If you believe your behavior is sane, that it is "wise, mentally sound, free from hurt and disease, without delusion or prejudice," then think further about your behavior. Do you have temper tantrums? Do you have any uncontrolled anger? Do you make the grand exit when you are angry? Do you use silence as a weapon with which to hurt people? Are you a compulsive talker?

Do you sleep too much? Are you not able to sleep, even though you are tired? Are you unable to get out of bed in the morning, even though you need to get up and do exercises that might save your life? Are you continually stressed? Do you continue to eat things like ice cream and candy when you need to lose weight for your health's sake?

Do you have excessive worries or fears? Do you drink or work to excess? Do you procrastinate, try to control people? Do you do any of these things in the face of the desire not to? And do you continue to have the illusion that you really are in control (or could get in control if you just "made up your mind to" and took the time)? Unless you can see the insanity of your thoughts and behavior, you may find it impossible to take Step Two and get in recovery.

The Personal Effects of Taking Step Two

When I came to Step Two I realized that although I was a committed Christian and I really believed in God, my problem was that in some very important respects I was living a frantic, highly stressed existence as a Christian professional speaker and writer. I knew that something was not right: I was teaching about grace and freedom, on the one hand, and my life was anxious, stressful, and overcommitted, on the other. But I was in denial and couldn't see how bizarre the contradiction was. People in this program have helped me to realize that anything I do or think that is destructive to me or to my relationships with other people or with God is a kind of insanity, especially when I keep doing it month after month.

I finally saw that to replace an all-loving, powerful, affirming, and wise God with my own self-centered and self-destructing will can certainly qualify in itself as an act of insanity.

After several years of living with a tiny minority of people in Twelve-Step groups I realize that it may be okay for others to live the way I was living my life, which was trying frantically to get control of my wife and children, my irrational behavior, and my success, but this is an insane and destructive way for *me* to operate. I don't want to live that way anymore, even if everybody does it, even if it is "normal."

As I saw and heard people share their pain and their reality in Twelve-Step groups, something happened to me at an unconscious level. At first I felt uneasy when they spoke about their "insanity." Then I could smile as I heard people tell about their own irrational way of continuing behavior that was obviously bizarre and "dumb." I shook my head and laughed as I realized that they were describing me as well as themselves. I saw that our painful craziness is normal and healthy for Twelve-Step people. My training in the Church did not prepare me for this sort of frankness. I had never really felt all right about being in the Church and still being so stressed and anxious, so crazy inside sometimes. I thought that the rest of the people I saw at church either had it all together somehow or were out of touch with their true feelings. They didn't seem to be subject to the stressful, frantic feelings that could come over me in the middle of the communion service or at home in prayer, the fears of not being able to cope with my relationships and of not being able to make people happy, no matter how hard I was truly trying to make them happy.

In the program I began to see that there are a lot of people, many of them Christians, who have this strange, stressful craziness. But in places where I have lived there has been a conspiracy of silence about such fearful feelings—especially in the Church. However, in Twelve-Step groups, such insane, self-defeating thoughts and behaviors lose their power as they are brought into the light. They are not secrets anymore. As people begin to share honestly, they are living in the light of the group's presence, and others start having the hope that maybe God can restore them to sanity. They have hope because they have seen that God is already restoring people in the program whom they know! The Christian expression of this phenomenon is, "If we walk in the light, as he [God] is in the light we have fellowship with one another" (1 John 1:7). It is in this fellowship in the light that we find freedom in Christ from our Sin.

As I indicated earlier, I finally felt enough pain and discouragement to go for help. I had tried to "think things through" and had used all my old techniques to "get things under control." I had blamed my problems on inadequate finances and started killing myself trying to make a better living. I had prayed for God's help both in vocational and financial ventures and for relief from the compulsive working and the pool of stress in which I was drowning. So I thought I'd tried Christ, tried God, and for some reason that hadn't worked.

But when I finally faced my powerlessness and the unmanageability of my life in Step One, I began to see that I had not been behaving in a rational, healthy way at all. I was working all the time, and although I was exhausted and had some uncomfortable emotional and physical symptoms, I kept working harder, hoping I'd get some sort of financial break that would bring me security and peace. I was lonely and confused and obviously needed help, yet not only did I *not* go for help, I tried to increase my control over those closest to me, telling them all what to do (even though I didn't know what to do myself). I made it almost impossible for them to give me the love and support I so desperately needed. Yet it was not until I finally admitted my powerlessness to fix my own life that I began to see the insanity of my thinking and my behavior with regard to others.

At that point my approach to God and my prayers changed from an attitude of "Please fix me financially and restore my relationships so I can have peace" to a belief that God could restore me to sanity if I would *live* the Twelve-Step program I was in.

At that point I had taken Step Two.

TAKING STEP TWO

Step Two

Came to believe that a Power greater
than ourselves could restore us to sanity.

If you are interested in proceeding with Step Two, the first act is to ask yourself if you are willing to believe in a Higher Power, a power greater than yourself that can help you. You may not be able to describe or put a name to the Higher Power (if you are a Christian you may have no problem with this), but the question here is, Because of what I have seen and heard from the people in this program who do believe and are becoming more nearly whole and free people, am I willing to accept the hypothesis that there is a Higher Power who can help me?

If the answer is yes, write out a statement to that effect in your notebook. This may sound simplistic and unnecessary, but in the Twelve Steps, thoughts that do not become objective actions don't seem to help much. Because I am a Christian, my own statement might read, "I, Keith Miller, am willing to believe in a Higher Power who can help me. For me, that Higher Power is the God of Jesus Christ."

Now you have taken the first half of Step Two. To continue, read and do what follows.

"Came to believe that a power greater than ourselves could *restore us to sanity.*" Below are listed some behaviors that do not fit the dictionary definition of sanity: "to be free from hurt or disease; having mental faculties in such condition as to be able to anticipate and judge the effects of your actions on other people" and "being without delusions or prejudices . . . 'wise.'"

If you want to finish taking Step Two, describe briefly or give an example of how the following, and other dysfunctional and self-defeating behaviors, operate in your life (asking how "sane" these behaviors are).

1. In what areas (i.e., personal, vocational, faith, etc.) do you have recurring fears that aren't grounded in sound evidence?

2. Whom do you continue to resent periodically or constantly, and how does your resentment manifest itself? How does it feel?

3. What self-defeating behaviors do you continue to engage in even though it is not in your best interests to continue (e.g., overeating, using drugs or alcohol, entering destructive relationships, gambling, compulsive talking, procrastination, etc.)?

4. Give examples of decisions you have made or things you have done that were "crazy"—that is, things you did even though you knew the consequences could be harmful to you (personal/sexual, financial, relational, emotional, etc.).

5. Give examples of not getting help when you needed it (e.g., medical/dental care or help with compulsive-addictive problems, control-Sin-relationship problems, etc.).

When you see that your self-defeating behavior is insane and you believe that a Higher Power (God) can restore you to sanity, it is helpful to write it out. My statement might be, "I can see that my self-defeating behavior and my refusal to get help to change what I am doing is a form of insanity, and I believe that God can restore me to sanity."

Write your statement in your own words.

You have now taken Step Two.

Chapter 4

STEP THREE

*Made a Decision to Turn Our Will
and Our Lives Over to the Care of
God as We Understood Him*

Biblical expressions of the principles
of Step Three:

*You shall love the Lord your God with all
your heart, and with all your soul, and with
all your mind, and with all your strength.
Mark 12:30*

*. . . they left the boat and their father,
and followed him. Matthew 4:22*

Most thinking people have enormous resistance to turning any significant control of their lives over to *anyone,* even God. Why is this?

The Big Book describes the alcoholic's most basic problem not as alcohol but as self-centeredness and the need to control. The picture given is of an actor trying be producer and director of the whole show, trying to direct all the other actors, telling everybody what to do, how they should say their lines and play their parts. Such a person might be intelligent and even gracious, the book goes on to say, but people get angry because they don't want someone else to tell them how to play their parts, especially just another actor. So as the angry people resist, the controller tries harder to direct their lives. Only now the controller is baffled and angry, unable to see his or her actions as controlling but instead seeing them only as attempts to help the other actors do their parts as they *should* be done, that is, as the controller thinks they should be done (p. 62).

People coming into the Christian faith are told that they need to surrender their lives to Jesus as Savior, to renounce all sinful desires that draw them from the love of God, to put their whole trust in his grace and love and to follow and obey him as Lord. (See the baptismal commitment in the *Book of Common Prayer,* p. 312.) But I don't remember ever being told as a new Christian that my desire to control the people, places, and things in my life constituted Sin and was part of that surrender to Jesus Christ (unless my actions were immoral in some specifically enumerated way). So although I committed my life to Jesus and later asked God to fill my life with the Holy Spirit, it never occurred to me that I might be very sinful and get my life all snarled up by trying to "help" everyone (that is, get them to live the way I thought they should). And there was no Christian discipline in the groups to which I belonged that showed me how to face the control issues of my Sin-disease.[1]

So I became a "caring Christian" committed to Jesus Christ, and I continued to be a manipulative controller without even knowing I was doing it, much less that some of the helping/controlling was abusive, self-centered (I needed to fix them so I'd feel all right), and sinful (putting myself in the center where only God should be and orchestrating other people's lives—including those of Christians in church programs).

Since my book *Hope in the Fast Lane: A New Look at Faith in a Compulsive World* came out, I have had many Christians tell me that they too are miserable because of their unconsciously controlling ways and other people's reactions to them. They report discovering in themselves a determination to direct the lives of the people around them. When their loved ones won't cooperate and see the light—the controller's light—things get worse. Finally, if the controllers are fortunate, they see that they are powerless to change anyone and that their whole life has become unmanageable and confused—though they may be deeply committed Christians—even ordained ministers.

Christians who are frustrated and blocked by their denied Sin despite their conscious commitment to God and Christ need a way to bring their control tendencies to God so they can be freed, find reconciliation and serenity, and get on with growing spiritually in Christ. If they discover a Twelve-Step program and take Steps One and Two, they are told that the way to unsnarl this tangle of worms and to get well from this disease is to make a decision to turn their "entire lives and wills" over to God, to let God be the producer, director, and healer of their lives and the lives of others around them.

Surrender? No Way!

But this idea of surrendering, of releasing authority and control of outcomes to another, is a very difficult notion for thinking persons. Not only does surrendering go against all our childhood injunctions to "do it yourself" and "don't give up," but as long as we can keep our minds churning, we can keep from facing and understanding our own part in causing our painful feelings. Some Christians have additional difficulty at this point because they think they already understand this process thoroughly and have already *done* Step Three: committed their lives and their wills to God. But there is a strange paradox here.

Evidently some people try to control even the processes of healing by "understanding" them. I am one of these. But this so-called understanding is often a way to avoid *experiencing* the emotional meanings and release involved. Paul Stern, a psychiatrist at Harvard University, said twenty-five years ago that the most difficult defense to overcome in therapy is "intellectualization," that is, attempting to control therapy by analyzing our problems and articulating the reasons for them.[2] Therefore, a person who thinks he or she really understands how Step Three works may have greater difficulty actually *taking* the step. And many of us Christians fall into that category, thinking we have made a commitment to God already through Christ because we have "said the words" of commitment. We tend to think that because we have thought it or said it, we have done it. But if this were true, Christians certainly wouldn't worry about the future, our finances, or our families, the way some of us do.

The Belief That God Is Supposed to Do Our Will—A Stumbling Block to Surrender

There is another stumbling block for Christians approaching Step Three. Many Christians live their lives as if God is *their* servant and will help them attain their goals. They believe that when we pray, "Lord, help me to do this thing (whatever it is)," he will do it if the request is moral and not aimed at harming another. I evidently believed this for years, and I would get very angry with God when he didn't show up and do the thing I prayed for—especially if it was a prayer for someone else. But that sort of praying and living is very different from "turning my life and my will over to God."

Some people try to do Step Three this way, as if God runs some sort of "emergency crew" we can call on when all else fails or when our control of a specific situation or person starts slipping. We say, "God gave me all these abilities, and I'm going to do what I can to solve each problem first. I'll turn my problem over to him after I have done all that I can." There is a truth in that approach that is helpful. We try to solve a problem, but can't; then we turn the problem over to God. I had always used this approach in one form or another until recently. And often that kind of surrender *will* bring release. Any time you turn things over to God, the *process* of doing so can clear your head. Often you can then walk through some sticky situation and get the problem solved.

As we continue to try first, fail, then go to God for help, we begin to develop real faith, because going through this process does work to release things and turn them over to God. But then, after a while, a change takes place. You work hard on a problem, a compulsion, or a relationship, and you turn the problem over to God and go back to work on it. But this time you fail to be able to either solve the problem or turn it over to him, and the release doesn't come!

As I began to look at this unexamined prayer process, I could see that I'd gotten things all turned around. I hadn't been turning my *life* and my *will* over to God at all—except in some general, abstract way. I had been making use of God as a sort of cosmic employee to help me do what I had already decided needed doing—which was *my* will for other people and myself.

A Christian entrepreneur with this way of praying might get into a business deal, for example. The businessperson puts together a team to get the deal done: an accountant, a lawyer, a tax adviser, a banker, and God—and uses them in that order. When everyone else has done his or her part, the team captain calls on God to come through with the victory: the business goal of the entrepreneur. The bottom line is that the entrepreneur is telling God what to do.

Many of us are in denial, and our lives have been so messed up that we don't know God's will, so when we're asking him to bless ours we aren't even aware that that is what we are doing. In our denial we have the honest delusion that we are praying for his will. And we get very discouraged when, for instance, a sick child dies after we have prayed for the child to live; or we get very angry at God and full of pain when somebody leaves us after we have prayed that they wouldn't, regardless of our part in their going. God's sort of sporadic answering and refusing to answer our prayers can be very confusing to a Christian. It is especially confusing when God does not choose to answer pleas to get one out of an addiction or to heal a bruised marriage relationship or to bring home a runaway or alienated child.

What Kind of Surrender and Prayer Does God Desire from Us?

It's as if when the pain, failure, and alienation caused by our Sin-disease and denial have gone so far, God has to show us the extent of our repressed need to control—even him—by not answering prayers that would *not* lead us to recovery but only back into trying to control our lives. A classic illustration is the alcoholic male who prays to learn to "drink like a gentleman" so he doesn't have to stop drinking and be cured of his underlying control disease. In our Sin and denial many of us have unwittingly made God the agent for our will to heal us in *our* way (so we can still be in control). But through the Twelve Steps God shows us that his way is for us to learn to do his will and to quit striving for control, to let him heal us and deal with our lives and relationships *his* way.

And the first three steps constitute the beginning of a lifelong turning process in which we change the direction of our lives from the way we think they should go (in our stress and Sin) to the way God thinks they should go, in serenity, humility, and loving obedience to his will as we can begin to determine it beyond our denial. Traditionally Christians have called this change of direction conversion. But unfortunately the absolutely revolutionary nature of the change called for in conversion has often been lost, and new Christians are not taught the extent of their Sin and denial. Therefore, after a Christian honeymoon period new Christians often unknowingly continue to try to get God to do their will by the way they pray and worship him. And they get very discouraged, and sometimes leave the Church, when they don't get "answers to their prayers." The problem is that many of us are operating with a twisted view of the nature of God.

Firing Old Gods and
Embracing a New God

One day I heard a new man in the program talking to an old-timer about the Third Step. The new man said, "No way I'm going to turn my life over to God! He'd ruin me—and I'd deserve it." He went on to say that for him God was a giant policeman, and the man's life had been such that his experience with the police was not at all positive.

The old-timer, a strong, quiet man, listened to the new man's description of God and then in all seriousness said, "You ought to fire that God; you ought to fire him! You've got the wrong God for this program, friend. The God who operates here is loving, forgiving, and gives you all the chances you need to get the program; he is honest and will always be there for you. I had a God like yours when I first came in here, but I had to fire him and get me a new God."

"What can I do about a God if I fire mine?" the new man asked.

The old-timer thought a minute. "Well," he said, "you can use mine till you get on your feet."

All my theological buzzers went off. I thought, *"Fire God!* We're dealing with Ultimate Reality here, friends. You just can't *fire* God and get a new one!" But I kept my mouth shut and listened, and I learned another one of the many humbling lessons that I have learned while working the Twelve Steps.

As I walked away from that meeting I was thinking about what the gnarled old-timer had said about "firing God." I thought, "Fire God, indeed! Maybe I ought to leave this program. I can't stay here and listen to that." Then I began thinking about what the old-timer had *meant*. And I realized that after thirty years of being a speaker, eight years of graduate school, most of it in theology, being on the staff of a seminary, and later a writer about God, *I* needed to do exactly what that man had suggested so colorfully. *I needed to fire God!* At least, I needed to fire my concept of a God who promises he will be with you and then really doesn't come when you count on him. I needed to fire the God who says he loves you but is gone out of town or too tired to show up and teach you to be a man and teach you how to grow up. No wonder I didn't want to turn my life and will over to God, because that was my unconscious operational image of God—an image I realized was a picture of my human father as I experienced him, not the God of the Bible at all. My father had not been there for me when I felt I really needed him as a little boy. And I (like most people) had not understood that my relationship with an imperfect human parent was the unconscious foundation on which I had built a wonderful theology of Grace. So even though I consciously believed God would take care of my financial security and my family, my stomach churned with fear and doubt when they were threatened.

When I came to this step I thought I had already surrendered because I'd verbally given God control of my life; I was confused. I said, "There's something wrong here, because I've done this 'turning my life and my will over to God' in church, in evangelical meetings, and now I'm supposed to do this again in a Twelve-Step program?" Yet somewhere inside I knew my faith was not working. I could not seem to stop overcommitting and working all the time, and I was compulsive in many areas of my life. And yet I prayed every day for relief and change. I could not understand why my prayers were not being answered, because I knew I'd be able to serve God better if my compulsive and addictive behavior were stopped. I was baffled; I believed, had faith, yet was frantic and evidently didn't trust God at all with the important things in my life, because I was worried about them all the time. Yet I still resisted surrendering my life and my will to God.

The Personal Effects of Taking Step Three

Because of my lack of trust I'd been trapped in the "control" disease. If *I* didn't control my family, my finances, my intimate relationships, God might. I might fail or live a modest life or lose my family. And although I consciously wanted to let God teach me and help me, the idea of surrendering my life and my will to him in these areas was really anxiety provoking. So I fired that God who was made in the image of my father and decided to believe in the God I saw living in the lives of recovering people in the Twelve-Step program, a God who operated exactly like the God of Jesus Christ in the Bible. At that point I made a decision to turn my life and my will over to the care of this God, and that "turning over to God" included my codependence and the bruised childhood from which it came.[3]

A strange thing has happened to me as I've kept going to meetings and working the program. I am being renewed in my faith in Christ, and I am also being reparented by some of the people in those Twelve-Step rooms who have loved me and been there for me through some of the hardest days of my life. I've gradually begun to trust a "new" God. Of course, it's not a new God at all, it's the God of the Bible, but it's a new God for me inside, a God who loves me and *is* there for me, who's honest and dependable and cares enough to confront my denial and my lies and my subtle attempts to get everybody to do it my way. Now the God of my emotional spiritual reality and the God of my head are much more the same. I see this God as being more dependable; I feel that I can trust him with my future while I seek his will today.

Several years ago when I began this Twelve-Step journey, I was afraid of many things, and my fears have subsided. Some of them may be back tomorrow, but that doesn't frighten me now, because I have some effective tools and caring support with which to face them.

How to Take Step Three

How do you take this step? It says, "Made a decision to turn our will and our lives over to the care of God as we understood him." Although that sounds like a simple statement, there is a lot of controversy about what it means. The writers of the step were wise and gentle, as Jesus was. He let people walk away and wait until they were ready to come to him, and this program does that too, at each step. But when you are ready, some people say that you just *do it* right then—turn your life and will over to God!

But other people say "making a decision" to do something is only the first part of doing it. For example, if I make a decision to buy a house, I haven't bought the house yet, and I certainly can't move in this afternoon. There are a series of things I must do after making a decision to buy a house before I have actually bought it. I have to find a house, get a realtor, a lawyer, a banker, check taxes, check a certificate of title, and do all kinds of other things. Then finally, at the end of the process, I've bought the house, and I'm living in it. In taking Step Three, if you make a decision to turn your will and life over to God, you're *deciding*. You're committing to "buy the house." You're committed to turning your life and your will over to God. But you haven't completed the transaction when you say the words of commitment.

Contrary to my early Christian training, the *words* of decision do *not* get one's whole life and will turned over to God. When I was told this in the program, and I realized it was true—otherwise why would I spend so much of my time trying to get control—I asked my sponsor, "If saying the words doesn't turn my will and my life over to God, how do I do it?" He smiled and said, "That's what Steps Four through Twelve are: the way to turn our whole lives—past, future, and present—over to God. Christians often do what we call the 'Twelve-Step Waltz': One, Two Three, One Two, Three, One, Two, Three. They see that they need God, see that their lives aren't working, and they commit their lives to Christ, again and again. But," my sponsor paused and said thoughtfully, "not many of them go on to get spiritually well. They just keep making verbal commitments of their lives to Christ. Thank God we have the steps to keep growing spiritually!"

Once you decide to give your life and will to him, the other steps are designed to remove the blocks, the things that keep you from surrendering your bruised, self-defeating past and becoming that person God made you to be. Steps Four through Twelve slowly reveal to you the things that have always kept you from being happy and free, from having good boundaries, from being creative and loving, and from doing God's will, and they show you how to surrender these things to God.

My experience is that doing Step Three involves a paradox. After I decided to turn my life and will over to God, I asked my sponsor what to do next. He suggested that I look around in my life and simply "do the next right thing," whatever that might be. I was reminded of the wonderful Zen saying, "After enlightenment, draw water, chop wood." The next right thing for a parent might be to buy one of your children some needed clothes. If so, you would go shopping with the understanding that you are trying to do this the way God would have you do it. At first most of us really didn't know how to do things differently, but in taking Step Three we opened our minds to the possibility that God would let us know—and that we didn't have to have all the answers. Gradually we are becoming more teachable, instead of being people who already know the answers. So we may buy the clothes the same way we always have, or we may get an idea about the kinds of clothes we buy our children or the way we relate to them while we are buying their clothes. But we become aware that we are trying to turn our whole lives and our wills over to God and do all things the way he would have us do them.

As I go through each part of my day, something may begin to "nudge" me, to tell me what to do next. If I'm in doubt about where the nudge is coming from (God or my disease), I ask my sponsors or bring it up in a meeting. We attend meetings, then go out to try to live what the program says. Then we carry the group in our minds with us (the communion of saints, in Christian terms). We begin to carry in our minds a group of people who have been living this out longer than we have. When a situation comes up, we remember that Fred talked about it, and we ask ourselves, "How would Fred do this?" The communion of saints is all about this—a cloud of witnesses, people of faith who have traveled ahead of us through life helping us know the mind of God. (See Hebrews 11 and 12:1.) Carlyle Marney called these spiritual companions our "balcony people."[4] I suppose a good sponsor is a little like a "guardian angel" God gives us to watch over us as we work the steps.

We begin to know the mind of God as we begin to live with him and see other people doing the same. As we see them learn in specific situations what God's will is like, we begin to understand how God may work in our own lives and what his will may be in more and more specific instances. I don't understand exactly how it works, but after you are around people who are trying to live for God for a while, you automatically begin to do things differently, and the loving, caring and honest results tell you, and others, with reasonable clarity whether it is probably God's will or your own disease you're following.

TAKING STEP THREE

Note to the Reader: If you have decided to work the Twelve Steps and are contemplating doing Step Three, it is very important to realize that if you give up controlling those around you, one or more of them may step into the power void and attempt to control you. Because this is often true, it is important to learn about how you may develop healthy "boundaries" to protect yourself from being controlled and to keep you from inadvertently controlling others.

I have described what boundaries are and how they may be used to help one in recovery in appendix B, and I suggest that if you are working the Twelve Steps, you stop and read that material before taking Step Three.

Step Three

Made a decision to turn our will and our lives
over to the care of God as we understood him.

A Look at Your Own Background

1. Can you remember being given the following kinds of messages? "Take care of yourself." "Don't bother other people with your problems." "Don't give up." If so, describe the way you remember getting those "do it by yourself" messages. What were the circumstances?

2. What do you feel when you consider really putting your life and your will, your whole future, in God's hands? (Describe your feelings about doing this.)

3. What are the specific fears that come to mind when you consider taking Step Three? What might happen to you? What might God do to you? (Or what natural consequences might God allow to happen if you "give up control"?)

4. (Read appendix B concerning boundaries.) What kinds of boundaries did your parents help you develop (none, damaged, walls, or

intact)? Describe the way you experience boundaries or lack of boundaries in your relationships.

5. Can you believe that God can help you develop healthy boundaries if you turn your life and your will over to him? (If you happen to have been raised in a church that violated your boundaries you will want to distinguish between turning your life over to God and turning your life over to the Church.)

6. Can you see how turning your life and your will over to God could help you say no to people and circumstances that are not good for you? (Give examples regarding your family, vocation, social life, and personal growth and development.)

God as I Understand Him

1. Can you think of areas in which you do not trust God (e.g., finances, family matters, intimate needs)? List them here.

2. Can you see the roots of any of these areas of fear and lack of trust in your childhood relationship with parents? Describe these beginnings, if possible.[5]

If after doing this exercise, you feel uneasy, you may want to discuss the things you discovered with your sponsor or a counselor. This exercise is not to try to blame anyone for anything but to see if your fear of surrendering may have its root in a skewed view of God, an unconscious identification of him with your imperfect parents (and all parents are imperfect).

3. Have you used God as a servant to do things you ask for and been disappointed when he hasn't done them? Give some examples if possible.

Making the Decision!

If you have already made a commitment of your life to God or Christ, are you ready now to put your life and your will in his hands to do the changing you'll need to do to defeat the compulsive and painful results of the Sin-disease in your life? If you are ready to make this decision, here is the commitment prayer from the Big Book (p. 63) that has served as a model for many people:

"God, I offer myself to Thee—to build with me and do with me as Thou wilt. Relieve me of the bondage of self, that I may better do Thy will. Take away my difficulties, that victory over them may bear witness to those I would help of Thy Power, Thy love, and Thy way of life. May I do Thy will always."

If you are ready to make this decision you may want to write out your own commitment prayer, or if the prayer from the Big Book says it for you, memorize it, copy it, or make it your own by changing or adding to it in any ways that feel right for your situation.

Chapter 5

PREPARING TO TAKE STEP FOUR

Made a Searching and Fearless Moral Inventory of Ourselves

A biblical expression of the need to deal with our inventory material:

If we say we have no sin, we deceive ourselves, and the truth is not in us. If we confess our sins, he is faithful and just, and will forgive our sins and cleanse us from all unrighteousness. 1 John 1:8–9

(Also) *Rend your hearts and not your garments. Joel 2:13*

What we have done in the first three steps is to get in touch with God in a way that allows us to access *his* power in overcoming Sin and its consequences in our lives.

In Step Three we decided to get out of the driver's seat and move ahead into the rest of the Twelve Steps with the protection and guidance of God; we are now willing to risk stepping out of the self-centered Sin position and inspecting our Sin-diseased personalities. This prospect is so unsettling that most of us would only do it to find relief from the intense pain brought on by our character defects that have been such troublesome mysteries to us and to our families.

Working Step Four can be the beginning of lasting character changes. We've committed our life and our will to God to the extent we can, and now we are going to clean house spiritually to find out why we are at war within ourselves and with the people close to us. By doing the next few steps we can uncover denied Sin-behaviors and character defects that have blocked our spiritual growth. This same Sin is at the root of our dishonesty and our critical, intolerant spirit and our exaggerated feelings of anger, guilt, self-pity, pain, shame, grandiosity, and jealousy. I never saw that these inner problems were what were making me miserable. They were just "invisible" discomforts that other people sometimes saw and were affected by but that I couldn't isolate as being problems caused by *my* behavior and attitudes.

How Steps One, Two, and Three Prepare Us for Step Four

Now, if seeking out your character defects seems a bit too much to you, it may be because you are not troubled with the Sin-disease. But because of denial, the character defects we have trouble identifying in ourselves or that cause us to be angry when people suggest that they may be ours are often the very ones we need to concentrate on.

If you honestly took Steps One, Two, and Three, yet don't feel you have any serious problems to list in Step Four, you may be experiencing a strong case of denial or delusion. If you take Steps One, Two, and Three and then say, "I don't need Step Four," you may do well to ask yourself why you decided you were powerless in Step One. Why is your life unmanageable? Why do you need to offer it all to God so he can help you? You might ask yourself why you "are so bothered by the speck in your brother's eye"; such projections point to our own denial. Usually there are some semiconscious habits or some behaviors bothering us that keep us controlled and powerless. We may have fleeting memories of being critical, or of eating desserts when we promised ourselves we wouldn't, or of committing to read the Bible every day and neglecting to do so.

The fourth Step tells us how to begin to get at the specific character defects that cripple us, the character defects that because of denial we have trouble even seeing as ours.

A Moral Inventory

Imagine you are transferring the ownership of your life to God in the same way you would transfer ownership of a business. One of the first things you would do in negotiating to sell a business would be to take an inventory to discover the damaged or out-of-date goods that are no longer salable. In Step Four we call it a "moral" inventory because we compile a list of traits and behaviors that have transgressed our highest, or moral, values. We also inventory our "good" traits and the behaviors that represent them. In our life's moral inventory the defects or dysfunctional behaviors might include some that once worked; some dysfunctional behaviors may have saved our lives as children, but they are now out-of-date, self-defeating, and cause us a great deal of trouble when we use them as adults.

For example, throwing tantrums or "hitting" may have produced the desired result when you were three, but these tactics do not work so well when you are thirty. Maybe you were really good at flirting when you were sixteen; maybe it got you lots of attention and affirmation and made you popular. But now as a parent with three children, you find flirting creates problems in your marriage. Most of us don't realize that we are still doing many such self-defeating things that keep leading us into painful situations and complicating our attempts to control other people, ourselves, and God. In our Step Four inventories, we see, besides these self-defeating behaviors, specific abusive things we have done to be listed and described.

The second part of the inventory is to find the useful things, the good or positive traits that strengthen us in this new life. At first I thought an inventory was only about damaged or out-of-date material. But as some of us began to look at our own lives, we found a whole new sense of creativity emerging and an ability to risk trying our creative wings. We found some *good* character traits emerging.

Some of us are learning a new kind of assertiveness in our intimate relationships. In the past we had not been very direct and then got mad if you didn't guess what we wanted. We are learning to say what we want and to risk the rejection of somebody saying, "Well, that's not what I want." Others, who have been bossy and inattentive, are learning to listen to people and not "straighten them out." Learning such things is normally part of a child's growing up. But nobody ever taught us how to live without manipulating. We learned how to "perform" and "win" but not how to live honestly. For example, I thought it was more polite to hint about my needs or wants in a subtle way so that people could "guess" them and give me what I wanted without my having to ask directly. The healthy way of "asking for what I want" was considered rude and ineffective.

Setting out to do this inventory is not always simple. Lurking at every turn on this adventure is denial—a dark cloud that comes over us and blinds us to certain things about ourselves and what we do or have done. Therefore most of us have approached Step Four by actually listing what we could see about our character defects and our good points, which may have been very little. But as we become willing to own each item, our awareness grows, and gradually more and more of our inventory becomes known to us.

The rest of the chapter gives nine guidelines that many people have found helpful while working on Step Four.

Guideline 1
Understand the Purposes of Step Four

I believe that preparing to take Step Four begins with understanding the purposes of this step. With better understanding comes increased motivation for doing it honestly and thoroughly. There are at least three important purposes to Step Four that I can see:

- To acquire deeper self-knowledge that can lead (by continuing in the Twelve Steps) to self-acceptance and even self-love
- To face the truth about our behavior
- To identify our behavior patterns so that we are prepared to surrender them and ask God to act in our behalf to make lasting changes in us

To Acquire Deeper Self-Knowledge. Step Four leads us into an adventure of self-discovery, as we begin to know and love the person we are underneath all the outward image and acquired trappings. We can now take the risk of seeing our negative aspects because we have decided to believe that God (along with some perceptive people) has accepted us in our self-centered powerlessness. This experience of self-acceptance begins to change our view of God, who we see as being more accessible when we face our hidden issues openly.

To Face the Truth About Our Behavior. The Sin-disease creates emotional and spiritual barnacles that collect inside us and infect our character with rationalizations and deceit, crippling our lives and relationships. These emotional barnacles are caused by behaviors in the past, and even though we may have forgotten them, if we don't deal with them, they "stay alive" and affect us and our present relationships in an insidious way. It is almost as if we are doomed to compulsively repeat our harmful habits until we *notice* what we have been doing and face the truth about our behavior.

The Sin-disease causes us to see our relationships and behavior through a self-justifying lens. We may either think the problems in our lives are all outside ourselves and that it is other people who keep hurting and abusing us (perhaps by rejecting our well-meaning attempts to help them), or we may take the polar opposite view and think that *we* are the sole cause of *all* our problems and in our grandiosity believe we are the most awful and most sinful of people. In both cases, denial and the Sin-disease are in charge. Neither those who see others' problems as causing their own nor those who believe that they themselves cause all the problems can find the true source of their misery.

In his book *Letting God,* Philip Parham says that many young teenage criminals can't see that they have done anything wrong.[1] They see the problems as being in society and other people. Until they can see that they themselves have committed a crime, they feel almost no guilt and can't be helped. And until *we* can see what we've done, we can't be forgiven and reconciled with society or the people around us.

Through Step Four, God gives us a method for beginning to revitalize our twisted conscience. We begin to see the truths about ourselves that the world and the Church see but either cannot or will not reveal to us. This step leads us to the truth that can make us free that Christ was talking about (John 8:32).

To Identify Patterns.   A third purpose of Step Four is to begin to identify the patterns in our behavior. The Twelve and Twelve (pp. 42f.) and the Big Book (pp. 64f.) offer a structure for sorting through these behaviors that we will follow in taking Step Four in the next chapter. They cite three basic human needs or instincts that affect our happiness: (1) the sexual instinct, relations that affect our manhood or womanhood with regard to sex, (2) financial and emotional security, the need for sufficient money and the emotional security of a personal place in life, and (3) the social instinct, or the need for companionship.

These three basic instinctual drives would make us happy if we just experienced them in a reasonable way: if we were satisfied with a moderate sex life that was satisfactory for us and for someone with us or with getting a reasonable amount of affection as a man or woman, if we tried to make only a moderate living, and if we tried to be only a person among people. But when we have put ourselves instead of God at the center of our lives, we begin to behave in distorted ways with regard to these instincts.

When my inflated instincts collide with somebody else's, and we both want something strongly, we've got automatic war and serious emotional problems. The same sort of warfare breaks out inside us when we do things that go against our highest values in order to satisfy our swollen instincts. As A.A. declares in the Twelve and Twelve, "Nearly every serious emotional problem can be seen as a case of misdirected instinct" (p. 42), a case of trying to control more than our share of life's goodies. When others want what we consider to be more than their share, we are likely to feel anger, frustration, or depression; we may then either attack them or use addictive or compulsive behavior to try to cover our pain. The residue of these collisions of instincts is often resentment and fear.

The Big Book also points out that these two character trait manifestations (resentment and fear) are apparently universal. They follow collisions of instincts and cause most of the trouble for people in working the steps. These two traits are the most destructive "barnacles" in lives of people who come to Twelve-Step programs. Resentment, as I am using the term, is different from anger. Normal anger is a healthy response to threat or abuse. It mobilizes our strength for fighting or legitimate defense. But resentment is anger focused on punishing the offender or getting revenge—and it usually includes continuing emotionally loaded fantasies of doing so.

How These Swollen Instincts Push Us into Control.   As our thinking about our needs becomes distorted, we try to get what we want when we want it—and that necessitates gaining control. Trying to satisfy inflated natural desires creates the character defects and the misery that eventually may lead us to powerlessness—if we are fortunate. I say that we are "fortunate" to arrive at a sense of powerlessness because it is only the admission of powerlessness that leads us into the spiritual healing found inside the Twelve-Step program.

Guideline 2
Expect to Rely on a Higher Power to Do Step Four

The theory is that once we see that we are not God and cannot change the people, places, and things in our lives to control our happiness, we may also understand that in fact we are powerless to heal our spiritual sickness and "make things right" for everyone—including ourselves. And when we know that we can't "solve" this Sin problem, we are told that as we offer our lives and our will to God and begin to work the steps, then our denial begins to recede and we receive God's power and God's insight to do Step Four's searching and fearless moral inventory. Richard Grant once reminded me that for Christians it has always been important when walking out on the waters of the unconscious to keep our eyes on Jesus and not simply on the "violence of the wind and the waves," or we will sink like Peter and stop the process of recovery. This advice has helped me stay focused on God's power to hold us up as we enter this frightening space.

In taking Step Four we begin the process by which our swollen basic instincts are restored to an uninflated, healthy level, and we leave behind grandiose and greedy behavior for lives led with serenity, sanity, and happiness. First we examine our lives in the three basic areas (sexuality, security, and social needs). Most of us are never taught what is appropriate in any objective sense in these areas. We either adopt our parents' values uncritically or rebel and turn 180 degrees away from their views. In neither case do we learn what "normal" might be. While doing Step Four, we become conscious of the values and behaviors we have been controlled by in these areas. We can now see some of our swollen instincts and the dysfunctional aspects of our behavior and make new choices as we move on through the Twelve Steps.[2]

Guideline 3
Feel Your Feelings as You Go

How do we deal with all the pain and guilt that might come up if we write an inventory? I've heard many people say, "Well, I really need to do Step Four, but every time I write, I start crying." And some people do start crying. They start writing, and they wallow in the pain because they are already depressed.

But it is very helpful to realize that you are doing Step Four with your sponsor as a guide and supporter and within the context of a group of people who have already done it or are in the process of doing it, and it is wonderfully reassuring to know that they have encountered the pain and survived, that they have found serenity on the other side of the pain and fear. People often come to Twelve-Step meetings in tears one week and a week later look radiant. You can see why the expression "born again" came into the Christian experience as the early Christians saw all of life with new eyes. It *is* like a new life. In working the steps, the new-life experience happens again and again in different areas of life and at different levels of spiritual awareness.

Guideline 4
Get the Support of a Sponsor

If you haven't found a sponsor yet, I strongly recommend making that the next item on your agenda; you should do it before you start seriously working on Step Four (see appendix A). Most people who have taken this step report that they don't think they could have done it without the support of their sponsor.

A sponsor can help with the pain that sometimes comes up as denial recedes during certain steps. He or she can assure you that you're no worse than anyone else. Your sponsor helps by telling you things he or she has done that are similar to those you are discovering. People who think they are World's Champion Sinners often believe they have more resentment, guilt, or shame than anyone else. The sponsor may say, "Listen, let me tell you about resentment," and tells about his or her own. And the person taking Step Four may then realize, "I'm *not* the worst person that ever drew breath," and get some balance. As a matter of fact, one of the great discoveries of the program for me has been that I'm not all that different from other people. I'm not weird and strange and a special case who's hard to "cure." In fact, I am a regular sinner who is special because God loves me, but my pain and fears are very similar to everyone else's. *What a relief!*

Guideline 5
Attend Meetings Regularly

Let's imagine you came into a Twelve-Step program feeling isolated and filled with fear and resentment. But in meetings people welcome you and begin to listen to you and trust you, and you hear men and women revealing past and present behavior and feelings, behavior and feelings more shameful or fearful than yours. You take the first three steps.

You begin to notice that the other people in the group face the same resentment and fear that you do, because these are things that come up in meetings on Step Four. As you see other people coming out free and serene when they have taken the fourth Step you may realize that someone with your problems is forgivable. You may say to yourself, "Wait a minute, I could forgive this person, and he (or she) is like me. I see that Jesus was right when he indicated that everybody is sick with the Sin-disease, not just me." This insight changes the whole problem of doing Step Four. As Paul put it, "All have sinned and fall short of the glory of God" (Rom. 3:23). This awareness that we are all in a similar boat gives us the security and courage to sail into the frightening waters where others have gone.

And one day *you* begin to share in a meeting things you have done that hurt people around you. As you share and watch the people's faces who hear you, you realize more fully that this fearful, shameful reality is only evidence of your humanity, that you are *not* worse than other people. Gradually you become convinced that God can indeed forgive you and clear up your life, that you can find rest and peace within yourself as well as with the people around you.

Often as we listen during meetings we also gain insights into new kinds of "hidden" behavior that we can add to our growing list of material about ourselves that is our Step Four inventory.

Guideline 6
Banish the Myth That You Should Have Been Perfect

I believe that shame and guilt come up during Step Four because we think, "I am a bad person, and somehow I should have been able to avoid these sins and be perfect on my own." But eventually we realize that if we are "sinners," there are thousands of us in the program and in the Church, and it's great to be home again where Christ reigns over recovering sinners. We've not only joined the human race; we've joined Christ's people. And when you have accepted your humanity in Step Four, the rest of the steps teach you what to do to deal with the garbage of your past and the guilt and shame connected to it.

Guideline 7
Resist the Urge to Focus on What Others Have Done to You

As you begin your inventory you may find yourself focusing a great deal on all the things people did to hurt you. You may have a strong desire to go tell them what they've done to you. You may say, "Well, I have done this, but he (or she) has done that." The list about the other person will often be longer than the one about you.

But as my sponsor told me, I am doing *my* inventory, not anyone else's. It was hard for me to resist justifying myself; everything in me wanted to make sure everyone knew that "anyone would have done the 'bad' things I did under the circumstances." I finally saw that self-justification is one of my major character defects and is part of my need to control other people's opinions of me so I can be "right."

But I was told that to get well spiritually our job is to set aside our resentful feelings about "them" in order to get *our* side of the street cleaned (which is all we are responsible for). If while doing your inventory you get stuck on a particular resentment, you might just say, "I am going to set this resentment aside for now and finish this inventory. I will do my resenting later." Use any way you can to get through it.

Guideline 8
Write Your Inventory on Paper

I strongly recommend that you write each item on paper. Some people have wondered, "Why write it down? Can't God read my mind?" But to get healed through the Twelve-Step process we must *see* and *own* our character defects and our sins. I believe God already knows what they are and has known all along. This exercise is to help us break free from our own denial and to begin to become responsible. Making a list of our sins is a good way to start this process. It's harder to deny your sins and defects after you have written them on a list.

Guideline 9
Don't Rush; Step Four Takes Time

There are many phases to the process of writing Step Four. Sometimes people find that they're not ready to begin because they haven't really done Step Two: they have not really come to believe that God can do anything about their problems. Or perhaps they haven't really made a clear decision to trust God with their lives in Step Three. Other people need some time—weeks to months—to think about their lives, to listen at meetings, or to get a sponsor relationship started before they can begin to write anything meaningful. Other people, for whatever reason, are able to start writing at once when they get to this step.

The important thing to remember, I believe, is that this is not a race with anyone else in the program or with some cosmic timetable you may have concerning how long it "should" take you to finish each step. We each have a different past and different character defects. Some may work harder than others but find their progress slower. The speed of doing the steps is not always a measure of how hard someone is working or how intensely he or she *wants* to work the steps. Other factors—the depth of denial, the intensity of the disease and the amount of past abuse, a person's emotional resilience—may affect the process. It has continued to be helpful to me to realize that this program is one of progress, not perfection.

As long as you are keeping the Step Four objectives in mind, going to meetings, reading the Big Book, developing a relationship with your sponsor, and praying along the lines of the Third-Step Prayer and the Serenity Prayer for "the serenity to accept the things I cannot change, the courage to change the things I can, and the wisdom to know the difference," I believe you're making a sound beginning toward working on this step.

With a clearer understanding of the purpose of Step Four, and prepared by taking the first three steps, we can move toward actually taking a searching and fearless moral inventory of ourselves.

Chapter 6

TAKING STEP FOUR

Made a Searching and Fearless
Moral Inventory of Ourselves

There are many approaches to taking Step Four. Several are described here, but no one is expected to do all these things. Each person taking the steps is advised to decide, with the help of a sponsor, how he or she will approach Step Four and how much detail will be included. As you approach the beginning of your own "searching and fearless moral inventory," start at whatever level you can. Let's say you can't think of anything harmful or abusive you've done to others, but in spite of your efforts to resist, you find yourself absorbed with what people have done to you. You might decide to list these problems of others. One man said, "I only have three things wrong with me: my wife, my mother, and my oldest son." Whatever you can think of, get it down on paper. Even that much will help, because when you take that list to the fifth Step you will have somebody around to give you feedback and help you interpret what you have written. Most of us, however, will be able to think of specific things we have done sometime in our lives to hurt others.

Begin with Resentments

Resentment is the result of a collision between our actions, fed by our swollen instincts, and either the actions of other people or our own highest values. The author of *A Day at a Time,* a daily devotional book for alcoholics in recovery, says that resentment causes violence in violent people and illness in nonviolent people. If you are a person who expresses your resentment openly, you may have had some violent feelings or may have taken violent action. Any incidents you can recall should be listed in your inventory, along with a description of the situation. Often facing these resentments in Step Four relieves one of having to be violent or have crippling feelings later.

Some of us fear that we might react violently if we faced our feelings openly or that our violent reactions might cause others to reject us or retaliate in a way that we couldn't handle. We may, therefore, keep our resentments buried inside, where they often express themselves as depression and physical illness. Before you can see the actual resentments you have buried, you may need to start your inventory with

descriptions of your experiences of depression, when they have occurred, what happened before they started (if you can recall), and any
accidents you have had or physical illnesses that are known to be stress
related. Any resentments that come to light as you work on this, listen
at meetings, and talk with your sponsor can be added later.

Try to recall and write about incidents that may have happened clear
back in childhood. These include resentments of people (relatives,
friends, or enemies), of institutions (schools, churches, the government,
and so on), or of principles by which you have lived. An example of
resentment of a principle might be a woman who was taught as a child
that if she took care of herself she was selfish. Her mother never taught
her as a child how to take care of her basic physical and emotional needs
and wants. As an adult this woman may resent feeling guilty when she
does the normal things to take care of herself. She may feel resentment,
for instance, because lacking training regarding dental hygiene she has
lost many of her teeth from neglect. The principle "to take care of yourself is being selfish" caused her a lot of pain.

The inventory begins with a list of the incidents we can recall that
created resentment in us. The Big Book (pp. 64 and 71) suggests that you
write these resentments in three columns (or, as here, three sections):

1. The person or object of my resentment
2. What happened to cause the resentment
3. The effects in my life

I have added a fourth section or column, and I suggest trying to
recall what you did *before* the incident listed as "a possible Cause" that
may have caused the other person's action.

Here are a few examples of resentments. It's helpful to write your
inventory with this kind of detail. (Some incidents may also have affected you with fear or wounded pride. List as many effects as you can.)

I am resentful at Bill Smith [my partner].
The cause: Charging big personal expenses to our partnership
account. Bought an airplane and charged it to the company. Does not
repay the company and treats the plane as his own property.
The effect in my life: resentment, pride, fear (instinct involved:
security)
What I did earlier to cause the behavior: Dumped business on Bill
during a crisis and went on vacation.

I am resentful at Bill Smith.
The cause: Flirts with my wife—a lot!
The effect in my life: resentment, fear, pride (instinct involved: sexual relationship)
What I did earlier to cause the behavior: I insisted that my wife work at the office with Bill, and without consulting Bill, because I thought that she was lazy and getting a free ride.

I am resentful at Larry Lane [goes to my church].
The cause: Spoke against my financial plan just before the vestry election. I was running for vestry and didn't get elected because he spoke against me.
The effect in my life: resentment, pride, fear (instinct involved: social security)
What I did earlier to cause the behavior: Turned report in late. Embarrassed him in public situation, since he didn't have a chance to prepare by studying my financial plan.

I am resentful at my wife.
The cause: Judges and nags me. Talks about what an attractive man Bill S. is. Makes jokes about how I snore.
The effect in my life: resentment, pride, fear (instincts involved: emotional security, sexual security)
What I did earlier to cause the behavior: Manipulated wife to work for me. Set her up to be with Bill all day.

Focus on Our Part in the Painful Transaction

Next focus on your own part in the painful transaction between you and the person (or institution or principle) you resent. As one concentrates on the other person and what he or she did, denial goes up about one's own defects. As one builds up anger and other feelings about what "they" did, those feelings blot out one's own responsibility.

After seeing our own Sin and watching other people in the program face theirs, many of us have a very different feeling about the causes of the problems in our lives. I can now see many of the reasons that I am very hard to live with. I couldn't see them before because I was focusing on what "they" were doing to me. I kept hoping and praying *they* would change. When I began to look at *me* and my own self-centered controlling and my powerlessness to stop it, I could see how other people could be trapped too by their compulsive behavior, and I could feel a lot more compassion for them—and less resentment.

Go back to your list, and as the last item (column four) write what you did that may have set up the behavior you resent. Do this regarding each one of the incidents you recorded. Write what *you* did specifically that stemmed from your being selfish, dishonest, self-seeking, or frightened. You may again start dwelling on what they did to you, but force yourself to say what it was that *you* did that may have caused the collision of instincts and don't concentrate on the other person and what that person did wrong that hurt you (which may have been a lot).

In the first situation with Bill Smith on my list, for instance, I might look at my part and say, "Well, I dumped the business on Bill and went to Europe for two months because I had planned that trip. And I already had my tickets. He worked himself half to death to get through a crisis while I was gone." So then I would put beside that item in section (or column) four on my list "selfishness, my inability to put off my own gratification, and my unwillingness to change my plans once I had made them." And I might begin to see what my part was in the trouble between us, why Bill could be mad at me, why he would buy an airplane after my dumping on him that way and leaving him to save the business.

Regarding the Larry Lane item I might see that I turned my financial plan in to Larry late, just before the vestry election, knowing full well that it was his responsibility to discuss my plan with the people (who were going to vote on it before the election). It never occurred to me that with no chance to look my plan over he might not be too enthusiastic about it and might be embarrassed at not being prepared. He might have bad-mouthed my plan out of his embarrassment and anger. Setting him up that way has to do with *my* insensitivity, *my* selfishness, *my* procrastination, and *my* manipulation of people, thinking only about getting elected: the Sin-disease again.

With regard to the item about my wife: I might recall that I got my wife to help Bill with accounting because I didn't think she should just "lie around the house"; I thought she needed something to do. My Sin-disease, my need to run my wife's life, led to my jealousy. I set them up to visit with each other almost daily while I was busy working other places.

Take an Inventory of Our Fears

After listing all the resentments you can remember for your whole life, you then list all the fears that you can remember since childhood. Then ask yourself about each incident, Why was I afraid?

Most fear is because our faith failed and our self-reliance failed and we felt that we were not going to get something we wanted or were going to lose something we had. For example, if I have a certificate of deposit at the savings and loan (which is guaranteed) and I trust the company with my money, I don't stay up late at night worrying about my money. If I *am* worried about my money, it indicates clearly that I do not trust the savings and loan or the insuring agency—regardless of how much I say I do. If we are worried about something, it indicates that we are not trusting God with that area of our lives. Many of us Christians are in denial about our lack of trust in God; we really do *not* trust God about many of the important things in our lives, even though we say we do and often believe in our heads that we do.

I have experienced a great deal of financial fear. I know that with my education and background I can make a living of some sort, but I'm afraid I won't be able to make the kind of living I want to so I can have the things and do the things certain people do. This fear has to do with my pride and my inflated sense of what my social standing should be.

Through this inventory process in the fourth Step I discovered that I have been fighting my battles on the wrong battlefield. My problem was not money; it was false pride. I believe that one of the main reasons I have not wanted to look at myself closely is that I might have to change my life. But once I'm willing to adjust my standard of living, I am free. If I am willing to live in a modest place and have a simple life-style, I won't be intimidated by the fear of not having enough money to support a grander life-style. This decision is a matter of faith, of trusting God, of putting my reputation, my sense of worth, in God's hands and getting my life in order. With my insecurity and feelings of low self-worth, that took courage for me. But in the Twelve-Step program I am learning that trust is what courage is all about. If I have trust in God, then I can truly risk at a more significant level.

Take an Inventory of Each Swollen Instinct

After making this list of resentments and fears, inventory your specific instincts, the three primary trouble areas: sex, security, and social acceptance. I suggest going back to birth again, although some people just write what they can remember, not trying to start at birth.

The more specific you can be, the better. At first a person might try to be too general and say, "Well I have always had a little problem with the opposite sex." That will not do it. The "general confession" in a worship service assumes that each penitent person will make his or her own specific confession. When people try to do this step as if they are doing the general confession in the worship service (which says nothing specific about our behavior and attitudes) they miss the benefit of this step.

The idea here is to clean house and *face* the specific ways you have allowed each instinct to get out of proportion because of your self-centeredness in the Sin-disease.

The Sexual Instinct. "Sexuality" is not just about being in bed with somebody. Sexuality here includes the nature of the relationships you have had with members of the opposite sex, including but not limited to explicit sexual experiences.

The Twelve and Twelve has a good picture of this part of the inventory process (see pp. 42f.). First, it suggests that you ask yourself what sexual incidents you can recall that have hurt you or other people. Now, take a blank page and divide it into to two columns or sections, labeling them "behavior" and "attitudes." My inventory might look like this:

Behavior:

When I was a young boy in grade school I used to kid girls, sometimes in a cruel way, because all the guys who were popular with the boys kidded the girls. Later I always tried to date attractive girls to bolster my own self-image.

Attitudes:

A pattern all my life with women has been to operate out of the attitude that females were to be used to make me feel better about myself as a man.

As I wrote these things on my inventory list, including specific names and details, I realized that as time passed I'd learned to kiss girls instead of kid them. But that was also a way of using them. I had to get to this level of honesty in doing Step Four before I began to see this pattern of using women to make me feel better about myself as a man. I had never known this about myself, yet this "unseen" behavior had caused a great deal of pain in my life and relationships.

If you're married, look within your own marriage. Have you been selfish and demanding? Write these things under behavior. Have you wanted sex on your time schedule, your way, or did you withhold sex as punishment or as a weapon? Did you tell your mate you didn't feel sexual and then resort to masturbation to punish him or her? Did you pretend not to notice your partner's sexual signals?

Outside your marriage, did you flirt or make your mate jealous? Did you have emotional affairs and excuse them because they weren't physical? Many Christians have emotional affairs and say, "We didn't *do* anything." Sometimes emotional affairs are more serious than physical ones; they can bleed off intimacy and keep people from facing the conflict in their own marriages.

Concerning your children, did you kid about sex when they were small? Did you make inappropriate sexual suggestions or advances to any of your children or have sex with them? Did you take the time to give them appropriate sexual instruction, or were you too embarrassed?

Under Attitudes, examine the following things: How have you responded to sexual pressures? Did you make excuses or lie about your sexual selfishness? When your sexual advances were not accepted at home, did you feel depressed and rejected as a sexual person? Were you vengeful? Did you get back at your spouse in some way? Did you use this rejection as an excuse for outside sexual relations, saying, "Well, I'm not getting enough time and attention and love at home; I'll just find someone else. I'm justified in this, after all." If you had an affair, did you claim that you were pursued, that you really didn't want to, but it "just happened"—you couldn't help it? Did you blame your spouse for causing you to "stray" because he or she didn't satisfy you sexually in some way? List everything that comes to mind about your reactions to any or all of these things.

Financial Security.   When you inventory your life regarding financial insecurity, ask yourself, What character defects drove me to exaggerate my financial needs so that I got absorbed and obsessed with making money? If you are not absorbed with *making* money, perhaps it is your spending of it that is out of control. If that is the case, ask yourself, What character defects propel me to spend money beyond my income? Perhaps your problem is the reverse: you have a distinct distaste for or fear of spending money to the point that you and your family are subject to unnecessary deprivation even though your family's income could provide more comforts. Ask yourself what character defects contribute to your need to hoard money, not spending the necessary money to provide for yourself or your family.

A character defect often found with regard to financial insecurity is pride. We want more than other people, so we may either compulsively work to amass money or compulsively spend beyond our means to appear more wealthy than we are. Pride can also influence us to hoard what money we have so that we never risk having to ask for financial help from anyone.

Fear is another defect that often heightens financial insecurity. If you have fears about financial matters, write about the first time you recall having such fears. What form did your fears take?

As I was doing this step, I remembered that during the Great Depression in the early 1930s my father had owned an oil company. He lost it, and our financial situation changed drastically. When I was about three, I remember one Sunday playing on the floor behind the chair where my father was sitting. Not realizing I was in the room (or ignoring the fact), he began discussing finances with my mother. My father, whom I couldn't remember ever having cried before, sat and sobbed because he had "lost everything." Although we never lacked the essentials of life, I realized that it's no wonder I am afraid when I think of possible financial failure.

Ever since I saw clearly the memory of my father's financial fear, I am beginning to detach myself from that memory. Now I see that worrying about finances has been a pattern in my life no matter how well things were going, and I see where this fear came from: I have been carrying some of my father's fear. But I had never seen that connection clearly until I did Step Four.

Ask yourself what character traits have contributed to your financial insecurity and how they affected you. Specifically, were you guilty of lying? Cheating? Copping out on a responsibility? Griping? Acting like a big shot? Gossiping about associates? Being dishonest on expense accounts? Not paying loans back promptly? Cheating on income tax returns? Gambling beyond your means? List these and/or tell specifically how you did them.

Emotional Security. The obsession with emotional security can lead one either to be overdependent and controlled by some stronger person or to start controlling other people in order to feel secure. Either condition often arises from codependence, a very painful "disease."[1] Overdependent people may get jealous if the one they depend on steps out of sight (and out of their control) either physically or emotionally. Such jealous persons seldom grow spiritually while in the disease and may wind up very confused, because in their own minds all they are trying to do is love, rely on, and help the other person in various ways. The behind-the-scenes indirect (or passive-aggressive) control exerted by an overdependent person is hard to recognize but can be very powerful. ("You can't go hunting with the guys. What will I do here alone without you? I'll miss you so much" "You can't go visit your sister, Honey. I don't know how to cook! I'll starve while you're gone.") But the tragedy is that the "protector" the overdependent person is leaning on often runs away (or dies). They cannot stand being made responsible for the dependent one's happiness (and being controlled by the responsibility). They may either run away emotionally while sitting right in the house or run out of the house and leave the relationship.

An obvious authoritarian-style control artist may experience the same result—the ones being controlled finally leave. If they don't leave, then the controller may nevertheless feel resentful all the time, because these people are "hardheaded" and won't listen to "constructive suggestions." The controller's resentment may come out in overtly abusive behavior or surface sideways as sarcasm, hostile jokes, gossip, or other passive-aggressive behavior toward those around him or her.

Our emotional insecurity is often greatly increased by the bruised, twisted, and broken personal relationships in our lives. This is where the majority of us have suffered most because of the Sin-disease. Our emotional insecurities lead us often to fear, worry, depression, anger, and self-pity.

To inventory your emotional security issues, list all your personal relationships in which there have been recurring emotional problems. Just list every relationship: this child, this friend, my mother, my father, my brother, whomever. Beside each person's name put the feelings the name calls forth (e.g., pain, fear, anger, shame, guilt, joy, or sadness).

Next, go through the three areas of instinctual need with each person. Is the painful emotion caused by a sexual anxiety or frustration? Is it caused by a financial situation with this person? Is it caused by an exaggerated need for material success? Is it caused by emotional insecurity regarding social needs or sexual passion?

It may seem strange to examine one particular instinct using all three instincts as a guide. But this exercise is to help us break free from our own denial and to begin to become responsible. Writing down our sins and defects in Step Four is a good way to start this process. It's harder to deny your defects after you have written them on a list.

The Social Instinct.   With regard to the social instinct, instead of simply wanting to be a regular member of a group, we want to be president of the committee. Or we want to be the smartest, best-looking, holiest, so that we can be considered one of the "special ones." If we become power-mad, we try to control things financially, politically, and socially. We may ruin our chances for intimate personal relationships because we are always jockeying for social position and trying to get someone to do something that will help us fulfill our plans.

Several years ago I discovered that I had some heart trouble that could be fatal. My wife and I decided to change our lifestyle, as I wanted to get out of debt before I died. Before we made this change we had an office with two employees working in it and Andrea had an office down the hall. Within a one-year period, we had closed both offices, let our employees go, moved to our beach house, sold our other house, sold one car, and purchased two bicycles. Theses changes represented a large cut in our expenses. At first, because of my exaggerated need to be considered a financially successful person, I didn't want anyone to know how we had cut back; I felt some shame about having done so. Later, in doing Step Four, I learned that this shame about not having a lot of money was a part of my family history. And I saw that there was nothing shameful about the changes we had made. In fact, given our circumstances, we had acted very wisely. By becoming willing to change our standard of living and risk the return of my swollen social instinct, I gained the emotional security I needed about our finances during that period.

Because of social insecurity people spend large sums of money to buy things that they can't afford in order to make themselves appear more affluent than they are. Some go to absurd lengths to get in a certain club or organization, or to get elected to a church or civic office. All these overkill behaviors are evidence of a swollen social instinct.

I spoke with a man not long ago who said that he wanted so badly to be considered successful that he saw everyone as a potential customer for his business—everyone. He was so obsessed with succeeding that even the people he loved became objects whom he thought of in terms of their net worth. He felt terrible because he couldn't have close, sharing relationships with them. For years he wasn't aware that he tried to control people in this way. This sort of social/financial ambition is very common. Unfortunately, it ruins people's personal and spiritual lives because it makes intimacy impossible.

To inventory your issues regarding the social instinct, list the social connections you have had that have been painful in some way. Consider whether your pain comes from not receiving a position you wanted, the recognition you believed you deserved, or the attention you wanted. Then list the harmful or dysfunctional things you did as a result. What character defects and feelings were involved in these situations? If none of these fits, then ask yourself why your affiliation with that particular group or organization has been painful.

List the names of any people with whom you have close personal relationships now or have had in the past. If a relationship is over, write about how it ended. Write about any conflicts you had with that person during the relationship. You may begin to see patterns in your past and present relationships.

TAKING STEP FOUR

Step Four
Made a searching and fearless
moral inventory of ourselves.

If you want to take Step Four you may want to use your notebook or take blank sheets of paper to inventory your resentments, fears, and swollen instincts as described in this chapter. When you have finished listing the "damaged goods" in your inventory, take some time to list the positive things that you have realized about your past behavior, character traits, and attitudes since being in the program. For example, "I am an intelligent, sensitive person. I'm a good listener. I am really trying to work this program. I want to learn to do God's will."

The following forms may be used as many times as you need them to examine various aspects of your life.

Chart I: Resentments

I Am Resentful at
The Cause
Effect in My Life
What I Did Earlier to Cause This Behavior

Chart II: Fears

I Am Fearful of
The Cause
Effect in My Life

Chart III: Sexual Instinct

Behavior
Attitudes

Chart IV: Financial Security

Behavior
Attitudes

Chart V: Emotional Security

Behavior
Attitudes

Chart VI: Social Instincts

Behavior
Attitudes

Chart VII: Character Defects
Behavior
Attitudes

Chapter 7

UNDERSTANDING STEP FIVE

Admitted to God, to Ourselves, and to Another Human Being the Exact Nature of Our Wrongs

A biblical expression of the need to do Step Five with another person and its connection with healing:

Therefore confess your sins to one another, and pray for one another, that you may be healed. James 5:16

Even a quick reading of this step reveals that it is a form of confession. This way of confessing is one of the remarkable aspects of the Twelve Steps: the recovery of an incredibly healing and restoring Christian practice.

From the beginning Christians have believed in confessing their sins to other Christians not trained in theology or (more recently) psychology. The author of James stated it clearly as a part of the healing process, "Confess your sins to one another, and pray for one another, that you may be healed" (James 5:15). Why did the early Christians believe that it was so important to confess their sins to one another? The reason is twofold, it seems. First, as the passage from James indicates, we confess our sins so that we may be healed, made whole. But there is a deeply theological reason for confession also.

Christians believe that God "is light and in him is no darkness at all" (1 John 1:5). The author of the First Letter of John tells us that God can't stay in relationship with darkness or sin. If we are to stay close to God and have fellowship with him, we must find a way to get the darkness or sin out of our lives and keep it out. The promise of the New Testament is that "if we confess our sins, he [God] is faithful and just, and will forgive our sins and cleanse us from all unrighteousness" (1 John 1:9). In other words, once we are connected to God through surrender in Christ, we are cleansed of our darkness (or sin) and can walk with God in the light. But to *stay* in God's presence—in the light—we must continue to confess so that God can continue to "cleanse us from all our unrighteousness" (i.e., character defects and Sin).

The author goes on in the second chapter to spell out the basic purpose of Christianity. He says, in effect, if you do sin, don't worry! Now you have Someone who has opened a passage to God, and you can be forgiven; the sins of the whole world can be forgiven (see 1 John 2:1–2).

The language of the New Testament can be difficult to comprehend, and it doesn't always seem to relate to what happened to me this morning or last week. But the Twelve-Step program puts into the language of "what happened this morning" these same basic New Testament principles on the necessity of dealing with the sins and darkness that have bound us to our need to control (and to our addictions when we cannot). The Twelve Steps do this in a way that allows us to use the principles in our own recovery and spiritual growth. Steps Four and Five give us practical, concrete ways to see our sins, confess them, and be healed and made whole. We can then get back in fellowship with each other and be at one with God again as he forgives us of our sins and shows us a new meaning and purpose for our lives. Moreover, after we have worked the first five steps the power of God has become more immediately accessible to many of us on a daily basis.

Many Protestant believers think that the Protestant Reformation is all about *not* having to confess anymore, that Calvin and Luther put a stop to confession. But that's simply part of our delusion, the way the disease works.

As I wrote in *Hope in the Fast Lane—A New Look at Faith in a Compulsive World,* Luther and Calvin were both in favor of confession; they were just against selling it. Luther said in the thirty-sixth volume of his works,

> Confession is useful, even necessary. I would not have it abolished. Indeed I rejoice that it exists in the Church of Christ because it is a cure without equal for distressed consciences. For when we have laid bare our conscience to a brother and privately made known to him the evil that lurks within, we receive from our brother's lips the word of comfort spoken by God himself. And if we accept this in faith, we find peace in the mercy of God speaking to us through our brother.[1]

Many non-Christian men and women in A.A. might be surprised to hear that, because it is the same experience they have had in the Twelve-Step programs, without seeming to be part of a religion.

The Purpose of Step Five— Spiritual Dialysis

In the previous chapter I talked about Step Four as a way to look at the effects of our swollen instinctual needs for material and emotional security, for sex, and for social acceptance. Step Five can be considered to be a spiritual filter for the toxic memories, thoughts, and behaviors of the past that continue to sabotage and poison our lives and relationships in the present. Just as a kidney dialysis cleanses our blood by filtering the poison from our system and leaving the healthy fluids and tissue to keep cleansing us, Step Five helps us filter out the hidden, crippling behaviors and character defects from the past that are poisoning our relationships with God, with other people, and with ourselves.

We need to go through this specific separating and removal process because the self-defeating habits we discover during Step Four are so much a part of the bloodstream of our lives that we have had trouble even seeing them, much less separating them out, alone. Many of us Christians have, by ourselves, been able to recognize and admit some of our big faults and confess them without the Twelve-Step program. But during the past few years I have become aware that the denied, deeply controlling character defects that, alone, I couldn't even see have been the ones that continued to poison my everyday life and close relationships.

We may have had flickering moments when we recognized some of these denied faults in our lives, but then we went on ignoring them. Because we had to protect our image of adequacy, of perfection, our Sin-disease worked constantly to blur our awareness of these abusive, controlling behaviors and help us maintain our nonabusing, good-person image. But once I started taking Step Five I began to recall more clearly that flickering awareness of having to be right and get things done my way. And I started to see behind the walls of my denial.

Our adequacy image may include being seen as intelligent, sincere, pious, laid back, hard-working, masculine, or feminine. Some people's images and walls develop from being abused as children. Many of us early on got the idea somehow way down inside that we were really shameful and had to hide our "true selves" for fear we would be rejected "on sight." [2] Many of these turbulent feelings are buried in our unconscious minds, but they cause us to develop tenacious images to hide behind—even if the image is one of being "laid back."

If we can't eliminate the behaviors we fear might reveal our inadequacy and show our imperfections, then the Sin-disease brings in denial, and presto, the offending habit or behavior "vanishes" from our sight, and we can no longer *see* the self-defeating behavior that contradicts our image.

If I am trying to control my wife, perhaps at first I can see that I am being controlling. But then when denial comes in and we argue about my controlling, I might say, "Look, I'm not controlling you, I'm just trying to make you happy. I've been through this problem you're facing, and I'm going to show you how to get through it better than I did so you won't have to face the misery I had." The controlling behavior is the same, but I have put a different, a more "Christian," interpretation on my attempts to control so I won't contradict my image of being a noncontroller.

This process appears to be almost universal. We unconsciously set up images of what we want to be and censor any contradictory evidence in our behavior and thinking. But it's not a very efficient system for living, because the Sin-disease is progressive. As we get older we get careless, and the cracks in our images and the inconsistencies they reveal may start showing to more and more people. In order to help bolster or "enforce" our shaky image we depend more and more on what the Twelve-Step program calls "character defects": lying, criticism, advice giving, and gossiping. These character defects help us shore up our image from the inside by denying our defects and highlighting those of others. We do this, however unconsciously, to keep from being "revealed" and losing the respect we believe our image has brought us. Without our image we feel we'd be destroyed or deserted. But our efforts to maintain our fine, adequate, sincere image so we will feel as though we are "enough" become increasingly difficult.

Some Specific Character Defects That Come from Perfectionism

Complexity—Keeping All the Image Balls in the Air.   Coming into the program, my emotional life was so complex that it reminded me of the role played by Dick Van Dyke in the movie *Mary Poppins.* He played a song as a one-man band, beating on a big bass drum with his elbows, clanging the cymbals with his knees, playing a horn that stuck out of a holder on top of the drum. In my case I was like a man wearing a football helmet and three Brooks Brothers suits over a Superman outfit. I could take them off real fast and be whatever color or shape you wanted. And then sometimes I tripped and fell, and people said, "You are not what you seemed to be." I thought they had a judgment problem, but they just saw the real me trying frantically to look perfect and adequate to everyone.

Being the "Supreme Court" in Our Own Home.   Because we perfectionists can't relax our control over this image, we have to be a walking court of law, complete with judge and jury, to straighten out our families or our colleagues on the job and remake them according to our values and the expectations that support our image of life. And when we fail, we are often harder on ourselves than we are on anyone else.

No Room for Gratitude. True gratitude, the mark of humility and serenity, is almost impossible for us perfectionist controllers. We are constantly trying to reshape life all around us and make it work the way we think it should for us and others and to keep people close by convincing them to believe our perception of us; all this leaves little room for gratitude. How can we be grateful when other people just won't stay put and behave the way we want them to over the long haul—*and* still think we are wonderful? So even if they "mind" us outwardly, they won't vote for us as lover/king of the world whose "name is wonderful." We mutter that we will be grateful to God when *they* change to the extent that things are under control in our lives. But gratitude eludes us, moving ahead like a mirage across the desert.

With all these interwoven defenses and diversions from the truth about who we are, it's no wonder that we perfectionists approach confession and Step Five with guilt and fear. We have spent a lifetime building an image that we are not even sure of (because a lot of it is in our unconscious mind); we suspect that there is something not secure about it. And therefore, to keep from being revealed for who we are, we Christians have attacked specific confession over the years and have almost eliminated it from the life of the Church.

Step Five Begins a Profound Kind of Change, a "Conversion"

The minute people quit defending their image and take Step Five, they often can start being intimate in meetings. They can begin to reveal out loud in front of others something of who they really are today. This kind of honesty turns everything around; the energy once used to enforce denial starts working toward uncovering, discovering the very defects we attempted to hide, and moves us toward honesty instead of toward dishonesty. A person taking Step Five is like a train going into a roundhouse one way and being turned around so it can come back out going the opposite direction.

Christianity calls this kind of change "repentance" and conversion. Repentance (in Greek, *metanoia)* is a "turning." An army is going one way, and at a signal the army changes direction and goes a different way. The army converts. And in taking Steps One through Five, we change. We start to see our denial, our unreal images, and go in a different direction—toward dismantling our painted facades and becoming the person God intended us to be. All of the Twelve Steps guide us toward this changing, this going a different direction.

I said to a friend who is a Catholic priest in a Twelve-Step group, "You guys have kept confession, at least." He said, "No, we really haven't. I do about three a week, and I've got a big church. And they are pretty much a mechanical thing with many parishioners these days. It's certainly not what you are talking about in Step Five."

Why Does Our Honesty Have to Include Another Human Being?

People often have a real objection to sharing their character defects with another human being. They say, "Wait a minute. The purpose of this step is to get right with *God,* and he already knows my character defects. I don't have to tell another person." But the person listening is not the object of your confession; God is. We need the other person as a witness so that when our disease tells us that we didn't really confess, and we start to get back into our guilt and shame (as we often do after a solo, silent confession), we can remember that someone was with us and heard our confession. It concretizes what we have done.

Besides, confession involves an interesting paradox. Let's say that a couple are good friends with their next-door neighbors. The four of them often barbecue together and play dominoes. One time the husband is away on business and comes home about five hours early. Just as he is opening the front door he glances at his neighbor's house. He can see through the bedroom window, and there is his wife in the arms of his neighbor. The husband knows what she has done (he has seen her), and his wife knows it. But can they ever have a close relationship again, even though both of them already know about the adultery, unless she confesses it to him? No chance. It's the same way with God. Even though he knows our Sin and our sins, the magic of confession is that when I tell God what he already knows, then our relationship can become clear again; the block, which was in me, is removed.

Some people seek an easier and softer way by doing a "general confession" to God alone. They are not about to name specifically the humiliating, "awful" things they have done out loud before another human being. But this very act of specifically confessing things is what often leads to serenity. The more afraid you are to tell about a certain act or thought in your fifth Step, the more likely it is that confessing that particular thing will put a new crack in your denial and free you in a new area. There doesn't seem to be an easier, softer way, and people who seek one apparently don't understand the tenacious and tricky nature of this spiritual disease we are facing. Step Five is to help us to see, to grasp, to understand specifically how the disease has permeated our lives in ways we usually cannot see any other way. And confession before another person (to change the metaphor) is like lancing the boil of Sin and beginning to let the poison out of our inner lives.

The Twelve-Step program points out that without an admission to God of our defects in front of another human being, we cannot get in recovery from the disease process. Nobody is more obnoxious in a Twelve-Step program than somebody who has quit using a chemical or overeating and isn't working the program. In just the same way nobody is more discouraging or obnoxious in the Church than a Christian who has stopped committing the obvious sins and joined the congregation but doesn't "work the program" by facing his or her controlling, God-playing ways. In the Twelve-Step programs such people are called dry drunks. In the Church they are called hypocrites.

Confessing to God alone is a beginning, but experience in the Twelve-Step program indicates that if we just confess to God alone, that is all that will happen. Nothing changes. People in Twelve-Step programs know that if you are not willing to do Step Five sooner or later, you are not really serious about cleaning up your life. That is certainly a broad generalization, but that seems to be the consensus of people for whom the Twelve Steps have brought serenity and hope.

You Can Discover "Good" Things, Too

Besides revealing and dealing with our sinful behaviors we can begin to uncover and own our positive character traits and abilities. Denial has caused many of us to bury our positive abilities along with our character defects. Some of us were afraid that if we owned our abilities, people wouldn't think we were humble. We would also be responsible for living up to our potential perfectly. We were afraid that if we admitted our dreams and tried to implement them publicly, and they didn't work out successfully, this failure would blow our image of adequacy. Because of this image problem we often keep ourselves from the beautiful, creative things God has for us to do with the abilities he's given us.

Healthy Human "Perfection"

The Twelve-Step program says to us that true perfection as a human being is not about being "errorless." Human wholeness is about being honest, having integrity, and, as Pia Mellody once told me, about being "perfectly imperfect."[3] In this Twelve-Step process we learn that we are imperfect and that this condition is universal for real human beings. But we also learn that we can be forgiven for our mistakes, our sins, and can learn wisdom as we face them and make amends. Each of these imperfections and sins can be an occasion for character development and spiritual insight about how to give and receive love. As we face our hidden selves, we develop much more compassion for those trapped as we have been. And as we begin to face and deal with the denied, controlling, Sin-filled defects in our lives, we are told that we are beginning to grow in humility and genuine spirituality. But we would never have connected the need to deal with our very "unspiritual" denied character defects with clearing the decks for true spirituality.

Steps Four and Five constitute a powerful strategy to dismantle our false images by locating and getting rid of the character defects that support them like buttresses holding up a building. These defects support unreality in all aspects of our lives and cripple our relationships. And these self-serving, Sin-diseased behaviors are what separate us from God.

God's love has appeared to many of us to be like a tender mist coming close to us, always present, waiting, so that if there is an opening it will rush in, a fresh yet gentle breeze. In my experience there is an urgency without force on the part of God. When, through Step Five, we unplug the windows that have been stuffed closed with our character defects, the Spirit of Healing himself comes in.

Now that you have your written inventory in Step Four and have examined Step Five, you are ready to move into the specific actions called for in the fifth Step.

Chapter 8

TAKING STEP FIVE

*Admitted to God, to Ourselves,
and to Another Human Being the
Exact Nature of Our Wrongs*

The process of taking Step Five has three distinct phases:

- You choose a person to whom you will admit "the exact nature of your wrongs."

- You meet with that person and tell him or her what you have learned in Step Four.

- You listen to any feedback the person you've chosen has for you and take it in.

Choosing the Human Being
to Hear Step Five

Choose the person you share Step Five with very carefully, just as carefully as you would choose a sponsor. Keep listening in meetings, and ask around to find out who might be a good person with whom to do Step Five.

He or she needs to be someone whom you trust to keep what you say confidential. Also this person needs to understand the Twelve Steps; ideally it should be someone who has done Step Five. The one you choose should be trustworthy and nonjudgmental, but for many of us, *nobody* seems trustworthy enough to hear our truly private defects.

If you can't find somebody "perfect," don't worry, your Step Five experience will be beneficial with almost anybody who has compassion and integrity and can keep matters confidential. Remember that the Step-Five listener is primarily a "witness," watching you tell your inventory to God.

When You Choose Someone Outside the Program.   If you choose someone who isn't familiar with the Twelve-Step process, you will need to tell that person certain things about what to do. You can choose a total stranger who is qualified, like a minister or counselor, if you are afraid to choose someone you know or a nonprofessional listener. You don't have to be "Tarzan," the strong person, in this program. Just do the best you can. Doing an inferior Step Five is better than doing none, and your first Step Five will be incomplete and imperfect in any case.

When you meet with someone who isn't familiar with the Twelve Steps, explain that you are going to tell him or her your resentments, fears, and character defects, and about the harmful or abusive behavior you've discovered in your life. Ask the person not to interrupt until you are finished so that your listener won't try to minimize your faults or try to stop you from confessing your character defects because of his or her own discomfort. Tell the prospective listener whether or not you want feedback regarding what you share, what he or she heard you saying. State clearly that what you are going to reveal must be kept totally confidential, and make sure that is clearly understood.

If the person says something like, "You don't really have to do this. God already forgives you," then *don't* share your fifth Step with that person. Just say, "Thank you very much, maybe I don't," and leave. Find another person. Whether other people realize it or not, it is very important for you to do Step Five with another person present. That is why it is easier with people who have done the step themselves.

When You Choose Someone in the Program.   Often your sponsor is a good person to do Step Five with because he or she can help you from then on with the issues you have discovered. Many people are too shy to do this step with their sponsor right off, however; perhaps they fear their sponsor might not like them anymore. You may find someone else in the program to read your fifth Step to and then discuss part or all of it with your sponsor. There are no rules about this. If one thing doesn't work out for you, try another. But it is important not to quit until you do the fifth Step with someone.

The Procedure and the Meeting

Once you've chosen someone and that person has agreed to hear your step, review the following guidelines other people in Twelve-Step programs have found helpful. First you make an appointment, then have the meeting. During the meeting you not only share with the person, but you silently check your feelings as you go. Ideally you hold nothing back, but get out before this other person, yourself, and God everything you possibly can.

Make an Appointment.   When you make an appointment to do your fifth Step with someone, allow plenty of time. It may take several hours. If the person you approach says he or she doesn't have that much time when you'd like to meet, ask if you could reschedule at a better time. You are asking somebody to give you their valuable time, so it's good to be very respectful of that person's schedule and make the appointment well in advance. People who have taken Step Five will have a good understanding of the time issue.

Prepare Yourself for This Meeting.   You may want to pause before you go to your Step Five appointment and go through the first three steps again, admitting your powerlessness, believing that God can cure your insanity, and offering your life and your will to him. Then you are ready to surrender yourself to God along with the outcome of whatever happens in Step Five.

Take Your Written Step Four to the Meeting.　　Most people use what they have written in Step Four as notes with which to begin Step Five. Having notes in some form is helpful because of the way denial works. Many times people have gone to a counselor about one specific thing, spent an hour in the session, and then arrived home and said, "My gosh, I spent the whole hour, and I forgot all about what I went to tell." This is the way denial works, so it's good to have some notes for Step Five. Some people find it helpful to check off items in their notes as they are saying them.

My sponsor told me that in his Step Four he wrote 134 pages of resentments, things he'd done that hurt people, character defects, immoral and illegal acts, and anything he could remember that might reflect who he was and what he'd done to others, God, and himself, starting with his childhood. I didn't write nearly that much. There are no rules about this. Just be as thorough as possible

Listen to Yourself.　　It was helpful to me to approach Step Five with the attitude, "I am going to try to hear what I am saying to this person." This attitude is helpful because, listening to ourselves, we can begin to hear our own arrogance, fear, self-pity, and attempts to minimize our faults or "explain" ourselves. This other person becomes a sort of sound monitor like those in a recording studio. It is as if you have earphones on. While you are talking, you may also hear some things about your Sin-disease.

As you tell your fifth Step, you may catch yourself doing the same kind of self-justifying you did in Step Four, saying things like, "And I did this to hurt this person, but in all honesty I think that person set me up by doing such and such to me. I wouldn't have done what I did, which I admit was wrong, if he or she hadn't done that." In that moment you have forgotten *your* Sin or minimized it as you tried to justify your behavior. Self-justification has no place in a fifth Step.

If you're like most of us, you'll catch yourself explaining to the listener *why* you did some awful thing; that's not what Step Five is about either. You are to ignore what other people did to you and any extenuating circumstances. This is *your* inventory, and you are to stick to your sins and character defects and not take other people's inventory or try to justify yourself.

Just seeing how often I was tempted to point to extenuating circumstances or justify my actions in a dozen ways showed me how deeply ingrained the Sin-disease is in my own life.

You may hear your self-pity. I know my voice gets a certain "feel sorry for me" sound as I say dejectedly, "Well, ah, it was a really hard time for me." And when the listener gets a sympathetic look on his face, I can quit talking about it. The person now knows my behavior was justified because my circumstances were so difficult; I've won my listener over—and lost the healing reality of facing my own Sin.

You may pick up the sound of your own resentment or anger as you share an incident, and this will let you know that there is something going on beneath you words. These are some of the things we use to hide our faults—self-justification, self-pity, and resentment.

Examine Your Feelings as You Share Step Five. When doing Step Five it is helpful to tell not only the facts about your harmful or abusive past behaviors but what your feelings were as well. When we tell the facts without the feelings it doesn't mean as much. Of course many of us are out of touch with our feelings. That's a serious symptom of the Sin-disease (and part of the effect of codependence or any addiction). We are using the compulsive behavior or the addiction, in fact, to cover or hide those feelings that are uncomfortable.

Some of us are so out of touch with feelings that all we can say is, "I feel bad." But "bad" is not a feeling. Fear, pain, sadness, anger, guilt, shame, joy are feelings. These are like the primary colors in the spectrum of emotion. There are other feelings, like "unhappy" and "hurt" and "resentful," but they stem from "sadness" and "pain" and "anger" combined with other things. As the primary colors of red, blue, and yellow in combination make up the other colors, these basic feelings combined with other things make up such feelings as "unhappy" or "resentful." I found it helpful to stick with the "primary feelings" as much as possible when checking my feelings during the fifth Step.

Examine Your Relationship Patterns. Besides becoming aware of hitherto buried feelings, you may begin to see how for years the same patterns and habitual behaviors have affected your relationships with the people close to you.

You may see your part in marital and family problems that you hadn't been able to understand before. I began to see how people could have been angry with me for years for my continual and intense need to be "right" in every argument.

Many of us have become aware that we have been fighting the spiritual battles of our lives on the wrong battlefields by trying to straighten out *other people.* This happens in very simple ways. Let's say you want to do something your mate does not want to do: go to a movie or cook hamburgers or make love, whatever it is. You are too good a person to be mad about the refusal; that would blow your image as a good Christian marriage partner. You have been thinking about doing this proposed activity all day, and when your spouse doesn't want to participate with you, you are very disappointed. But you say, "That's fine. It doesn't bother me at all. I'll read." And you get a grim look on your face.

The next morning you find a place to express your anger, a place that points to your mate's imperfection, not yours. The next morning your spouse makes some minor mistake like setting the alarm a half-hour too early. You feel *rage* and throw the alarm clock clear across the room. It is obvious that that reaction is a little strong for a mistaken alarm setting. But it is not the alarm we are talking about here. It is the ego. It happened last night when you didn't get your way. The fight that ensues is on the wrong battlefield. It's the wrong time; it's an inappropriate amount of anger for the present situation. But because we are out of touch with any feelings we have that might hurt our good-person image, we experience the anger as if it were all about the alarm clock. We (and those around us) live through a lot of baffling arguments in this way in patterns caused by our Sin-disease.

Hold Nothing Back. We are urged to hold nothing back in doing Step Five. But if a certain sin comes up in your mind and you think, "I just *can't* tell that," and you can't, that's okay; go ahead and do your Step Five and don't tell it. Do the best you can. But try to hold nothing back. Nobody is perfect, and recovery is not about perfection, it is about progress.

Remember, though, as in writing your fourth Step, the things you are most afraid to tell—shameful acts of abuse, financial dishonesty, or sexual thoughts and acting out that you are very ashamed of—are often the most important things to tell in Step Five and may lead to the greatest freedom.

Listen to Any Feedback from Your Listener

A listener who has been through the fifth Step will tell you experiences from his or her own life similar to those you have revealed. Hearing these is like having warm oil poured over you. The things we think are the grubbiest and most individual about our sins are often the most similar to those of other people. We don't usually know that because these most personal failures and abusive behaviors are hardly what people ordinarily talk about!

In Christ we have a family who can understand that we all have sinned, and if we pretend we haven't we are "liars and the truth is not in us" (see 1 John 1). The tragedy is, often in our own families we can't share our reality. We are afraid (with good cause, often) that they will straighten us out or be critical and rejecting. Unfortunately sometimes the people in the Church do that too. But in sharing a fifth Step or even telling appropriate parts of your story in good Twelve-Step meetings you can usually share your real feelings and the drama of your life without fear of being "fixed" by controllers. If people do start giving you advice when you haven't asked for it, go to another meeting; they've missed the basic point. Often when you have very personal things to share that might make you particularly vulnerable, it is better to wait and share them in a fifth Step or with your sponsor, one on one. (See appendix A on sponsorship.)

My Step Five Experience

The man I happened to choose to hear my fifth Step was a Catholic counselor who lived over five hundred miles from my home. I assumed he had probably never read my books or heard of me, which was just what I wanted. With a lot of fear, I told him what I wanted to do. I knew he was in a Twelve-Step program and had done a fifth Step himself.

I told him my story and read from my Step Four notes, keeping my eyes on the page as I read much of the list. Although I had a basic Step Four written out, I also told him some other things I remembered along the way that weren't written down. When I was finished I was weeping with shame and relief. At last I had "told all" to another person. I waited to hear his response, fearing that he would say, "Don't even worry about thanking me, just *leave.* You are so bad!" But when I finally looked up

I saw that he had tears in his eyes too. He looked at me and said, "Your list is just like mine." He began to tell me some ways in which his story was very similar to my own.

And then he said, "I haven't been quite honest with you. I have read some of your books." I cringed and wanted to die! And then he said, "No, no, wait. You are real to me now, and I can understand what you have tried to say in your books." And he thanked me. I could hardly believe it; I was so grateful. It was a powerful experience of acceptance. Here was someone who saw me as I really was (warts, sins, and all!), and not only did he not run away from me, but he identified with me in his tears and in his words.

After You've Done Step Five

People have reported different outcomes and experiences after completing Step Five. A sense of being loved by God, a sense of overwhelming gratitude and relief, a more balanced attitude toward material possessions, freedom from loneliness and isolation, increased self-acceptance, freedom to play, and the opening of a door to a new kind of spiritual growth are some of the things I've noticed in myself or heard from other people.

"Being heard" by the fifth-Step listener often comes across to the person doing Step Five as an experience of love and acceptance *from God.* As you experience love and understanding from somebody with a human face who hears and cares for you, the door opens for you to be able to grasp what God's love in your life might mean: that God does love us and forgive us—not just theoretically, but actually in the nonreligious pain of our lives. In the fifth Step we can see this compassionate acceptance in the eyes of another human being. It is often a tearful experience of gratitude, of "I can't believe this person is giving me this time, is giving me this attention, and is not rejecting me or trying to fix me after hearing the awful truth about me."

After doing Step Five some of us have realized that we no longer have to do more than others or have more attention than others in order to feel *equal* to them. We can look anybody in the eye. Many people come into this program feeling depressed and discouraged, as if life were over. Taking Step Five is like a fresh beginning, overturning the verdict that life is too much and that we will never be happy.

If I tell all that I am, and in response I am loved, that is a spiritual experience. I had never done it. I had only told parts, because I suspected that if you really knew all about me you wouldn't love me. I (as many people do) felt relieved beyond measure when I finally got it all out. This is another place in the Twelve Steps where it is common to hear people say that they feel as if they had in some inexplicable way joined the human race. They are no longer different, set apart, lonely. They have told it all, and they feel a dawning awareness that they are just like other people, instead of isolated strangers.

Although a "spiritual awakening" can come at almost any point when doing the steps, many people report a deep change after taking Step Five. Some experience a spiritual awakening like a conversion experience. Some call it a new spiritual birth (see the discussion of spiritual awakening in chapter 15). But whatever the experience, for many people taking Step Five seems to lead to having a stronger grasp on reality—the reality that they are going to be alright and that they are, in some real sense, acceptable and loveable.

In the third chapter of the Gospel of John, there is an account of Nicodemus, a very intelligent man, coming to Jesus and saying, "What is this faith you are speaking of?" Nicodemus evidently was a devout man with an intellectual understanding of the biblical faith.

Jesus gave him a little picture by saying, "Nicodemus, you must be born again."

Being a good intellectual, Nicodemus said, "You mean I have to go back into my mother's womb?" He was looking through a logical, rational lens.

And Jesus said, in effect, "No, you missed it, Nicodemus. The life I am trying to tell you about is very different from the life in your head that you have always known. This new experience of faith is as if an old man like you were born again into a new way of life. And that's what this life of faith is all about." A sense of having been brought out into a new experience of life and faith is one of the most common reports from people who are well into working a Twelve-Step program.

In doing Step Five many people have found new hope in their vocational lives. They start new jobs. Several people I know have stopped doing what they were doing and are taking new vocational directions they were blocked from before. Because of their inflated-shame they thought they didn't deserve to have happiness, and their buried secrets became blocks keeping them from even thinking about pursuing their cherished dreams. But when they got their shameful secrets out, they were free to work productively on fulfilling those dreams.

At this Step Five point, some people lose the terrible feelings of loneliness and isolation they have known all their lives as they feel a sense of belonging to an understanding family they never really had. The acceptance by the fifth-Step listener and those in meetings as we reveal our newly discovered defects is, in fact, an experience that most people only dream of—of being accepted by a nonjudgmental family that doesn't "straighten you out" when you share your real feelings. That sort of "family" is what many Twelve-Step groups have become in our time.

Self-Acceptance and the Changes It Can Bring

For some people Step Five is the beginning of self-acceptance, often a by-product of taking this step. They no longer have to carry and defend an eight-foot image that they couldn't relax with. The person they really are is "enough."

Some report that their fears of being known begin to subside at this point. I *want* my wife, Andrea, to know me now. When I first began to tell her about myself, I was afraid. But her reaction was anything but what I would have expected had I not been in this program. I still didn't trust easily, but as I claimed my pain and fears and shared them, she seemed to be grateful that I would share at that level instead of thinking I was awful. It seemed to make us closer instead of driving us apart.

Another surprise in doing Step Five concerned the freedom to play. It has always been an absolute mystery to me that some people could play without guilt or shame. They apparently enjoyed it and did not grit their teeth and do it only because "smart people" play (and then hurry up and get back to work). Many of us in the program have become playful in meetings and at home.

As some of us compulsive workers finished the first five Steps, we began to be more in touch with what we liked. We realized that many activities we had participated in, things we had eaten or drunk, and people we'd been with had been a part of our lives because of our image of who we thought we were supposed to be. Because we were out of touch with who we really were, we didn't know much about what we liked or who we liked being with. As our denial cracked open we began to realize who and what we like and what we want to do and be.

A New Kind of Spiritual Growth

For people who have taken the first five steps the doorway to a tough kind of spiritual growth is now open. Evidently we can only grow and change spiritually as we can see our character defects and controlling habits. As we begin in Step Five to reveal where we are, we have also started to build on that foundation. As the resulting taste of freedom is savored, spiritual growth through vulnerability and sharing can become a natural way of life for Twelve-Step pilgrims.

Not long ago, I asked a man who is a recovering alcoholic, "What do you think happens in these meetings?" He said, "Well, I was telling my little boy that I used to drink in order to cover up my painful feelings, and now I go to these meetings and talk about the painful feelings instead of drinking. I told him that when we go into the meeting and say our feelings, the pain floats away, and we don't have to cover it up with anything. We leave with the same effect that the alcohol was supposed to give us, only we don't have headaches and feel bad. Besides, we often learn what we're doing to cause the painful feelings."

"My little son looked up at me and said, 'Daddy, you did good.'"

And I thought, "Wow! It's so simple." When we share our real feelings, the pain does not all disappear, but some of the pressure is alleviated, and we can often see the meaning of our pain. But even if we don't, the telling itself is healing and gives relief. It is like the lancing of a boil. When we first come into the program, however, the *last* thing we want to do is this sort of confession of who we are.

I used to have a recurring dream that I was an actor in a movie or a class play and I got up before the audience and didn't know my lines, or I would be coming into a final exam that my whole life depended on and I wasn't prepared, or I'd be missing a plane or a train I had to catch. In my case the dreams were about my separation from what is inside me and my fear of being revealed as not being enough. But since I have been facing my Sin-disease and denial, I haven't had these dreams. (I'm almost afraid to tell you this for fear I might start having them tonight.)

Such Relief Doesn't Happen to Everyone

In all honesty, I must tell you that some people don't feel relief after Step Five; they feel terrible. They may experience shame or anger or fear and wish they hadn't done it. Often these reactions are due to the fact that they haven't really seen their powerlessness. In other words, they need to go back and do Steps One, Two, Three, and Four.

If this is your experience, you may need to talk to your sponsor, work on the first three steps, and take a hard look at what you may be afraid to face in your Step Four inventory. As you do these things you can continue to go to meetings and talk about the feelings of anger and fear you have about Step Five. If you have really done the first four steps, then Step Five is usually a great relief.

A person who has reached this point is entering a new spiritual dimension and is ready for what I consider the big spiritual steps in this program: Steps Six and Seven.

TAKING STEP FIVE

Step Five

Admitted to God, to ourselves, and to another human being the exact nature of our wrongs.

In your notebook write the following:

1. The name and phone number of person you choose to hear your fifth Step
2. The date of your fifth Step
3. As you told your fifth Step to your chosen listener, what feelings did you experience?
4. What behavioral or relationship patterns, if any, did you discover during this step?
5. Describe how you feel now after having completed the fifth Step.

Be sure to save your written fourth Step and any additional notes you made for your fifth Step. These may be helpful when you take Steps Eight and Nine.

Chapter 9

STEP SIX

*Were Entirely Ready to Have
God Remove All These
Defects of Character*

A biblical expression of the need to be entirely
ready to commit our whole lives to God in
such a complete way that he may transform
not only our character defects but our entire
minds so that we can know and do God's will:

*I appeal to you brethren, by the mercies of
God, to present your bodies as a living
sacrifice, holy and acceptable to God, which
is your spiritual worship. Do not be
conformed to this world but be transformed
by the renewal of your mind, that you may
prove [know] what is the good and acceptable
and perfect will of God. Romans 12:1–2*

(Also) *Search me, O God, and know my heart!
—Try me and know my thoughts!
And see if there be any wicked way in me,
—And lead me in the way everlasting!
Psalm 139:23–24*

As we completed Step Five, many of us experienced a new energy and freedom to begin again. In Steps Six and Seven we are offered something altogether different from the way many of us have been instructed to live in relation to God: an impossible goal—and a way to achieve it.

There Is More to Step Six
Than First Appears

Christians often approach Steps Six and Seven saying, "Well I can do these two steps together. They'll be easy. What Christian *doesn't* want his or her sins and character defects removed? After all, we want to be better Christians, don't we?"

And it's true that almost everyone I know wants the glaring defects to be taken away. As the Twelve and Twelve points out, "No one wants to be so proud that he is scorned as a braggart nor so greedy that he is labeled a thief. No one wants to be angry enough to murder, lustful enough to rape, gluttonous enough to ruin his health. No one wants to be agonized by the chronic pain of envy or to be paralyzed by sloth" (p. 66). And what alcoholic doesn't want the compulsion to drink removed? What sinner-controller husband whose wife has offered to leave him if he won't straighten up doesn't want this compulsion to control removed? What mother whose grown children will hardly speak to her and won't come home to visit doesn't want this compulsion to control removed? We think we can do Step Six easily because in our lingering denial we think we want to change *everything* to God's way of living.

But when we think that way, we have forgotten that we didn't get in this program to please God. The only reason we agreed to do the Twelve Steps in the first place was that our attempts to control our own lives and the lives of others brought us such *pain.* We had to admit we were powerless and our lives had become unmanageable. It's healthy to remember that we didn't want these things removed primarily because we wanted to be better Christians but because we wanted the pain to stop.

If we do manage to refrain from some of these pain-producing behaviors, there is not much cause for congratulations as "spiritual seekers";

our motivation was to stop the pain. Most of the reason I haven't done some of the sinful things I've refrained from doing has been self-interest. For years I consciously wanted to do God's will because I loved him and was grateful to him. But in the program I have seen that many times I have been "good" because I was afraid to be "bad" or because the consequences might be too painful if things didn't work out. I feared I would get caught and it would ruin my life in some way. Often I didn't really *want* to have all those temptations removed and never think about them again; I still liked to think about some of them.

Step Six Refers to *All* Our Defects of Character

What about the destructive character defects that we *enjoy?* For some, it may be smoking or drinking too much; for others, eating too many sweets or worrying about other people and trying to fix them. How about our sexual fantasies? How about feeling superior? I like to feel superior, a little smarter, a little better than other people. And when somebody else errs I get a small feeling of warmth along with the sympathy I feel for them—one of the character defects that reflect my ambition and my insecurity about being "enough." Also I've discovered that ambition can be greed in disguise.

What about self-righteous anger? Many people love to remind certain family members for twenty years of the abusive things they did back then. And what about gossip, or economic hoarding? These, too, are a part of the Sin-disease. Whenever our desires exceed their natural purpose, we are involved with Sin and character defects. If we are honest with ourselves, we must admit that there are many of these things that we really don't want to quit doing.

Although it may seem that I am advocating perfection, I am not. The only Step we can do perfectly is Step One, that is, admit we are powerless. The rest of them we can only aim toward doing perfectly. But the authors of the Twelve Steps knew that our disease causes us to be very slick and evasive, and that if we don't decide to let God remove *all* our defects of character, then we'll make *any* character defects we still want to exercise "an exception" and continue to be in control. So it looks like Step Six is impossible.

A Word for Those Who Think
This Process Is Too Difficult

I once spoke about the Twelve Steps on a Christian radio program in Arizona. The talk show host said, "Some of these listeners are not going to go for this. What do you say to the ones who think it's too tough?"

"I tell them to forget it," I said. "I'm not saying that you *have* to do the Twelve Steps to be a good Christian. I'm saying if you are sick enough of being miserable and want to get over the pain and confusion of the Sin-disease, this is the best way I know to do it. There isn't an easy way. We are dealing with spiritual cancer cells here.

"If people say, 'It's too tough,' I don't argue with them. Even if actual cancer were their choice, they would have the freedom in Christ to stay in it. It would make me sad, but no one else can make that choice for them. My job is to share my experience, strength, and hope with them and then put them in God's hands. This may sound harsh to some Christians, but denial of how serious is the choice to follow Christ has led many of us Christians into apathy or despair. The more direct Twelve-Step approach leads people to confront the need to *choose* to 'go for it' with regard to spiritual growth, or to realize that they are choosing not to. God's view of the failure to choose is alluded to in Revelations 3:15, 16 of the *Living Bible:* 'I know you well—you are neither hot nor cold; I wish you were one or the other! But since you are merely lukewarm, I will spit you out of my mouth!'

"When I try to control other people into making the 'right choices'— even to save them from what I am calling spiritual cancer, I am *operating in the disease*. Only God can save people from Sin, and my experience is that the principles included in the Twelve Steps provide a biblical way to recover from the disease Sin causes. I don't want anyone to have the disease, but I now recognize that everyone has the freedom to choose whether to enter recovery or not. I know that unless I had chosen for myself to get well and myself claim my powerlessness, I would not have had the motivation to seek out and work the Twelve Steps. In my lifetime I have chosen both spiritual cancer and recovery, and I like recovery a *lot* better."

But there is a problem here. Those of us who are compulsive perfectionists know that we have already tried and can't remove even those sins and character defects we can see. Now we're talking about removing *all* our sins. Obviously the old ways of spiritual discipline and dedication won't cut it with that assignment.

Our Part Is to Become "Entirely Ready"—A New Attitude Toward God

We have arrived at a crucial and often overlooked spiritual principle of healing and growth. Our part in the removal of our character defects involves a new attitude toward God and how he works to change our lives in the practical struggles of living.

A lot of us have always wanted to do things right, even perfectly, right down to the daily practices of the faith—prayer, Bible study, good works, tithing, and so on. Our spiritual teachers implied that if we "paid the price" in terms of prayer, scripture reading, and meditation, God would give us the strength to win in our struggle with our character defects and the compulsive temptations they lead to. But we have always failed to be perfect. We couldn't see the extent of this failure clearly, however. We kept thinking we were doing okay because we partially succeeded, and the disease used these successes to blind us to how controlled we still were by our Sin.

When I got my prayer discipline down and could pray every day and have a quiet time of a certain length, I'd see progress. At last I was praying daily, and for forty-five minutes. I would think, "At last I am in control of my prayer life!" Then I would start concentrating on getting my work under control, because I was overcommitted and my compulsive working habits had taken over. I would then become so intent on my work that I would find myself focusing on what I had to do at work during my prayer time. I would be thinking and praying about how to "get control" of my work—a Sin-disease approach—instead of facing my addiction to work.

When someone would accuse me of being a workaholic, I'd hide out, and through superhuman effort and ridiculously long hours "get caught up" to get my work under control. If I happened to get my work and time commitments under control (which I did only periodically through these work binges), then I might fall into financial fear or impatience to get more done or get it done faster.

In other words, whatever contemporary personal problem I *hadn't* solved would jump in and fill my life. I had the illusion that I had "solved" a particular problem when it was superseded by a problem more threatening to my image of adequacy. Because some areas in my life remained "quiet" I thought I had solved those problems "for good." In reality, by the time I got to financial fear, after going through all the other issues I've just listed, my prayer time would have slipped from seven times a week to three—or some days a fifteen-second, "Haven't got time today, God, see you tonight," and I was gone.

Yet when anyone asked me at such times, "Do you pray?" I would confidently and sincerely say, "Oh, yes, I pray every day." But unseen by me, my prayer life had eroded, changed in character and importance along with the quality of the rest of my spiritual life. All the while I had the illusion that I was living for God.

If I ever did overcome some habit I became grandiose and self-satisfied, unconsciously looking down at people who wouldn't pay the price to do whatever I had done to change. Noticing other people's weakness in a given area kept me from focusing on my other glaring character defects—about which I was in denial. Many alcoholics in recovery tell how really hard they were on other people in their families who hadn't stopped drinking (after the alcoholic had stopped), yet the recovering alcoholic continued to control and judge until confronted by the Twelve Steps.

When we tried to clean ourselves up with our own power and "discipline" we kept ourselves agitated, confused, in denial, and worn out, and we were in almost constant emotional pain. We were like the man who tore the scab off his arm every morning to see if his wound had healed.

Spiritual Growth—A Different Game

But it was in doing the sixth Step that I saw why I had become so exhausted. I'd been trying to do *God's part* in the spiritual growth and healing process. In the program I was told that my part was "being entirely ready," being ready to *let God* be the controller and life-changer of myself and others. When I did that, my sponsor said, I would see how God's power is released to flow through our lives to clean them only when we quit trying to control the *how* and *when* he is to use that power. Then I remembered that Paul too discovered that Christian salvation and growth came through grace not works. It is not works that we do toward our own perfection, Paul said, but our willingness to receive his grace

(Eph. 2:8–9). At first this sounded like a call to complacency—until I got into Step Seven. This attitude of readiness to let God reach into our lives and uncover and remove the things that make us spiritually and emotionally sick is paradoxically the doorway to active and effective change of specific lifelong habits and sins. But it means turning loose of control—even of our healing.

This is a very tough program, but the question that was asked me was, "Would you like to be free after years of being frustrated and anxious? Would you like to walk down that street and feel that you're living in the present and that your past sins and mistakes have been laid to rest?"

In the fifth chapter of John's Gospel there's an interesting passage that describes a cripple who waits by the pool of Bethesda, which was reputed to have healing powers. Bruce Larson helped me to a new insight about this passage when we were standing by the site of the pool in the Holy Land. For thirty-eight years this man has been waiting for someone to lower him into the water when the surface is disturbed so that he would be healed. When Jesus saw the man, he had a conversation with him that went something like this: "Do you want to be healed?"

The man was incensed. "What do you mean? Thirty-eight years I've been lying here on this pallet!" Then the man blamed other people: "I waited, and nobody would throw me into the water at the right time. My behind is flat from lying on these stones, and you're asking me if I want to be healed?"

And Jesus said, "Yes, that's what I'm asking. Do you want to be healed?" (And for all of us that's a very real question.)

The invalid had to think it over. His whole identity was wrapped up in being crippled. Everybody knew him and came by and said, "Hi, Joe," and Joe didn't have to work, didn't have to take on any responsibilities. He was a cripple, but he was in control of his life.

Jesus knew that if the invalid by the pool took him up on his offer to heal him, he'd have a whole new life. Once healed, we can't complain in self-pity anymore or tell other people it's their fault that we are not fulfilling our potential or being happy.

This process of "being entirely willing to let God" gives us something new to pray about. My old prayers used to be "God give me the power to overcome this problem"—whatever it was. Then I'd attack it. Now whenever I come to God with a character defect I ask a different question: "Am I really ready to give this to you, Lord?" And if I can answer yes, I am ready for Step Seven.

TAKING STEP SIX

Step Six
*Were entirely ready to have God remove
all these defects of character.*

1. Consider which religious behaviors you have engaged in that you now realize you used in the hope of fixing yourself (e.g., longer prayer time, more intense Bible study, doing volunteer work). Describe your feelings about doing each of those things at the time (joy, impatience, hope, frustration, boredom, anger, fear, etc.).

2. In what ways have you tried to fix yourself with your own power (e.g., stuffing feelings such as anger to "prove you had faith"; trying harder to resist a temptation or a character defect such as impatience, sarcasm, or resentment; criticizing yourself harshly whenever one of your character defects was active)?

3. What character defects have you recognized that you need to become willing to let God remove?

4. Are there any character defects you have discovered that you enjoy and are not sure you want God to remove—or know you don't want him to remove? If so, name them (e.g., greed, grandiose thinking, lust).

5. Describe how you have attempted to use your own power to fix others (e.g., giving advice, giving them books or tapes they have not asked for so they can get fixed, withholding communication or money or sex until they do what you "think best").

6. Write in your own words your statement to God that you are now ready for him to remove all your defects of character.

Chapter 10

STEP SEVEN

Humbly Asked Him to Remove Our Shortcomings

A biblical expression of the nature of the radical shift that can take place through Step Seven, from an anxious, material, or intellectual faith to a spiritual life of trust in God:

Truly, truly, I say to you, unless one is born anew, he cannot see the kingdom of God. . . . That which is born of the flesh is flesh, and that which is born of the Spirit is spirit. John 3:3–6

On completing Step Six, we were on the brink of entering the world of spiritual living, on the brink of growth at new and deeper levels than most of us had ever imagined. Approaching Step Seven we had experienced at least the beginnings of readiness to let God take over the work of healing us!

Taking Step Seven was for many of us the greatest act of authentic humility we have ever been asked to commit: to transfer control of our recovery to God. Although this step sounds simple at first, it is an amazing spiritual watershed. Where we had once asked God to *help us* get out of our pain and get our lives back on track, now we are telling him that at last we are putting ourselves in his hands so completely that we want *God* to remove *any* defects that stand in the way of our being the person God wants us to be—letting God decide what these defects are. In a paradoxical way we are going to quit trying to fix ourselves. When I was first told that, I said, "That's irresponsible! For me to quit wrestling with my character defects would be a moral cop-out." But what I said only showed my sponsor how little I knew about humility and the spiritual world.

What Is Humility?

The word *humility* has received bad press in recent years, and I can see why. I was taught that being humble was acting as if I were unimportant, inadequate, of no value. I got the idea that it was an outward attitude of "I'm lucky to be here breathing good air when other more worthy people could have it" (when in fact I am thinking, "I know I can get out there and succeed if I can just get the chance!"). Humility was acting as though I "knew my place" and wasn't going to be too competitive.

But my family's motto was, "Do it yourself, don't bother other people." "Bothering other people" (asking for help) was a sign of inadequacy. My father taught me that I should do everything myself, so I could be proud of my own victories over life's problems. I don't think he was unusual in his philosophy. In America it is common to believe we are supposed to be self-sufficient, both as individuals and as a nation. I thought that if I had to ask other people to do things for me, I was "being humbled," meaning that I was inadequate.

But according to the Twelve and Twelve, humility is a clear recognition of who we are followed by a sincere attempt to become what we could be. That is, humility is *seeing ourselves as we actually are,* good and bad, strong and weak, and acting authentically on those truths. This is not a naïve attitude suggesting we have in some way already "arrived." It is a sincere attempt to state the positive truth that when we face the truth of our shortcomings and the fact that we are powerless to change and begin to let God take our defects away, we have entered the pathway of humility. For the reality is, only God can take away our Sin, our deeply entrenched addictions, and our lifelong character defects. It is on this pathway, where we humbly ask God to remove all these defects of character, that the tools of recovery bring the healing, happiness, and security we have dreamed of. But once more it is only powerlessness and pain that can force us to take the seventh Step into humility.

Depending on Our Own Strength
Blocks Spiritual Growth

The experience of many of us in this program is that we want more than our share of romance, security, and prestige in the worlds we live in. And the Twelve and Twelve indicates that this is our Sin. We have to control people, places, and things to get more than our share, because other people are reluctant to give up part of their share. It was only if and when we got "enough" more than our share that we thought we would have the good feelings we dreamed of.

But as long as we felt that we could get these good feelings by our own strength, intelligence, and power (even with God's help), we couldn't have a faith in God that really worked for us, because we were replacing him as the deciding, controlling center of our worlds. That isn't the way things really are—we are not the central controlling power in life. That most basic ingredient of all, humility, was missing at the practical, everyday feeling level of our lives. And because it is humility that leads to a desire to seek and do God's will, our spiritual growth was impaired.

In our heads we wanted God's will, but our daily decisions said we wanted our own will. We'd say to God that we trusted him with our finances, our marriages, our children and that we only wanted his will to be done. Then we worried and worked compulsively to try to make everything work out just the way we wanted it. And when that way was threatened, we would become afraid and upset. Although we knew many moments of success and the brief happiness that getting things accomplished brings, we were often on the edge of being out of control, frustrated and lonely, depressed and anxious, and vacillating between fear and elation.

In the midst of this intense confusion many of us performed on the outside like angels. We were committed to "doing things right," and it certainly didn't seem phony. It *wasn't*. We weren't aware that this was what we were doing until we got to Step Seven and looked back. We just assumed that was the way life is in the fast lane. Today I know that this having to control at an operational level—even if we have consciously given God control—is the way the disease works in my life and in the lives of many people who come to the program.

Long-term Change Begins to Occur with Step Seven

Finally, before coming to the Twelve Steps, I went through some humiliations: broken relationships, divorce, failures. These events put me in a position to let God crack the delusion of my grandiosity—even as a "Christian leader." When our pain gets severe enough and our denial cracks open, we are shocked to see the deceptive nature of our lives and faith. As a result of that shock a lot of us have then watched God slowly turn our way of living and believing upside down through these Twelve Steps. For many of us the long-term change began with the humility involved in Step Seven as we "took our hands off" and asked God to make us into his kind of people, in his way, and on his timetable.

Humility acts as a lens through which we can begin to get a practical grasp on our own reality and our own part in the pain around us. Humility puts us in a true relationship with God as the Higher Power in our lives, because with it comes the stark knowledge that we aren't God and don't have the power to be. As we do these Twelve Steps, facing and confessing some of our worst sins, we begin to know islands of peace. We can see that humility, this facing, validating, and dealing with our own character defects, is the true road to self-acceptance and acceptance by God and by other people. Many of us have sought this acceptance intensely all our lives, down the wrong roads of grandiose dreams and compulsive attempts to work for God, to control people, places, and things "out there."

For years I was afraid that I would speak somewhere and somebody would say, "You're a phony. You don't know what you're talking about." I didn't feel like a phony, but I was afraid that I wasn't very smart. I didn't feel dim-witted, but I was afraid I was. As I began to do the steps and to see my grandiosity, I realized that the reason I have always been afraid of being "exposed" is that I have wanted to be *more* than I was; I felt that I had to know something wise about practically everything. And of course I didn't. I was afraid my dishonesty, my pretending to know more than I do, might be revealed. It was taking the steps and living into the reality that I don't have to be more, because I am accepted by God with all my limitations and the sins of my past, that was my first taste of humility—and peace.

Grandiosity—The Opposite of Humility

People in the Twelve-Step programs have taught many of us that a large part of our unhappiness has to do with this grandiosity and this pretending to be more than we are. We have laid expectations on ourselves that no one could have fulfilled and then felt unhappy when we couldn't fulfill them.[1] But as we become more honest, the situation around us changes. We are not under so much pressure to do the impossible. At the same time, though, it is scary, because sometimes we don't get as much done as we did and we have irrational fears that we may starve or "fail" if we don't drive ourselves as we always have. We worry that if we say, "I don't know," in response to questions, people will think we are not on top of our field. But now every day in meetings, I hear very wise people admit they don't know something. When they make such admissions, I feel grateful to be in this program where humility and reality are live possibilities when we let God be God in our lives.

Gradually (some days) my grandiose expectations for myself are being replaced. I am seeing that although I am a precious child of God who has some gifts and does know some things, I am just another struggling person when it comes to living in relationship with other people, God, and myself. For me to pretend that I know more than I do is not only self-defeating in my recovery from the Sin-disease, it is dishonest and another subtle form of trying to control other people's reality, their opinion of me.

Our Deepening Relationship
to God—and to Ourselves

But the biggest change the humility of Step Seven brings is in our relationship with God. He is no longer the "helper" who helps us get our agenda back on track so we can accomplish what we want. He is the "owner of the business," and we are trainee employees, learning the business and our part in it one day at a time.

As I have suggested, my prayer life reflected the attitude that God was my "helper" until very recently. I would pray that God would fix whatever was out of control in my life or my family's. But now I have seen that my agenda is formed largely by my Sin and my character defects. All my agendas, financial, personal, vocational, are almost completely made up of plans to put me in control, to get things to go the way I think they should for me and for the members of my family.

But when we took Step Seven, when we put our whole lives and our recoveries in the hands of God, who put in us the spark of life, many of us were amazed at the new surge of hope and enthusiasm that occurred within us. We saw that *God can show us* what our buried aptitudes are, what our proclivities are, what we were made to do. As we let God remove that which we are not, and as we hear and try to be in fact what we potentially are, then we'll be more authentic. Living more in tune with the person God made us to be, we become free from the constant war that has gone on inside about what we should be and do in different areas of our lives.

We May Be Using the Right Aptitude
in the Wrong Place

I have a friend whom I'll call Jim who went out for the same basketball team I did in college. He was about six foot three, and his legs were unbelievably long. When we ran laps together, he would glide along in a smooth lope while I churned away beside him. He'd be fifty yards ahead of me in a few minutes; when we finished a long run, I was panting for air, and Jim was not even breathing hard.

But Jim just couldn't make the basketball team. Finally the head track coach watched him running laps and said to him, "Listen, why don't you come out for track? We need another distance runner and you're a natual for that."

Jim said, "But I'm a basketball player."

The coach said, "Why don't you just give it a try?" Within a few months Jim was traveling in Europe and Asia with the track team, a world-class distance runner. He had always been a world-class distance runner, but he had thought he was a basketball player.

A similar thing happens to people as they work the steps and begin to see who they really are. Many of us have been trying to do something that wasn't natural for us. Maybe it was our father's or mother's dream for us, or maybe we just wandered into a vocation because there wasn't anything else on the horizon at the time. But when our denial cracks open and we put our lives and recovery in God's hands, we don't have to spend all our energy, consciously or unconsciously, maintaining a vocational image of some kind. As time goes by we may relax and begin to recognize the God-given aptitudes that we have never let ourselves see fully for fear we might fail.

You may have buried dreams that you could fulfill. Perhaps you ought to start a small business, run a university, paint, invent things, write books, or teach. But in growing up you got the idea from someone, "You can't do that; don't try it." When we take Step Seven and humbly ask God to remove our shortcomings, we are not only giving up our grandiose aspirations to control people, places, and things around us, we are also saying that we are entirely ready to let God engineer our lives through the process of recovery to fulfill whatever natural potential he may have put in us. We are ready to be made ready to do these things on his time schedule. We are fully subjecting our lives and our wills to God as we understand him. We are saying, in effect, "I now believe you are real, that you accept me as I really am, warts and all, and that you have my happiness and best interests at heart. I believe also that as I am willing to face the ego-puncturing pain of walking through this humility-producing process, you will take away the impediments that keep me from being the happy, joyous, and free person you made me to be."

A paradoxical discovery is that when we admit our powerlessness, we can discover the latent power that God has put in us. In a mysterious way having this power is part of what it means to be "made in his image." This personal power of authenticity develops as we continue to let go and center our lives in this relationship with God. And this power also affects the way we communicate our faith. Jesus, and later some of his followers, spoke to people "with authority," with authenticity, "and not as their scribes" (Matt. 7:29).

This picture of the way a relationship with God works in a person's life is paradoxical in several ways. God can release us to use the freedom and creative power he put in us because we do not have our hands tied up in efforts to control him, his people, and the world he made for us all. And this kind of contact with God replaces exaggerated fear, weariness, and weakness with positive spiritual strength and understanding, all of which make the miracle of living the Twelve Steps and the gospel of Jesus Christ possible.

Unless We're Entirely Ready, God Doesn't Change Us

Some people become confused at this point, saying, "I don't understand. I told God I was ready to have him take this character defect, but he didn't take it. Why not?" My sponsor told me that it might be because they were not ready to have God remove *all* their character defects; they still wanted to stay in control and just get rid of the ones that impeded their progress toward their own goals. He also said that if God doesn't remove a character defect you have asked him to it could be because you aren't *entirely* ready to have it removed. When that happened to me (when a character defect was not removed), he advised me to go back and do the first three steps on that specific shortcoming: (1) admit you are powerless over it, (2) come to believe that God can restore you to sanity with regard to the area in question, and (3) make a decision to turn the problem and your whole life and will over to God. As you go back, walk through this process, and talk about what's happening about the issue in meetings and with your sponsor, you can often see where you are not ready. Then you may want to go back and do the fourth through seventh Steps, focusing on the specific defect in question.

For example, a friend wanted God to take the character defect of "impatience" out of her life. She thought he would take the problem away from her, but instead he began by giving her lots of opportunities to *practice* patience. His strategy was evidently to provide opportunities for her first to look at the inner character defect that causes the impatience.

Finally, by working the steps, my friend saw the underlying reason she is impatient; "In my grandiosity, I think that I and the people who work for me or with me can do much more in an hour or a week than is possible, given the natural interruptions and limitations in a working period. For years I kept giving superhuman effort to meeting impossible commitments and trying to get other people to do the same. By looking deeper into my impatience and seeing my grandiosity, I am learning to make fewer commitments and allow longer deadlines for myself—and for those around me. And because I couldn't even see that *grandiosity* was the problem, my impatience was unyielding. I just thought I and others were not working hard enough or efficiently enough."

We become able to stop abusing people (including ourselves) in this way when we allow God's power to overcome our shortcomings. When he does remove a lifelong character defect the experience is incredible; it may free you to become what you have always wanted to be. My friend says she can't believe that she's patient with herself and the other people who are working with her. She said she recently requested a six-week extension on a project deadline instead of going into her usual "kamikaze completion frenzy" to meet the old (and impractical) deadline.

The Words of Surrender

This is the suggested prayer in the Big Book for taking Step Seven the first time: "My Creator, I am now willing that you should have all of me, good and bad. I pray that you now remove from me every single defect of character that stands in the way of my usefulness to you and my fellows. Grant me strength, as I go out from here, to do your bidding. Amen" (p. 76).

Since that initial prayer, whenever I notice a compulsion or character defect operating in my life (be it the desire to overeat, drink, resent, work compulsively, or control people), I say the words, "I am entirely ready to have you remove this defect of character." I imagine picking up the character defect as if it were a poisonous snake, putting it in a sack, and setting the sack on a conveyor belt going up to God. When the sack with the character defect comes back again later, I look in the sack, put it *right back on* the conveyor belt, and get back to what I was doing without engaging my mind with it. If you take the defect out of the sack and start trying to deal with it in your mind, it will win almost every time. Pretty soon I recognize the sack and plop it back on the conveyor belt without even looking inside. And then I go about my business. Every time the character defect comes up I do this. After days, weeks, or years,

I've noticed that some of them are gone and others hardly ever show up. I know that God has been at work while I've gone on with the program. It seems that he takes these tenacious character problems only when we are entirely ready to let him do so.

As my new attitude toward God developed by doing Step Six, I learned to go about doing what I think God would have me do. I learned to let him work in anonymity while I'm doing what I can to stay in recovery and love people.

It isn't that we "dismiss" the problem. We dig it out, we face it ourselves and with others in the program, and go to God and show him the defect; then in Steps Six and Seven we become entirely ready and ask him to remove it. Eventually God takes these defects, through the process of our seeing, claiming, confessing, and offering them specifically to him for changing. As we move on into doing the next right thing, God somehow drains off enough compulsive energy from our character defects that we can handle them. Hundreds of thousands of alcoholics know the amazing truth of having the compulsive craving for a drink removed this way by God.

Defects Involving Other People

I began to realize that healthy people really don't want us to *be* God in their lives and solve their problems. They want to tell us about their pain to have someone to share it with. Now that we know we are not God and *can't* solve the basic problems of other peoples' lives, we are able to listen and support them without feeling that we have to "fix" their problems. And we can turn the responsibility for solving their problems over to God, too.

Now when somebody tells me about a painful problem, often I can listen, keep myself out of their pain, and support them by saying things like, "That sounds painful, and I think you will make a good decision about this." Sometimes somebody tells me something that sounds to me a little like, "We're going to buy a live grizzly bear to play with our kids." That sort of thing used to cause an immediate and strong reaction in me. I'd say, "No, that's stupid," and proceed to explain all the reasons that would be a dumb move. Now I say, "A grizzly bear for the kids to play with? I feel a lot of fear when you say that." Then I don't say anything else. I've shared my feelings but haven't attacked or tried to control the other person with my "wisdom" and suggestions.

I didn't become aware that God had changed me in this area for months after I had been through Step Seven for the first time. Even though I had kept asking him to remove my character defect of being the Great Adviser and Fixer and had finally become entirely ready for him to take it away, I still saw the tendency arise every time I was with certain family members. But at a recent gathering we had an unusually good time. I asked the very wise woman God gave me to live with what had happened. She reminded me that nobody tried to control anybody. I was so happy I wept. I had not even *had the urge* to control them by giving advice.

I didn't realize, until I quit providing all the answers and solutions, that people around me feel more heard and understood when I don't "manage," and they are free to make their own sound decisions and to learn from their pain (to learn about "grizzly bears," perhaps).

Even in the past, my advice not to buy a grizzly bear never did stop any of them from doing so. But later if the bear ate one of the children's feet, they hated me. Why should *I* get hated because the grizzly bear ate the child's foot? When I tried to stop them from doing something they were dead set on doing, they didn't learn anything except to resent me. Also they didn't like me for controlling their lives. It seems that Philip Parham is right when he says about life in recovery, "Experience is not just the best teacher, it is the only teacher."[2] I know that may sound hard and uncaring, but I am speaking about my relating to people over eighteen who have not asked for my advice. It is not my job to step in and straighten out their lives. Even God doesn't do that to us, and he *has* the right answers.

What Will Replace Our Shortcomings?

Many of us, myself included, gave up certain personal and vocational dreams and choices years ago because we became stuck in our negative character defects and the negative atmosphere they created in our minds. But as we see that God's responsibility is the overcoming of our basic flaws, then we must choose something else with which to fill our thoughts (or they will snap back to the character defects and pain of the past or worries about the future).

People who begin the Twelve-Step program but don't follow through with it and don't put new things in their lives sometimes become sicker and more obnoxious and controlling than they were before—the only change is that now they don't act out their addictions (e.g., drinking, taking drugs, working or eating compulsively). As I mentioned, in A.A. these people are called dry drunks and in the Church, hypocrites (people who make the verbal commitment to Christ to become God's people but don't do anything about changing their own character and behavior).

In Luke 11:26 Jesus said that when a demon is cast out of a man, it goes away into an arid land. And then the demon gets miserable out there and says, "I think I will go home." So the evil spirit comes back to the person who has had his life cleaned out but doesn't put anything new in, and he brings seven more demons with him because he's got a clean place to go. "And," Jesus said, "the last state of that man becomes worse than the first."

If we clear out our shortcomings and addictive behaviors by giving them to God and don't put something positive in their place, we may become self-righteous prigs. The world dislikes us, with our judgmental lack of humility (unconscious though it may be), and the world shows sound judgment in not wanting to be around us.

As we continued to take these steps toward spiritual maturity, many of us decided to substitute for trying to fix ourselves and other people trying to find and do God's will. We put this new purpose in the vacuum where our self-absorbing compulsions and struggles to be perfect had been. As we become willing to let God take away our fear, we replace that fear with positive images. I was advised to tell myself each morning that I am a precious child of God; I am a wonderful person that God has made, and I want to become that person. I made a list of my positive traits and the things in my life that I am thankful for, and I read them every morning. In place of those worries, fears, and negative self-messages with which I started my days *for years,* I've begun to put in new positive information and a new agenda.[3]

We Are Preparing *for* Something

Someone once asked me, "If this program is about the Christian's life, when are we going to get to the part about helping other people?" The program's answer is that first we've got to get help for ourselves. Jesus said to "love your neighbor as yourself" (Matt. 19:19). But because most of us *don't* love ourselves, we have not had good results in following his teaching. If we don't love ourselves and accept ourselves, having seen our powerlessness and our denial, then it is virtually impossible for us to love other people with their Sin and their refusal to see their need for a Higher Power. The highway of church history is strewn with the bodies of those injured by Christians who have tried to "help people" and "create community" without having ever faced their own Sin-disease and realized that only God can heal and create authentic community.

So in the program we must begin by taking these first steps to face our powerlessness, turn to God and put our broken selves in his hands, and then finally in Step Seven ask him to clear out anything from our lives that will keep us from being who he wants us to be, anything that keeps us from doing his will. When we have given him permission to do those things, we will be prepared to relate to other people in humility and with his kind of love: "Love your neighbor as yourself." This first part of the Twelve-Step program is a way to let God teach us how to love ourselves. Later, if we want to keep what we are discovering, we will learn how to love other people.

We Americans are so impatient, however, that we want to whiz by this "facing ourselves" and go out to help change other people. Many of us have merely taken the control and subtle manipulation of the Sin-disease out on the streets in our Christian clothes; in our denial we are baffled that people don't respond, or if they do, that they don't stick around.

As we shall discover in Step Twelve, a prerequisite for keeping the serenity that we are finding and the new relationship with God *is* to carry the message to others. But the Twelve Steps, in their infinite wisdom, do not call for that until we ourselves are being healed, changed, and prepared to do this kind of message carrying under God's control, not our own. (This does not mean that we wait until we have done Step Twelve to help people. We start at once, but with great humility and the awareness that even our helping may be laced with Sin-disease, control issues, and denial.)

Having Experienced God's Changing Touch, We Can Move On

After we have begun to experience God's changing of us, it has dawned on many of us that now we can find the courage to go to others whom we have harmed, making amends and making a commitment to try to be different toward them. We now have hope that we *can* be different—not because we have found a new way to muscle ourselves into changing, but because we know that God can change us, remove our character defects that have harmed others, and accompany us through any pain we may encounter as we reach out. Now we are prepared to begin Steps Eight and Nine.

TAKING STEP SEVEN

Step Seven
Humbly asked him to remove our shortcomings.

1. What was your definition of humility before studying the meaning of the word in this chapter?

2. What does humility mean to you now?

3. Describe the ways your grandiosity manifests itself in your life? (Here are some examples: thinking if I could just get organized, I could accomplish a superhuman amount; thinking if I pleased my husband or wife enough, he or she would treat me with respect and love; thinking if I stopped being passive and stood up to my wife and "acted like a man," I could heal all the problems in our marriage by myself; thinking if I could send my son enough money, he would eventually get and keep a good job and pay his own way; thinking if I could calmly educate my roommate about the perils of smoking, she would eventually quit.)

4. Write down the date you prayed the Seventh-Step Prayer, or your own version of it.

5. Record what positive character traits could replace your character defects (listed in doing Four, Five, and Six). For example:

Defect: Fear
Positive Trait: Courage

6. As time goes on, you may notice that a character defect has been removed, and you felt or behaved differently in what used to be a painful situation. When you notice this, record these incidents in your notebook.

7. After asking God to take their *whole* lives, it has been helpful to some people to begin to get in touch with what they have naturally liked to do, realizing that God also touches us through experiences we are drawn to. Many of us have spent our lives filling roles unnatural to us to win some sort of love or approval, and part of recovery is to find God's will (the way he has made us) for how we are going to spend our vocational and recreational time. If you would like to get in touch with this aspect of your life, you can make a beginning by going back and listing things in your life you have enjoyed doing (e.g., hiking, doing math problems, gardening).[4]

Chapter 11

STEP EIGHT

*Made a List of All Persons We Had
Harmed, and Became Willing to
Make Amends to Them All*

A biblical expression of the need to see our
own faults, our part, and to forgive those who
have hurt us before going out to make amends,
hoping for forgiveness:

*Why do you see the speck that is in your
brother's eye, but do not notice the log that is
in your own eye? Or how can you say to your
brother, "Let me take the speck out of your
eye," when there is a log in your own eye?
You hypocrite, first take the log out of
your own eye. Matthew 7:3–5*

Now we are at a turning point in the recovery process. The moment we agree to have all of our own defects removed (in Step Seven), God turns us outward to prepare us to love others. However, before we can love others in a healthy way in the present, it seems that we must do what we can to heal the broken and bruised relationships of the past. The guilt, shame, pain, and resentment surrounding these relationships we have bungled is stored in the basements of our lives; this putrid, musty, hidden material isolates us and makes us want to keep our distance both from other people and from God. We are afraid of new relationships for fear they will be just as painful, or maybe afraid that if we get too close again people might discover the past results of our Sin and reject us.

This Part of the Healing Process
May Seem Reversed

In the past few years people have asked me, in effect, "Is this Twelve-Step program Christian or not?" This question arises out of a very perceptive observation: the Twelve-Step process is at several points very different from the model of spiritual growth many of us saw as young people at home and in Sunday school. Certain steps appear to be the opposite of the "natural impulses" we learned by watching what was actually done by those who taught us—as opposed to what we were taught about the way of confession and grace in human relationships.

Some years ago I heard a story about the chaplains at two Ivy League universities. As the story went, they occasionally exchanged pulpits. One year at graduation in the chapel of one school, the chaplain of the other preached to the graduating class. At the end of his remarks he told the following story: Years ago there was a husky thirteen-year-old farm boy who was very ambitious. He worked from dawn to dusk, and his father was very proud of him. For the boy's fourteenth birthday, his father bought him a secondhand Gravely mowing tractor. The Gravely company made very fine tractors, and the boy was thrilled. He began to earn extra money by mowing yards and fields for neighbors and the people in the nearby town. The boy took great care of his machine; he washed and cleaned the motor and shined the exterior.

One day he noticed the blade was dull. The boy very carefully drove the tractor into the barn and turned it over to take the bolt off that held the blade on. Having been around machinery a lot, he knew to loosen a bolt you turn it counterclockwise, so he put a big wrench on the bolt and gave it a turn. It only moved a tiny bit, and then it wouldn't budge. Now, this boy was very proud of his physical strength. He was a star lineman on the school football team. But he couldn't move that bolt at all, and he wasn't about to ask his dad for help on such a routine matter.

Just then he remembered what his father had told him in a similar situation. "Get a longer piece of pipe, and put it over the wrench handle to get some leverage." So he got a pipe and put it over the handle. Then he pulled on the pipe. Nothing. Then he got under the pipe with his back and tried to lift it. But the bolt would not move. Finally, in humiliation, the young man took the tractor in the family pickup to the Gravely tractor dealer in town. When he got there, the mechanic looked at the stuck bolt and said, "Wait a minute. Let me check something." And he looked up the model number. Then he said, "I hate to tell you this, but for several years the Gravely Company reversed the threads on that bolt. You've been *tightening* that sucker trying to loosen it. And don't worry about being strong, son, you've tightened it so bad we are going to have to burn it off with a torch."

The visiting preacher is said to have paused and then continued, "Everything you've learned at this school is like that—when it comes to dealing with your intimate relationships and your spiritual lives. If you try to use your mind to figure out your family, and if you try to control them the way you would a business deal or a scientific experiment, you are going to wind up tightening and ruining the very thing you want to free, blocking the very relationships you want to release."

And as we approach Steps Eight and Nine it is helpful to remember that in healing bruised relationships it is often necessary to do exactly the opposite of what we feel an urge to do and perhaps what we saw our parents and the elders of the church doing in their meetings and relationships. For example, when I have hurt someone's feelings in my family, my first internal response is to try to justify myself. If that doesn't work, I then try to bury the incident and pacify the person, perhaps doing something nice to make the person forget my thoughtless or abusive behavior.

But in Steps Eight and Nine we learn that the way out of the pain of separation is *through* that pain, not around it. Instead of justifying ourselves, we own our hurtful behavior specifically. Instead of burying what we find, we go to the person we have offended, confess the behavior, and make amends. For those of us who have always hated to be wrong and have been terribly afraid of rejection, this is a very frightening prospect. When I had been in the program long enough to be at Step Eight I had heard many people talk about the serenity and restored relationships that came from doing Steps Eight and Nine, and I was at least ready to do Step Eight. I was desperately afraid of Step Nine, but my sponsor reminded me that I only had to do one step at a time; I could wait until I was ready—even if it took years. So I began Step Eight.

When you first read about Steps Eight and Nine it's good to remember that you're supposed to have done Steps One through Seven first, which may have taken you as long as two or three years.

The Purpose of Step Eight

A man named Bill B. in a book called *Compulsive Overeater* said that the Twelve-Step program gives us a second chance to grow up; many of us missed the first time around with regard to our emotional lives.[1] The program gives us a second chance to learn how to live with God, with ourselves, and with other people. Bill B. says there is only one law for him, and that is to love, and only two sins: to interfere with the growth of another human being in any way and to interfere with one's own growth. He believes that such interference is blocking what God wants in the world (p. 106). Although my own definition of Sin is broader than his, I believe that Bill B. is right that the purpose of Steps Eight and Nine is getting rid of *everything* abusive or harmful that stands between us and other people.

My sponsor told me that this process is not primarily for the benefit of the other people. The purpose of doing Steps Eight and Nine is to get well ourselves so that we can be free to love people and do God's will. We're not trying to be perfect before the people in our past or even to get them to like us. We're trying to do our parts in getting rid of our own guilt and wiping our slates clean. If we feel guilty about some things others might consider stupid or immaterial, we may have to become willing to make amends for them anyway, because it's worth it for our recovery.

Our Need for a Mask of Adequacy Diminishes in Step Eight

By the time we reached Step Eight, it was fully apparent to most of us that the Sin-disease is a disease of denial and deceit, of distorting the truth. When we were immersed in the disease, much of the true meaning of what we did and said was not visible to us. When we are in denial, we are not fully aware of the dishonesty of our behavior, and we tend to defend our perceptions to the death.

This denial sustains the mask, the image of adequacy and righteousness (being right) that we supported with so much of our energy. Steps Eight and Nine go a long way toward destroying the need for this mask of adequacy or perfection.

When I first got into this program, I could not have said to you, "I lie." I could have said to you that I *used to* lie, but I could not have used the present tense, "I lie now," because my former religious teaching implied that when one commits his or her life to God and confesses about the past, one is then "cured" and doesn't do it anymore (though even a cursory look at the lives of many of us Christians would blow that theory). That way of thinking allows us to keep our current self-image of perfection intact—with the additional bonus of having been "honest" in the confession. I'm a good person who discovered my dishonesty and "gave it up." The incredible thing to me is that even though my behavior in this area has changed drastically, I still catch myself in this protective, defensive dishonesty; I still catch myself lying. And that is the difference: *I catch myself*.

Because of our new sense of self-esteem, of being good and worthwhile (because of grace) even in our imperfection, we can afford to catch these things. We are told that by doing Steps Eight and Nine we can begin to see ourselves, and how we run our lives by self-will, through the eyes of humility.

How Our Trouble Involves Other People But Hurts Us Too

Step Eight is a social housecleaning, just as Step Four was our personal housecleaning. In Step Eight we're setting out to clean up all the bruised relationships and the pockets of guilt, pain, fear, resentment, and sadness that are stored inside, stuck to our shameful past deeds. For this undealt-with material blocks us from loving other people, ourselves, and God in the present.

It's as if God were saying, "Okay, now you want me to take all of your character defects, fine. Then you can be free and serene and the person I want you to be. But first you must see that almost all your troubles involve other people. You've tried to control them one way or the other or fix them; you have guilty or resentful feelings about them; or you have been so preoccupied with yourself and your feelings, dreams, and plans that you have ignored them emotionally and caused them to experience some of their worst fears of being deserted. Now I want you to face what you have done and *own your part* in hurting each person in your life so you can move into the future I have for you unencumbered by the past and beginning to understand how not to keep repeating the mistakes of that past."

Steps Four and Five lanced the boil of pent-up feelings connected with our past actions and relieved some of the pain, but through Steps Eight and Nine God gives us a way to go back to the "scenes of our crimes" that we've been hiding from ourselves, a way to face more of the painful feelings at the point of their origin. In this way the infection can be healed, and the pain we feel over those past actions won't be necessary anymore. As we do this God can begin to heal our memories—even our denied ones—and quietly take away the guilt, resentment, sadness, and fear of discovery that has caused so much of the pain in our lives.

Facing this buried guilt and resentment is a major step toward being comfortable with ourselves. People who know me well are aware that I was never comfortable with myself. I never wanted anyone to see my weakness and imperfection and see the petty, selfish things that I had done. Now, on those occasions when I don't feel those fears of being discovered, it seems like a miracle to me.

When going through the Twelve Steps it's hard to remember that these sorts of changes take time. It took years for us to collect these painful denied regrets and bruised relationships. But we in the American fast lane figure if there's not a way to fix or solve a problem almost immediately, then the cure must not be effective, or we must be doing something wrong. The program, however, makes it clear that it takes time to undo the damage to trust that our diseased behavior has caused in the lives of people around us. One friend said that for him the speed of healing has been "agricultural." But Step Eight is a giant-step forward.

Making a List of People You Have Harmed

The first thing to do is to make a list of people you have harmed. You have a partial list from Step Four.

The Twelve and Twelve defines "harm" as "the result of instincts in collision, which cause physical, mental, emotional, or spiritual damage to people" (p. 80). Each person has to decide when he or she has done harm to another.

As you begin to list the names of these people and what you did to harm each one, also write why you did whatever you did. What were the consequences? What happened? How did the incident separate you from the other person? Did your behavior do obvious long-lasting damage?

If you're a perfectionist you may think you're going to go crazy doing Step Eight. You may need to ask your sponsor to give you feedback concerning how much to write and whom to include. Because there aren't any hard-and-fast rules, you will finally have to decide these questions yourself. But a good rule of thumb is that if something occurs to you that may have been harmful to someone else, write it down. You can ask about it and think about it later and get a better perspective.

One common thought that comes up for many people is, "I don't want to make a fool of myself confessing a lot of unnecessary things." But I suggest you suspend judgment about whether something is necessary or unnecessary for the time being, and just write it down if it occurs to you as a serious possibility. When you come to Step Nine you can decide whether or not to make amends about it.

Identifying When You Have Harmed Someone.   I have found it helpful to remind myself that there are two kinds of controlling. One is done by the outward controller who obviously controls everything, and the other by the sweet, "Christian" person who controls with caretaking deeds of kindness, love, sympathy, and tolerance, and runs the other person's life with gentle hints about what to do in every aspect of living. I had to ask myself if I was the kind of person who (for people's own good) is constantly giving them unasked-for suggestions so they can be more successful at their business, so they can become better parents to their children. This is sometimes just as harmful and abusive as the behavior of the obvious controller.

Other Harmful Behaviors.   Are you a bitchy gossip, whether you are male or female? Are you domineering, aggressive, sarcastic? Sarcasm hurts many people, even if they appear to laugh it off, excuse it, or claim to admire your "wit." Most people who do these things are in denial about doing them. A man came up to me not long ago and said, "I heard what you said, and I went home and started talking to my family. I asked if I'd hurt them in the ways you described." If that man has been controlling his family in the past, his new approach probably frightened them. But it is to their credit that they seem to have responded honestly. The man continued, "Do you know they brought up some of the most picky stuff, stuff that wasn't worth mentioning? It was all I could do to just keep quiet and not tell them it was the dumbest stuff I've ever heard." If that man had truly listened, he might have heard what his family was telling him about his "counseling" and the pain it caused them; he might have seen through his denial.

The things that hurt other people don't always hurt us; therefore, we sometimes have no way of knowing how we cripple the people around us unless they tell us. And when they do tell us, in our denial we tend to minimize their pain and our harmful behavior and blame them for being too sensitive. We often keep doing the harmful thing and think we're not guilty of harming anyone—based on the assumption that other people are like us, when they're not.

By the time many of us had reached Step Eight we were able to see some of the ways we had hurt the people close to us, and although it was painful to see ourselves and brought sadness and guilt, it was a great relief to be getting at the truth about our blocked relationships.

Ways Our Sin-Disease Leads Us to Hurt Family Members

I know people who have no idea that they've harmed anyone in their family. They believe they have been the best parent they know how to be, the best husband or the best wife, and they're bewildered by all this talk about making amends. If you find yourself puzzled this way, here are a few methods you might use to start finding out what you have done to harm people close to you. Keep a little notebook handy, and record what you discover with each of these methods.

First, when someone accuses you of doing something that hurt him or her, write it down and listen instead of defending yourself. If people said to me, "You're always late," I used to say something like, "That's not true. I'm on time much of the time. I was not late this morning. I was not late Sunday." I have three reasons they are wrong about what they said and can give specific examples to shoot down their arguments. But if you write down the complaint and don't defend yourself, later when you pray about your life and look at your notes, you may be able to see how you hurt people or made them uncomfortable, the times you were late, for example (perhaps more often than you knew), *and* how much you have hurt them and angered them with your self-justification.

A second method that is useful when a relationship gets uncomfortable is to ask yourself what you were doing just before the light went out in somebody's eyes. Were you being sarcastic? You may have thought of it as "just kidding." When accused, sarcastic people often say in disgust, "My gosh, I was just kidding! Can't you take a joke?" This throws the guilt and shame back on the person who's just been offended. That's a very abusive thing to do, especially to a child. The truth is often that you *were* being sarcastic, which is a form of abuse. When you become aware of these things, write them down in your notebook.

A third method is to notice how many suggestions you make to others about what they ought to do. You may say to a wife or child, "Look, if you'd just do what I'm suggesting, your life would be fine," and then wonder why the wife or child gets angry and strikes back or walks out. Write down in your notebook what you were doing when the fight started. If you can't see how you have done anything to hurt anyone, this writing in a notebook and praying about what you find may help crack through your denial.

Many times family members are afraid to talk to us honestly. Sometimes children are afraid of their parents (even when the children are adults), and the parents never know. If you already have a good relationship with someone, you may be able to say, "You know, I'm just realizing, I've got a lot of denial. Would you be willing to talk to me if I would be willing not to answer or justify myself?" A man in the program told me, "I had never dreamed anyone around me would fear me, but my son and daughter told me they were afraid of me. I've always seen myself as such a gentle person. But evidently there's some power in my life that I don't see, or maybe some anger." If that man's children had not told him they were afraid of him, he might have kept on hurting them and frightening them with his anger and watched, bewildered, as the distance between them and him grew.

It's not only the obviously abusive things that we need to make amends about. There are many subtle things that we don't recognize as harmful to others. For instance, do you have one child who's a favorite? When that child walks in the room do your eyes light up? If you have more than one child, chances are you have other children who feel angry, hurt, and rejected. To favor one unduly is to neglect the rest, even if we are not aware we are doing that.

My dad thought my brother was wonderful. He was named after my father. He was an outstanding athlete. He was ambidextrous; he could pitch a baseball or pass a football with either hand equally well. My dad loved my brother more than he loved me. I felt terribly rejected and thought I must not be much, especially much of a man, because my father spent a lot of time with my brother and didn't with me. As I mentioned earlier, at first I rationalized that I was just too young, but when I got big enough my brother was away at school, and my father didn't want to do the things he'd done with my brother—certainly not with me.

I don't think it ever occurred to him in his lifetime that he was neglecting me. But if my father had been in this program and had seen how hurt I was, and if he had come to me to make amends and said, "Hey, I've seen that I've hurt you by paying all that attention to your brother. I'm sorry, and I want to make amends," I'd still be crying with gratitude—and it's possible that I wouldn't have felt so insecure all my life.

Has your compulsive life-style kept your family in turmoil? If you maintain a fast-paced, intense life-style, you can cause a lot of pain to the other members of your family, especially when you dump anxiety on them by painting fear-provoking scenarios about how rough things are. Some of us were oblivious to the effect we had on other members of the family; people often can't rest when they live with someone who is always excited and in turmoil. Such a person can tell the family with great fear in his or her voice, "Don't spend any money. We're probably going to fail to make the income we need this year," and scare them to death. A man I know tells his wife about every business failure or bankruptcy in town, even though neither was a real probability for him. Other people dump their fears on their mate, then go to work and solve the financial problem, leaving the fear with the wife or husband or child. So even the way we share can be abusive.

We learn in the program to stop the dumping process by owning the pain or shame or fear as our own, which minimizes the probability that someone else will take it on. I say something like, "This is my pain (or fear, anger, etc.) that I'm describing, and I want to tell you so that I won't dump it on you for you to carry."

Other people abuse their families by erecting a wall of silence, telling them nothing about the family's financial situation, for instance, but just looking worried. People have a right to know certain basic facts so they can know realistically what the family can and cannot afford. The Sin-disease often causes one member of the family to control the others by frightening them or by withholding crucial information.

Three Parts to Step Eight

In *Twelve Steps for Christian Living*, Vernon Bittner divides Step Eight into three parts.[2] The first part is embracing the pain of our lives and relationships instead of running from it. We embrace the pain by writing down what has happened and staying with the painful feelings as we allow the harm we have done, and the harm that has been done to us, to become clearly conscious. Sometimes it is helpful to say, "So this is fear. I want to feel what fear feels like," and let it wash over you. So much of our training as Americans, and even as Christians, is toward quick answers, quick prayer to get rid of the pain, not seeing that the pathway to wisdom and understanding goes through pain.

My wife's attitude about this has helped me a lot. She said, "I learned that my pain is only pain; it will not kill me." As we stand in our pain we are frightened, and it hurts, but by knowing God can teach us through it, some of us are losing our exaggerated fear of pain.

The second part of Step Eight is writing down beside the names of each person with whom we have a bruised relationship our own part in what happened. By staying in the pain we can begin more clearly to see our part in much of our own Sin and failure.

Some of the people who hurt us may have been trying to defend themselves (even though their defense may have been unhealthy or abusive) against our controlling, fixing, advice giving, punishing, or interfering.

For instance, a woman told me in counseling that her husband had had an affair. She was furious, and she left him. As we talked I asked her if she could remember anything she had done to hurt or anger her husband *before* he had the affair. We talked a long time. Finally she said, "Well I did withhold sex from him for the six months previous to the affair to punish him for the way he treated my family."

This woman had not seen a connection between *her* punitive action and the unforgivable action her husband had taken to retaliate. She was adamant in saying that he needed to make amends to her, and she in no way saw any need for her to make amends to him. But in order to get into recovery this woman had some amends to make too. If she could forgive him for what he did, then maybe she could make amends for what she did and be freed from the intense pain she felt. That sounds very difficult, and it is, but that is one way God has healed people in the program from the irreparable sins of the past.

We begin to see the way the disease works in our life. That may sound morbid at first. But in going into surgery you take off all your clothes and get up on a table and let people look at you. That's not what you're going to do every day the rest of your life, but for surgery to save your life, it's necessary. Going back over the past this intensely is not going to be a way of life, but if you don't examine and experience the effects of the Sin-disease in your life and learn what behavior leads to the pain you continue to cause and experience in your relationships, then it's hard for even God to change those selfish and abusive habits. Jesus indicated that he came to help those who were aware that they needed a physician. Those who thought of themselves as "righteous" and wouldn't face their sin couldn't access the healing he brought (see Mark 2:17).

Finally, when we have looked at our list and lived with the feelings we had about what we did and what was done to us, we can become ready to do what we have to do to let go of our pain. We're told that what we have to do is be "willing to make amends to them all." Strangely enough, this simple process allows us to begin to get rid of those old movies about painful events that we have played and replayed in our minds, triggering past pain and resentment again and again—or at least learn to turn down the sound track.

Our Idea of What's Important in Life Changes

As we walk back through the pain caused by our broken relationships, many of us become aware that the important things in life are not striving for control, excitement, and being noticed, which a lot of us have spent our lives doing, but rather the love and intimacy of healthy relationships with people close to us and the serenity to enjoy living.

Some of us have been "getting ready to live" for sixty years. Intimate and serene living is like a mirage that has floated across the desert ahead of us. Some day "when things settle down, or when we get enough money, or when the kids are grown," we say. But we never get there. These steps can allow us to take stock of our lives, to file the destructive images from the past, and to put the focus of our lives in the present as the time to live. And to live happily in the present, we are told, we need to clean up the past, as we are led to do in Steps Eight and Nine. Because of our fear of rejection and all the energy it took to keep everything pushed down, denied, and out of sight, many of us were exhausted and had lost our love of life by the time we came into this program. This opportunity for a reassessment is welcome.

"Became Willing"—Humility and Forgiveness of Others

Finally, before going out to make amends, you will need to gain humility and to release your pain and anger about what others have done to you. This comes through forgiving them. As I said in the chapter on Step Seven, humility is not fawning. Humility is an accurate estimate of ourselves. By seeing and experiencing the pain caused by broken relationships we see that we are not the smooth social operators we thought we were. We see that we are ordinary people whose self-centeredness causes pain and chaos.

Seeing ourselves with humility can allow us to forgive our friends and enemies who have hurt us before we go out to make amends and hope for forgiveness from those we have harmed. Forgiveness in this sense means simply that we release our need to punish, to get even, to make the other person apologize or do anything. We release our need to continue to be hurt or be angry about what they did. In short, we get over the incident and drop it as an issue standing between us and the other person.

This forgiveness of others is hard. You may not be able to do it directly. In the first place, they may not know that they hurt you. I remember when they told me to forgive people who had hurt me, I thought of one man in particular and said to myself, "Wow, there is a guy who really hurt me. I'm going to tell that so-and-so just exactly how he hurt me, and then I'll be able to forgive him." But my sponsor said my job was not to use this forgiveness as an excuse to tell other people how wrong they had been.

The Twelve-Step solution to this strong urge to focus on the other party's fault is to realize that all these people are probably spiritually sick too, just as we are. They have the same Sin-disease. When I came to Step Eight and said I didn't know if I could forgive a particular person on my list, my sponsor asked, "Could you forgive that person if he had terminal cancer?" I raised my eyebrows as he continued, "The Sin-disease is like spiritual cancer, and he doesn't even have a program to recover from it." I thought a few minutes and then nodded my head as I realized that I could forgive him when I thought of the disease as spiritual cancer. And I began to forgive some of the people I had resented. This allowed me to go and make amends to a couple of people regardless of whether they even knew how much they had hurt me.

The main purpose of Steps Eight and Nine is to clean off *your* side of the street, regardless of the reaction of the other person to your amends. But I am so manipulative I wanted to couch my amends in a way that would almost guarantee that the people I had harmed would forgive me. I had to stop myself and simply become willing to just *go* to all the people I had harmed and make amends for the harm *I* had done. And then I was ready to look at Step Nine.

TAKING STEP EIGHT

Step Eight
*Made a list of all persons we had harmed, and
became willing to make amends to them all.*

1. Make a list of people you have harmed. Using the form below, describe briefly what you did and why you did it. Then describe the consequences in your relationship with that person, such as any strain or separation between you, and any damages or loss the other person suffered.

People I have harmed:
Person's first name:
What happened? (My harmful behavior):
Consequences (Separation and/or damages):

2. For each of the incidents you have described, write about any feelings you now have concerning your harmful behavior and the consequences.

Person's name:
My feelings today:

3. Make a list of the people who have harmed you, what each person did, and how you have felt about it up until now.

Person who has harmed me:
What this person did to me:
How I felt about it:

As you experience the feelings you have had about what these people did to harm you, become aware that the people whom you have harmed have probably had very similar feelings about you.

4. For each incident listed under item 3 that you would like to get over and drop as an issue between you and the other person, write out a brief statement of forgiveness for that person. If you are not honestly ready to drop one of the incidents you listed, do not write that statement. Just write the ones you can.

5. Write out your statement of readiness to make amends to the people you have harmed. To be rigorously honest, list exceptions, if there are any. If and when you become ready to make amends to the ones you excepted, come back to this page and write out your statement of readiness for each one.

When you are willing to make amends to them all, you are ready to take Step Nine.

Chapter 12

STEP NINE

*Made Direct Amends to Such
People Wherever Possible,
Except When to Do So Would
Injure Them or Others*

Biblical principles relating to the necessity of
making amends in order to better love God
and other people:

*So if you are offering your gift at the altar,
and there remember that your brother has
something against you, leave your gift there
before the altar and go; first be reconciled
to your brother, and then come and
offer your gift. Matthew 5:23–24*

(Also) *You shall not hate your brother in your
heart, but you shall reason with your
neighbor, lest you bear sin because of him.
You shall not take vengeance or bear any
grudge against the sons of your own people,
but you shall love your neighbors as
yourself. Leviticus 19:17–18*

Making amends is part of the process of reconciliation around which the whole Christian message centers. Being a Christian does not "require" that we do Step Nine, but unless we take the risk of being rejected and make amends, we do not become reconciled with those we have harmed, and we are blocked not only from relating to those persons but also from worshiping God. Jesus said that even when you are offering your gift at the altar and you remember that you've harmed someone, go right then and be reconciled to that person first and then come to offer your gift.

The Twelve Steps teach us that we can be healed, but that a part of this healing is to take responsibility for our lives and actions.

When we make amends we are simply telling the person we harmed the truth about our actions as we now see it, trusting that the healing, the self-acceptance, and the serenity we will gain is worth the rejection we may encounter. We are trusting that God and our fellow seekers in this Way can do more to bring us to happiness and intimacy than any negative opinion could hurt us. Although this risking of open rejection by those to whom we make amends is frightening, we have the experience of thousands of people who have taken this step before us to encourage and strengthen us as we go. After making amends to all the people we listed in Step Eight, we begin to experience the "promises of the program." (See "The Promises of the Twelve-Step Program" later in this chapter.)

Doing Step Nine correctly also takes courage, prudence, good judgment, and a careful sense of timing. If you are just coming into the Twelve Steps as you read this, remember that you're not ready to do Step Nine yet. You've got eight steps to walk through first. By the time you get to this point you may be amazed at the way you have become ready to trust God and do Step Nine. I would not have believed this until it happened to me. From the front edge of Step One, a rigorously honest Step Nine looked absolutely impossible to me.

Four Groups of People Who Need Amends

After completing Step Eight, a decision must be made about who to approach first. The Twelve and Twelve describes this approach in the following way. First, there are at least four general groups:

1. People you go to at once
2. People you make only partial disclosure to
3. Specific family members, friends, business associates, and other individuals in your past
4. People with whom you can't make personal contact

1. People You Go to at Once

The first group is made up of the people you tell about your entry into the program and your intention to get well. These are the ones you talk to as soon as you get into the program, usually family members or those close to you in continuing personal relationships. As soon as you make up your mind that you are powerless and your life is unmanageable and you really want to get well through these Twelve Steps, as you begin to recognize your own insanity and begin to believe that God will help you, you may see how abusive you've been and want to make complete amends. But it's best to start slowly. You can tell such people that you've seen your self-centeredness and your controlling ways and are going to try to recover through the Twelve Steps. The experience of the program is that it is better to save the tough amends to your family until later, after you have had some time in the program and seen more of your own denied manipulative "style."

Because of the strong need to feel justified that the Sin-disease causes, we tend to want to get back in control by teaching everyone else in our lives what we have discovered. The danger in making immediate amends is that our new "confessing stance" can be a new way for us to appear righteous, even while making amends. Moreover, our families may have heard before how *this time* we're really going to change. For these reasons, some people in the program recommend that we stay in it long enough to be sure it is going to stick before we go around trying to clear up past deeds specifically.

Other people want to make amends right off and get everyone in their families in a Twelve-Step program so they too can get help. Wanting other people to find help is good, but in working the Twelve Steps one must first do his or her own program, or the Sin-disease will win and the Twelve Steps will become only another device to control those around us. In the weeks and months between Steps One and Nine, I learned a lot about the ways I control people and operate in extremes and how my denied controlling kept me from relating in straightforward ways. I now agree that in the beginning you should tell your family only that you have recognized some things about yourself and that you are trying to learn about and recover from the character defects that cause you to behave in selfish and abusive ways. Most other amends and specifics can better be made after one has done the first eight steps.

2. People to Whom You Make Only Partial Disclosure

The second group is made up of people to whom you make only partial amends because complete disclosure might do more harm than good. The Big Book points out that this is especially true in the matter of sexual affairs. Many people get into this program and say, "I feel so guilty about my affair with this person that I'm going to go right now and tell her husband. I really need to make amends to him." But such a disclosure might ruin that couple's marriage. The wife would be frantic, because while you're getting yourself cleared, you're putting her on the griddle. Some amends need careful consideration. You are to go and make amends the best way you can, but *never* at someone else's expense.

3. Specific Family Members, Friends, and Other Individuals

The third group to which to make specific Step Nine amends might begin with specific family members. The Big Book describes the kind of unknowing damage a controller does to his or her family as follows (and I'm paraphrasing by adding the Sin-disease):

> The alcoholic [or controlling sinner] is like a tornado roaring its way through the lives of others. Hearts are broken, sweet relationships are dead. Affections have been uprooted. Selfish and inconsiderate habits have kept the home in turmoil. We feel a man is unthinking when he says that [refraining from controlling] is enough. He is like the farmer who came up out of his cyclone cellar to find his home ruined. To his wife, he remarked, 'Don't see anything the matter here, Ma. Ain't it grand the wind stopped blowin'? (p. 82)

There are two phases that I suggested earlier in making amends to families. Phase I: When you first start working the steps you might share your discovery of your denial about your controlling behavior (and your specific chemical or behavioral addiction if you have one). You now see you've been a controller and a manipulator; you don't know if you can stop, but you'd like to, and you'll try. You may want to tell them a little about the program you're in, not to convince them to join but to let them know this is not "just another good resolution."

Every book I've read on this subject says don't bother talking too much about how you are going to change (or have changed), because they're not going to believe your words anyway. Just get busy and live the program. People believe your life more than your words. As Jesus said (see Luke 6:43f.), if you want to know what kind of tree you are looking at, examine the fruit growing on it. That is the proof of the true nature of the tree, not the sign someone nailed on it. What you *do* in your life reveals what you really believe.

Phase II: When you make your Step Nine amends to family members, make specific amends. You can use your Step Eight list and check them off one at a time when you do Step Nine. Talk about the specific things you discovered by the various methods described in the chapter about Step Eight.

If you are serious about recovery and spiritual growth, you are trying to have integrity in your whole life now. When you're attempting to make amends, love people, and get your life straight, your relationships with them must have caring integrity, or your relationship with God won't remain in the light of his truth. "He who says he is in the light and hates his brother is in the darkness still. He who loves his brother abides in the light" (1 John 2:9–10).

Another area in which we may have harmed our spouse is sexual infidelity. Married people who are having an affair often see that they must stop if they are to recover. One who does the first seven steps will see that any kind of continuing deceit and dishonesty can be devastating to continued sanity and recovery. Such a "secret" can keep one from being honest at home or in meetings, makes one avoid intimacy in prayer, and contradicts the essential trust on which the program is built. For Christians there is the powerful seventh commandment against adultery, which puts an adulterer in the position of going against God's will as it is revealed to us (Exod. 20:14).

You must decide whether to confess disloyal sexual behavior to your wife or husband as a part of making amends. But this is a serious decision. Some people in the program say it is not wise. The Big Book says that it is a judgment call, but it also says that it is really hard to get well if you aren't *willing* to confess. To make a decision about whether to do so, you may have to go to your sponsor or a counselor who knows your spouse and you. The tendency is to think, "Well, he or she couldn't take it," but your spouse may know more than you think. And even if that's not true, to be able to confess and get clear of it is extremely important to your spiritual health, and possibly to your ability to be free in your intimate relationship with your spouse.

But the question that often comes up from the spouse who is told is, Who was it? The Big Book says you must make another careful decision there, because you're liable to put somebody else in a predicament in order to get yourself clean. There are no rules about this. Your sponsor or a counselor can be very helpful and supportive. The program only suggests that you must be *willing* to go to any lengths if you want to get well. It also says that we do not harm others to get our own side of the street clear. For Christians and members of Twelve-Step groups, the message that becomes louder and louder and deeper and more profound as they grow spiritually is that it is in facing God and the truth about your life that the truth shall make you free (see John 8:32).

Business Associates.   With regard to business associates and partners, I was in a small joint venture at one time, and in the middle of it I went off to seminary to work on a graduate degree. A group of investors had put money into the venture. The general partner in our partnership, whom I thought of as having the basic ability between the two of us, was the real head honcho. He was the guy *I* was counting on, so I thought everyone else was too. One of those investors later told me that he had counted on me and felt betrayed that I left; I didn't know that for years. But when it occurred to me that other investors might have felt that way, I didn't know what to do, until I got in this program and came to Step Nine.

I went back to the ones I still could contact twenty years later and said, "You made this investment, and it has come to my attention that you may have counted on my being a continuing part of the partnership (even though we had already invested the money before I left), and I want to make amends to you." One guy wrote back and just said, "Thank you . . . after all these years." Another man didn't write at all, and a third man said that he had understood at the time. You can't tell how anyone will respond. You just make amends and move on.

Amends Involving Money.   Making amends where money is involved is serious business too, especially if the amounts involved are large. You may have to go back and say you stole something big, and you may have to go to jail. But if it looks as though you might have to go to jail, be sure and talk it over with your family and business partner (if you are in a partnership) before you go to make amends. You are not to hurt other people in order to clear your own past. If you're supporting a family or contributing to a business that involves one or more partners, it may be very irresponsible of you to go to people in your past and say that you cheated them and they can take you off to prison. However, some families and business partners have said, "We hear your need to do this, and we want you to risk it, because we want you to keep on this path and get well." It is often possible to go to creditors or people you have cheated financially and make amends, telling them about the program and that you want to arrange to pay on the debt or obligation over a period of months or years.

As I've said repeatedly, though this is a very tough program, the questions that were asked me were, Would you like to be free after years of being frustrated and anxious? Would you like to walk down the street and feel that you're living in the present and that the ghosts of the past are gone? This idea of risking so much to make amends may sound bizarre, but we are dealing with life and death, spiritual and possibly physical life or death, and we are determined to go to any lengths to get well. As I have done this, I've found great release.

Not all matters of cheating involve large sums, however. I've got a friend who stole candy as a kid, and it still bothered her. She went back to the store in her hometown and said to the owner, who was by that time an old man, "Years ago when I was a girl I took candy from your store over a period of months, and I want to make amends." My friend gave the store owner a check for fifty dollars. But the owner laughed and said, "I haven't got any candy in the whole store that's worth fifty dollars." My friend said, "No, no, take it. I'm sure the interest by now would make it fifty dollars, and besides, I need to do this for me."

Christ's Call to Love Our Enemies

The more difficult an amends is to make, the more negative you may feel toward the person to whom you go to make amends—and often the more rewarding the aftermath. There's a spiritual dynamic here that is very powerful. Jesus spoke of it when he told his disciples, "Love your enemies and pray for those who persecute you, so that you may be sons of your father who is in heaven" (Matt. 5:44–45). What does loving them mean? It doesn't mean you have to "like" them, have warm feelings about them. *Love* for the Hebrew was an action word that seems to have involved moving into another's life space in goodwill, caring. In making amends you may have to go with the bit in your teeth, yet in a helpful and forgiving spirit. Anything the person has done to you, you are willing to forgive (or willing to be made willing).

When we pray the Lord's Prayer, we ask God to forgive us our sins *as we forgive those who have sinned against us* (Matt. 6:12). And in the program we are told to confess our abusive deeds and in some cases our former bad feelings. Some of us have simply said to the people we've hurt and offended, "I realize I'll never get over my disease and/or trying to control others if I don't make amends and do what I can to straighten out the past."

The Big Book advises against leading with religion. On the other hand, it points out that this may develop into a very good chance to witness to the person about your faith in God. It may be that as the conversation develops the person might say something like, "Where did you get the guts to come and admit what you did to me and try to make amends?" You might then be able to say something like, "Well, I'm in a program, and I've made a decision to turn my will and my life over to God so that God can help me live a sane and serene life. Making amends is part of the healing process of recovery. And this relationship to God has come to mean so much to me that I finally felt I could risk coming to you to make amends."

Actually the most convincing thing about making amends to people we know is not the words we say but the fact that we subsequently change our behavior and *quit doing* the abusive things about which we had to make amends. A changed life speaks with a clarity no words can match. And that's what draws people to the program, to the Church—and to God.

Making amends is a scary business, but many of us have found that the rewards are worth enduring the fear: an increased sense of self-worth and courage to be straight in personal relations.

Making Amends to Yourself

It sounds strange, but many of us have hurt ourselves worse than anybody else has. We have put ourselves down, punished ourselves abusively for failure to be perfect and for hurting others. We have not let ourselves enjoy life or have much fun, or we have made ourselves pay dearly when we've had a good time. In short, we have not loved ourselves at all. In the program one begins to see this not loving ourselves as part of the sickness and the insane thinking God is trying to free us from.

One of the things that can make the whole amends process so terrifying to some of us is that we're so afraid we will discover (and other people will discover) that we are not what we pretend to be, that when God peels the protective, defensive layers off our inner life like the skin off an onion, there won't be anyone of significance at home. But through the gospel and the Twelve Steps God says there is somebody very precious at home inside each of us. And that is the precious person God made in his image. We learn that the onion, those layers of protective and defensive behaviors designed to make up for what we fear we aren't, is not our true home. In fact, the onion, our unreal adaptive self, often smells bad, and its fumes get in our eyes so that we really can't see very well at all. In doing the first nine steps we become grateful that we are enough as we are, without all the trappings we've developed to impress people.

4. People with Whom You Can't Make Personal Contact

The fourth group to whom you may need to make amends is made up of people with whom you can't make personal contact. They've moved, or they have died. You may have to go to your sponsor and tell him or her what the problem is and what you've done to locate these people and then tell your sponsor the amends you would have made if you could have located the person you harmed. A sponsor can stand in for that person you harmed (but can't locate) and let you make amends. You can complete the amends in prayer if the person is dead.

Another way to make amends to someone who is lost or dead is to write and mail a letter, using only your first name and the person's first name and no address. A lot of people get great satisfaction out of that because they have actually done their part and tried to clean off their side of the street. And in some cases this unilateral kind of amends is all one can do. Surprisingly, since it's the best you can do under the circumstances, the writing of the amends and the willingness to make them where possible often removes guilt and negative energy from your heart, and you can move on in your recovery.

In the case of people who have died, be very careful about making amends to relatives. Be sensitive about not hurting somebody. For example, if you teamed up to steal some money or had some other kind of illicit involvement with the person who's died and you're planning to make amends by going to tell the deceased's mother or father, this could be an example of harming someone else in order to get the amends off your chest. But if it's a matter of money and/or you've cheated the deceased, you can pay the money back to the heir. The main thing I was told to remember is to make amends and restitution wherever possible, but always to remember not to clear your own conscience by harming someone else.

The Reaction of the Other Person
Does Not Control Your Recovery

Some people may not accept your amends. Some people have been so bruised in their relationship with you or with others that they can't believe you are sincere, or if sincere that you have the power to change. Or the people to whom you want to make amends may be parents who are going to try to control you; they're not about to go for this new program, because as you get free you're out of their control. But the amazing, wonderful thing is that whether your amends are accepted or not, you *can* get over the guilt, pain, and shame and become free from the unhealthy control of parents, spouses, and other people to whom you have given your power in the past.

One person I used to be very close to still sees me as the selfish, controlling man that I admitted I was in my amends. I feel very sad about that, because this is someone I love a lot. My mind used to go over and over that relationship continually, like a spider over a baseball, looking for a way inside that person's wall, looking for a way to get in and fix the relationship and make that person see that I'm really okay and not abusive now. But I have finally detached, and I don't insist on fixing that relationship (except once in a while). The program teaches me that I don't have to convince someone else that I've changed. God knows, I know, some friends in the program know, and I've made amends. If that person can't or won't see that my life is different, then it will have to be that person's problem. All I can do is to continue to get well and relate to the people who want to relate to me and can accept my love.

Avoid Manipulating the Person for Forgiveness.   If you make your amends to try to manipulate people into forgiving you, or forgiving a debt you owe them, or if you try to trick them, they will probably know. Even if they don't know, the experience of the program is that *you* will know, and your progress will be affected negatively.

When some of us came to Steps Eight and Nine we had friends we'd severed connections with because of resentments, pride, and real or imagined wrongs. Whether the wrongs were real or imaginary, the resentments were eating away at us. At Step Eight when we wrote our list of people to whom we needed to make amends, we included theirs, and we tried to see what our part could have been in the hurts. In Step Nine we wrote or called and went to see each of them. We told them about discovering our denial and that we'd realized certain things that we'd done to them, and we listed those things. Although these people had done things that hurt us, we didn't say anything about their actions. By standing in our pain and asking ourselves what our part was in the hurts in our lives, we had seen some of our actions we had repressed. And in the program we had learned that *we don't have to make sure that everyone else sees things the way we see them.* This is still very hard for me because I still have a strong need to justify myself. But when I got through with my amends, I felt great relief, and I liked myself a lot better than I had.

Avoid Manipulating to Resume a Severed Relationship.   When making amends, I was told not to promise to pick up or reenter the old relationship by saying something like, "Well now we're going to be friends again," or imply that you are going to see the person again. You may not want to be friends again. There has been a lot of pain, and you perhaps don't have anything in common now. You're trying to make amends and clear up the past, that's all (although in some cases people who have been enemies for years do become friends). Neither a positive response nor any continuing relationship is crucial to this process of making amends.

The Results of Trying to Make Amends

Sometimes people whose marriages have been distant and cold for years fall in love again after one of them makes amends. In other cases the cracked relationship shatters, and the couple gets divorced. If a couple gets divorced after one partner attempts to make amends as outlined here, it often means that the marriage was already over and neither party had the courage to end it. Although "fixing" the relationship is *not* the purpose of making amends, and all you are trying to do is clean off your side of the street, many relationships are in fact healed. People everywhere in bruised relationships have been waiting for years for the other party to acknowledge a hurt and say, "I'm sorry" (and really mean it).

The old saying "Love means never having to say you're sorry" is probably the worst and most untrue definition of love ever perpetrated on the public. The experience of the Twelve Steps and the gospel would indicate that love often flourishes where people *can* and *do* say they are sorry and make amends when they have hurt or abused each other.

Besides marriage relationships, parents and children and siblings have been reconciled following amends. There's a delusion, especially in the Church, that all family members, especially in Christian families, feel loving and close. Though this is true of some families, I wonder how many people reading this book have someone in their family they're at odds with? From my life and counseling experience, I'd bet almost everyone. Many of us don't talk about the pain in relationships with brothers, sisters, parents, or children, because we are ashamed to feel such intense anger, resentment, or even hatred toward members of our own family. Through the process of making amends, long-standing feuds in families may melt and disappear.

On the other hand, when you make amends you may get some very negative or controlling reactions from family members, because your recovery may threaten to break up the family system and leave them no longer in control. They may try to talk you out of making amends: "You don't need to do that. You didn't do anything wrong." But even if your family is still suspicious and distant after your amends or even if someone tells you off, you didn't fail. You cannot fail in making amends if you do it sincerely and with a humble, loving, and nonjudgmental attitude, because you have faced the past and you have done your part in God's reconciliation process.

The Promises of the Twelve-Step Program

After you do the first nine steps, you will find on page 83 in the Big Book what are called "the promises" that are said to come true about this time in the Twelve-Step process. When I first read them, I thought, "Well, Bill

W. (A.A.'s co-founder) got carried away at this point. Some of these will *never* be true for me!" But as I am writing these words all of them have begun to. These are the promises:

> If we are painstaking about this phase of our development, we will be amazed before we are halfway through. We are going to know a new freedom and a new happiness. We will not regret the past nor wish to shut the door on it. We will comprehend the word serenity and we will know peace. No matter how far down the scale we have gone, we will see how our experience can benefit others. That feeling of uselessness and self-pity will disappear.

In other words, we will see that all the painful experiences we thought were so bad in our lives, once we have faced them and made amends, can help other people as we share the program with them. The painful incidents in our past become like drawbridges we can let down into other people's hearts so that they can walk out into freedom over our experience and say, "I'm not alone." And we will see that nothing that has happened to us is wasted. The promises continue:

> We will lose interest in selfish things and gain interest in our fellows. Self-seeking will slip away.

I cried when I read that. When my denial cracked open I saw myself as being an almost totally selfish human being. But when I finished Step Nine and reread the promises, I saw that I am becoming interested in other people. My selfishness didn't mean I didn't help people. I've counseled and helped many people in my lifetime. But there's something different now. I'm a regular part of a group of people struggling along trying to make it. I'm not "the counselor" among the others who "need help." Rather, sometimes I go to someone to get help, and the next time someone comes to me.

That's what I think Christian fellowship is all about. As we share our lives, God is there. His Spirit is the real Counselor. We just give God's love to each other through our authentic sharing. "For where two or three are gathered in my name, there am I in the midst of them" (Matt. 18:20). Somehow the sharing has become different, not a do-good or "fixing" operation but a "walking down the road together" journey with each other and God.

The promises go on:

> Our whole attitude and outlook upon life will change. Fear of people and economic insecurity will leave us.

That is happening to many of us. In my financial fear I've fantasized winding up alone in one of those condemned huts scheduled for demolition, surrounded by a litter of tin cans and wearing a secondhand sweater with holes in the elbows and no patches, sitting there by myself looking out, hoping somebody will come along and give me a crumb. Today I don't have pictures of financial insufficiency very much. And after *years* of having them almost constantly, the relief feels miraculous.

The promises conclude:

> We will intuitively know how to handle situations that used to baffle us. We will suddenly realize that God is doing for us what we could not do for ourselves.

The Big Book goes on to say, "Are these extravagant promises? We think not. They are being fulfilled among us—sometimes quickly, sometimes slowly. They will always materialize if we work for them."

Some of these promises have come true to almost everybody I know who's journeyed through the ninth Step. And many people report that they all have come true.

Once we get a taste of these promises, the next thing we want to learn is how to keep the life we are finding. And Step Ten shows us how to bring the first nine steps to bear on the problems of living every day.

TAKING STEP NINE

Step Nine
*Made direct amends to such people
wherever possible, except when to do so
would injure them or others.*

List in your notebook or on a separate sheet the people you want to make amends to in each of the categories below. After you have made each of your amends write beside that person's name the *date* and the *method* by which you made amends (e.g., phone call, personal visit, letter, discussion with your sponsor) as well as your feelings about having made the amends. It is common for one's feelings to become increasingly positive as time elapses. You may wish to copy the following format:

Group 1: People you went to right away (people you have already made the initial amends to as described in this chapter)

Name	Date of Amends	Method	Feelings

Group 2: People to whom you do not think you should make full disclosure

Name	Date of Amends	Method	Feelings

Group 3: Specific amends to family members and close friends, business amends, amends about money, and so on

Name	Date of Amends	Method	Feelings

Group 4: People with whom you cannot make contact

Name	Date of Amends	Method	Feelings

Chapter 13

STEP TEN

Continued to Take Personal Inventory and, When We Were Wrong, Promptly Admitted It

Some biblical expressions of the need to continue to watch for our defects and to search out things that might hinder us so that we won't be tempted and slip, and of the need, if we do slip, to make amends:

Watch and pray that you may not enter into temptation; the spirit is indeed willing but the flesh is weak. Mark 14:38

(Also) *If he turns from his sin and does what is lawful and right, if the wicked restores the pledge, gives back what he has taken by robbery, and walks in the statutes of life, committing no iniquity, he shall surely live, he shall not die. None of the sins that he has committed shall be remembered against him; he has done what is lawful and right, he shall surely live. Ezekiel 33:14–16*

(Also) *If we walk in the light, as he is in the light, we have fellowship with one another, and the blood of Jesus his son cleanses us from all sin. 1 John 1:7*

The first nine steps contain the behavioral and spiritual reformation process of the program. The last three steps show the pilgrim how to maintain the new life that comes as a result of committing one's life and will to God, working the steps, and giving away what one is finding.

Step Ten is often considered by newcomers to be a throwaway step. People say, "Well, I'm going to continue the program. There's no need to do anything specific about Step Ten." And they pass over it as if it weren't there. But it's one of the most important steps of all to many of us who have been in the Twelve-Step process awhile.

Step Ten is a spiritual pocket computer to help us keep tabs on our behavior today and a cleanser to help keep our spiritual lenses clean. In this method of keeping an inventory every day, we ask ourselves questions like, Which of my character defects popped up as uninvited guests today? Am I using the tools of the program? Am I praying? Am I thanking God for all the good things he has done for me this day, and for any positive things he's freed me to do? Am I reading the Bible? Am I reading the Big Book? Am I going to my sponsor? Am I going to worship?

The reason this is so important is that the Sin-disease, with its denial and delusion, is always hovering "just a decision away" to throw us back into fear and confusion. Its tactics are to convince us in various ways, "You're 'well' now and don't need a stupid program to lead a normal life. You can and should operate on your own as a mature adult." The disease's "strategy" often works like this: When we begin to feel a little secure and happy and our relationships are more comfortable, many of us "forget" to have our quiet time. We forget to go to meetings and don't call our sponsor. We're too busy again, because the pain that drove us into the program has been alleviated. This is a dangerous place to be, because it is one of the major delusions of the spiritual life that we can "do it ourselves" without a daily contact with God and a daily look at the reality of what is going on in our own lives.

In Step Ten we learn to use the first nine steps as spiritual "tools" on a daily basis to keep our lives close to reality, to humility, and to God. All the steps so far are part of a process of cleaning up to get our human home ready for a new tenant. You might think the next line is, "The new tenant is God." But although God is certainly with us, that's not it. The new tenant is the precious child of God bearing our name, the person

God made in his image to be the occupant of our life. This childlike person has been buried all these years under the domination of the disease—the abuse, denial, pain, guilt, and broken relationships of our past. Many of us have gone around frantic for years because we have no sense of belonging, of being at home anywhere, even at church, our own homes, or indeed our own lives. Through taking the first nine steps, the house of our lives is made as clean as we can get it through our willingness and God's action. And that's clean enough.

In this Twelve-Step process we've signed over the ownership of the house to a Higher Power. We said to God, "I want to give this life to you." As we do this, God takes over the ultimate owner's responsibility for structural change. But we have the continuing job of daily maintenance. This change of responsibilities is an incredible relief; we don't have to be perfect, right, in charge, popular, and "totally successful." (Many of us had it backwards, trying always to handle the owner's ultimate responsibilities—which only God can handle—and trying to get God to do all the daily maintenance, which is *our* natural job.) In a quiet way each of us can relax and enjoy living our own life, inside ourselves and with the people around us and in the program, without the ultimate responsibility to make everything right.

A New Style of Life

Through these next three steps, Ten, Eleven, and Twelve, the Twelve Steps quit being a program for major surgery and become a way of life for ongoing recovery and spiritual growth.

Step Ten shows us how to keep our lives and relationships clear and uncluttered each day and to keep expanding our awareness and our gratitude. We are now well into the spiritual part of the program, and we have been ever since we grasped at Step Seven the understanding that only God can do the transforming work required for us to grow spiritually. A part of this growth is an expanding awareness of God's will. It seems that unless we can begin to evaluate life from God's perspective, we cannot grow, either in the program or in the Church. The Big Book says, "Every day is a day when we must carry the vision of God's will into all of our activities. 'How can I best serve Thee—Thy will (not mine) be done'" (p. 85). The diseased view of evaluating life to see how we can "get in control" is upside down and insane compared with the "surrender" perspective of a life of recovery. That's why Christians have always advocated reading the Bible devotionally on a regular basis: to learn to see all of life from God's perspective.

Some of us quit growing emotionally and spiritually years ago when the compulsions of the Sin-disease took over. But now, after doing the first nine steps, we can get back on a continuing growth track, and Step Ten tells us how we can face crises in our daily lives and learn to keep evaluating and examining so that our awareness of reality and God's will can continue to expand. But this takes practice.

Donn Moomaw, who was an All-American linebacker for U.C.L.A., was voted the outstanding college lineman in America one year. Donn, who is now a gifted Christian minister, told me once, "Football teams are not made or broken on the two-yard line with two minutes to play. They are only revealed. They are made or broken in the summer when the players are running alone on the roads and running the stadium steps, getting in shape, and learning the plays. The crises, the tight spots in the games only *reveal* how much they have already practiced and learned."

A great ballplayer doesn't have to think about the fundamentals when he is in a tight spot; they are a natural part of him. But he had to concentrate on the fundamentals in the beginning.

And that's true with regard to the Twelve Steps. What you've learned so far through the first nine steps will start revealing itself. Seeing the profound changes in people at this point, it's tempting to think they happened by magic. But it's not magic. People change because they have paid the price in their vulnerability and willingness to surrender to God, to pray, to do the steps, go to meetings, read the Big Book, clean up their pasts and their relationships, and offer their whole lives to God so he can change them.

Using Steps One, Two, and Three Daily

There are times when an emotional storm hits, and in our anger or fear we are vulnerable to moving back into our controlling ways of relating to people and into our compulsions and/or addictions. The first three steps can help us calm down and get out of our unmanageable emotional storm to do an inventory.

Let's say Steve, a friend, gets mad at me, and I react by trying to convince him that he is wrong. I get angry, and then Steve defends himself and gets angrier, and then we're into a "control or be controlled" situation. I can see his gritted teeth and blazing eyes and feel my hot face.

Since I worked the Tenth Step I try to do the following "moves" to get back to sanity: when I realize what's happening to me, I stop, back off, and as soon as I can I do the first three steps. I sometimes have to do that five or six times a day.

For Step One I say, "I'm powerless over Steve, and my life is unmanageable." Then I move to Step Two: "I'm so angry my face is red, and I'm acting as if I have the power to make Steve think differently about this by showing him how wrong he is, which I know is a form of insanity on my part. God, I believe that you can restore me to sanity." And then Step Three: "I am making a decision right now to turn my life and my will and the outcome of this encounter with Steve over to you." Almost always that process calms me and gives me some emotional space in which to deal with what's really happening. By the time I've done Step Three, the tornado of irrational feelings has often subsided, and I can see what's happening.

The first part of this process, then, is to recognize you're powerless, put yourself in God's hands, and start identifying which form of insanity from the Sin-disease is occurring. You may want to do a spot-check inventory after the storm subsides. The outcome may be that I see my part in the problem and want to make amends.

Three Kinds of Inventory to Use to Check on the Activity of the Disease and Get You Back to Reality

Though the descriptions that follow may seem complex and the activities they describe burdensome, remember, very few people do all three kinds of inventories on a regular basis. Each person chooses the kind of inventory most helpful to him or her. There are three kinds of inventory:

1. A spot-check inventory is situation by situation and can happen many times a day.
2. A daily inventory is a review of the whole day once a day.
3. A thorough inventory is done periodically.

1. A Spot-Check Inventory

A spot-check inventory is for situations like the one I described—a collision of instincts. If you don't do the first three steps prior to the spot-check inventory, the inventory is very difficult to do, in my experience. But after surrendering the outcome to God, you can more honestly analyze what has happened to you.

Another way a spot-check inventory can help is in catching old character defects as they are operating today. For example, one Saturday morning I had agreed to go to the airport to have breakfast with a representative from a publishing company. I got in late the night before from a meeting, and when my alarm went off the next morning, I turned it off, knowing my wife's alarm would go off in thirty minutes. I dozed off, but because my wife hadn't set her alarm, I overslept and was very late. When I got there, I was tempted to say, "Well, my wife usually sets the alarm, but she didn't," which was true.

The facts are, however, that I did not get up early enough to make the appointment on time, and it had nothing to do with my wife. Still, I was tempted to blame her because she usually sets her alarm. But to say what I was thinking would have been one of those "untrue truths" with which I used to fill the air when I'd fouled up. I stopped and took a spot-check inventory, which revealed my old tendency to justify myself by blaming others. Then I said to the person I met at the airport, "I really blew it. I turned off my alarm and went back to sleep. I'm sorry. I hope you can forgive me; there's no excuse." I shook my head and continued, "It's my Sin, and I want to make amends to you because I don't like to keep people waiting. That's not the way I want to live." She said, "That's what your book is about, isn't it?" I smiled, "Yes, that's why I was able to write it—because I discovered this stuff in myself." Afterward I felt clear of guilt and shame, and because of the spot-checking I did I could go on with the day instead of being obsequious and repeatedly saying, "I'm really sorry I was so late," as I have so often.

In doing a spot-check inventory about a face-to-face confrontation you can ask yourself, "Is what this person saying to me true?" Or "What am I really doing here?" This act of analyzing, instead of simply reacting, alters things, and often causes the emotional static to subside. You're in a different mode now, thinking rather than exploding or automatically lying.

If what the person is saying is not true, ask yourself, "What have I done to this person recently that has been thoughtless and abusive?" If you can see something, then move on to Step Five and admit it to God and yourself (and to your sponsor later if the incident stays in your mind). You may or may not admit it to the other person, depending on whether it would help. I try to admit any fault I can see by saying something like, "When you said that about me, I can see that you were right." Such admissions—when honest—go a long way toward resolving the conflict.

If you think it's the other person's fault, then try to be willing to forgive, hoping that he or she would forgive you if it were about you. In this way you can take many of the jagged cutting edges out of your relationships, edges that cut you and others up emotionally. This may seem to be going too far, but it is certainly in line with a similar radical biblical wisdom: Christ taught, "Love your enemies, do good to those who hate you, bless those who curse you, pray for those who abuse you. To him who strikes you on the cheek, offer the other also. . . . As you wish that men would do to you, do so to them" (Luke 6:27–31).

In the program they told me, "If you discover your character defects in action in spot-checking, be patient with yourself. You're *going* to blow it sometimes. You're going to go home and have arguments from time to time. Tell yourself, even if you have to do it ten times a day, 'recovery has more to do with progress than perfection.'"

That spot-check inventory takes the focus off of quick-tempered criticism or power-driven blaming, anger, pride, and revenge. The focus of your life shifts to seeking self-awareness and restraint and to finding out the truth about your behavior and your relationships so you can do God's will. The passage "You shall know the truth, and the truth shall make you free" begins to have a new meaning.

After practicing this tenth-Step spiritual process for a while, you will very likely begin to see the anatomy of the relationships around you. Sometimes now, in my close relationships, I can see what's happening to somebody else and to me, and we can talk constructively about it rather than blame and justify. The other person will often become calm and reasonable when I have talked about my part and not focused on his or her part.

In the past such conflicts were a blur to me. Once I got mad there was very little rational about the whole transaction. Sometimes I was so angry that I couldn't even talk, yet in my mind I always thought about how irrational *other* people were being.

As the Twelve and Twelve points out, we begin to see that "all people, including ourselves, are to some extent emotionally ill and frequently wrong." We begin to see that it's pointless and spiritually debilitating to get angry or have hurt feelings in talking to people who suffer, as we do, from the pains of imperfection and emotional immaturity. All of us are in some ways still growing up. In this program we're purposely trying to grow up by praying and following the guidance of the Twelve Steps.

Before I got to the Twelve Steps I was under the illusion that only occasionally was anybody mistaken in what they said (as compared to what they meant to say). And it usually wasn't I. But I've learned that most of us are wrong every day both about facts and about the way we try to communicate. We say things unclearly, and they are misunderstood, which irritates us (why can't other people get what we meant when it seemed obvious to us?). There's a lot about our behavior to be forgiven. If I'm always having to be right, I'm going to be miserable much of the time, and I'm certainly going to make the people around me uncomfortable.

Besides, when we get angry at somebody because "they're wrong," it makes *us* sick. That is not very smart. Some of us now do a lot to avoid that kind of indignant anger, not by stuffing our feelings but by realizing that if other people are doing something unpleasant or untruthful, it's more likely to be a character fault of theirs, not ours; for us to try to straighten them out is to throw us both into a self-defeating war.

By doing spot-check inventories we are learning that when we are tempted to rage or try to control people or when we fail in some way, we can respond more rationally by checking the reality of the situation. We try not to be doormats, but we're learning that courtesy, kindness, justice, caring, and not having to justify ourselves are marks of a spiritually mature human being. When we don't know what to do in a situation, we back off and say to God, "Not my will but Thine be done." We try to wait, listen, and acknowledge the other person's feelings. In other words, if we don't know what to do we start *listening* to the other person. When he or she says something that we can hear, such as being miserable about something, we can say, "That really sounds painful"—or frustrating or lonely or whatever the feeling is that we hear the person express. Just acknowledging the other's feeling often takes all the anger out of the situation and is very healing.

2. The Daily Inventory

The inventory at the end of the day helps us focus on the present. The spiritual life *is* focused in the present. Nothing creative or loving ever took place in the past or the future. The moment it happened was a present moment; God only operates in the present. Imagine that time is a long thread and the present moment is a button sliding down time. God is always present on the button, and all creative and loving acts take place in that moving present moment. In the Sin-disease, many of us filled the only real time we had—those present moments—with painful memories of the past or grandiose or fearful dreams of the future. In recovery, after we have done the first nine steps, we learn to trust God with the past and the future and to live in the reality of each day, each moment. We try not to fill the past with new unresolved issues or jump ahead with fear about tomorrow. As we live in the present, we are also living consciously in God's presence, and therefore that presence and the energy and wisdom of God are much more likely to permeate our words and actions in a natural, unaffected way.

Doing a daily inventory reminds us that each day we can focus God's power and watch him clear up the wreckage of that day. We can live in the present and go ahead and sort out the things we want to get rid of. Some people make a brief inventory of their day on paper every night. They list the character defects, sins, and abusive behaviors they remember from that day. Others do this in their minds. Next, they review the *good* thoughts they had today and the good things they did. For example, I might write, "I stopped and called my Uncle Jim, who's sick, and had a nice conversation with him," or "I wrote a letter to Joe, who's in trouble." Go through all the good things you can recall doing that day, and list them. Some people make a balance sheet on two sides of a piece of paper—writing the good things they did on one side and the dysfunctional and/or harmful things on the other.

A Checklist. Another thing some people find helpful is to make a checklist of their most common character defects. Here are some examples of things from the Big Book that you might include in such a list: selfishness, dishonesty, resentment, fear, jealousy, self-pity, greed, envy, depression, hatred, self-will, self-reliance.

As I've said before, the pain of failure in our lives can be the doorway to spiritual progress. So I check quickly and see if I can recall any selfishness, dishonesty, resentment, or fear. These are the character defects that get me in trouble. Did I follow my own self-will today? Did I insist on doing it my way? Self-reliance: did I insist on doing it myself when I should have asked for help? List any examples so you can make amends right away if necessary.

Self-righteousness is to claim a wrong motive to clear yourself. For example, perhaps I'm sarcastic to somebody, and the person says, "Oh, that really hurt me. Were you being sarcastic?" If I say, "No, I was kidding. Can't you take a joke?" (when I really was being sarcastic but want to keep myself feeling righteous, believing I'm too good a man to hurt somebody like that), that is claiming an untrue motive ("kidding" instead of "being sarcastic") to keep myself looking righteous. A person in recovery might say, "Yes, I was being sarcastic, and I'm sorry."

Jot down these character defects and failures so you can make amends the next day. You can lie in bed before you go to sleep and go over this list of "good" and "bad" things. If you feel you need to make amends, you can usually make a note right after your inventory. I make such notes because I don't like making amends and am liable to forget by morning.

This daily inventory helps keep the spiritual garbage out of our lives and the dead dogs out of the basement of the past. If you don't make these amends, they collect inside you and begin to block your relationships again. Trying to handle these things every day has been a great help to me in beginning the process of spiritual growth.

The truth is, I don't do a "formal" inventory every day now, though I did for a long period. But it has become a habit each night to go quickly through my checklist of common character defects to see if I need to make amends. This process of reviewing my day only takes a very few minutes, unless I run across some heavy denial or an issue I need to think about right then.

3. A Periodic Inventory

A periodic inventory may happen once or twice a year; you take Step Four again. Many people say if you take Step Four right the first time and do the spot-check and daily inventory, that's plenty. But others have found that every few months they uncover a new layer of painful or abusive incidents to inventory that weren't evident when they did Step Four the first time. If you were to take a fourth-Step inventory today, six months from now you might see some things you had denied earlier. Every week I'm finding more things that I've denied, more issues in my relationships, and so forth.

In these periodic inventories, we first reflect on our progress and spiritual growth and see what God's done in our lives, allowing us to be grateful. Often one changes from a complaining attitude to what the program calls an "attitude of gratitude." Gratitude is one of the most healing facets of spiritual recovery and growth. As we begin to feel like forgiven, accepted people with gifts to use, we step into a new experience of hope and self-acceptance. Gratitude is a natural response. When we list all the things we have to be grateful for, we are suddenly closer to God and long to serve him and be more loving. I don't know why or how this works, but for many of us it is true.

I thank God now, many times a day. I didn't used to take time to do that, because my mind was focused on the things I wanted that I didn't have.

As we take these periodic inventories, we also see dysfunctional areas we haven't touched, or reactivated character defects we thought we had dealt with. We may see how we have "taken back" Steps Three, Six, and Seven. In Step Three we said to God, "I've decided to give you my life and will." By doing an inventory we can see ways we haven't carried out that decision at all. So we do Step Three again.

When we see our true selves, confess, and are forgiven, we begin to accept ourselves as we actually are with all our imperfections. We gain freedom from guilt and shame and from the fear of being found out. Because God forgives us again and again, we can come right back and surrender to him when we see that we have taken over control again. The Christian expression of this truth about the number of times forgiveness should take place was expressed by Jesus (in Matt. 18:22) when he told Peter that one should forgive another "seventy times seventy" times (an infinite number). Realizing we have multiple second chances helps us to relate better to other people, because we know we do not have to be—indeed, cannot be—perfect. One by-product of this is that we don't feel so often that our pride is on the line.

How Steps Six and Seven
Can Be Part of Step Ten

In Steps Six and Seven we became entirely ready to have God remove all our defects of character and humbly asked him to do so. As we find new defects of character through these various inventories, we don't try to mobilize our strength and resolve to change and solve the defects. We go to God and say, "I'm entirely ready to have you remove this new shortcoming I've found." And we give it to him. This means that we stop "fighting" defects. We stop fighting people, trying to change them. We stop fighting ourselves, trying to become perfect. Instead, through the inventory process, as we try to face these shortcomings and make amends for the harm they cause, we offer the defects to God. And we return to living in the present.

The Christian message is that God's love and God's power, revealed in the life and death and resurrection of Jesus Christ, can reconcile us to God, make us "new creations," free us from Sin and the disease that it spawns, and send us out as ambassadors to spread God's truth about life. (See 2 Cor. 5:17–20.) Step Ten gives us practical ways to keep accessing that love and that power, one day at a time.

How Steps Eight and Nine
Are Part of Step Ten

Whenever we discover the abusive effects of our shortcomings or defects, a part of the process of releasing them to God is to go back and do what we can to make restitution, just as we did in Step Nine. Then our relationship with God becomes clear again. (See again Matt. 5:23.) To grow and to give our lives to God, we must make amends and attempt to be reconciled to the people we've wronged. Doing frequent eighth and ninth Steps on wrongs we discover is an essential part of spiritual growth in Twelve-Step programs.

Making amends can also be a powerful deterrent to repeating a sin or abusive act. For example, telling someone we lied or cheated or were disloyal or unfaithful is a painful experience for most of us. That pain becomes a real deterrent to repeating whatever it was we had to admit. I've heard people stand up in meetings and say, "I was so mad and started to let her have it, and then I remembered I had enough amends to make already. I didn't want to make any more." You actually find yourself refraining from doing certain things because you realize that you're committed to making amends.

We know we're going to fail. Some days we'll wake up in the morning and be angry or feel worthless or unworthy of being loved. But when that happens, we spot-check and say the first three steps. We remind ourselves that each of us is loved as a precious child of God, that this spiritual journey is a way of progress and forgiveness. And somehow this seems to be working for many of us. The promises of the program are coming true, sometimes sporadically, sometimes continually. We feel more comfortable with ourselves and, at last, more trusting, even of God.

The next step, Step Eleven, deals with the way we are to relate to God after doing the first ten steps.

TAKING STEP TEN

Step Ten

Continued to take personal inventory and, when we were wrong, promptly admitted it.

Using the First Three Steps

Did any incidents of conflict occur with anyone today? If so, how can you use the first three steps to regain serenity and clarity so you can decide how to respond?

For each incident, go through the following steps.

Step One: I am powerless over (describe).
Step Two: Describe any "insanity" (thoughts, exaggerated feelings, inappropriate behavior) from which God needs to restore you regarding this incident.
Step Three: Write out your decision to turn whatever you described in Step One over to God.

Doing a Spot-Check Inventory

For each incident described, take a spot-check inventory of *your part* in the conflict and make a decision concerning your need to make amends. If you need to do this, go to the person, or make an appointment, and make amends.

Doing a Daily Inventory

At the end of each day review your list of character defects, and note any examples of them that surfaced during the day so you can make amends tomorrow. The defects listed below are from the Big Book. Copy them in your notebook. Disregard any that don't apply to you, and add any of your own that are not included.

Character Defect	Example Today	Check When You Have Made Amends
selfishness		
dishonesty		
resentment		
fear		
jealousy		
self-pity		
greed		
envy		
depression		
hatred		
self-will		
self-reliance		

Doing a Periodic Inventory

Gratitude: List all the things you have to be grateful for that have happened since you did your original Step Four inventory (or your last periodic inventory).

Consider the decisions you made when you did Step Three. Is there anything in your life today that indicates you may have "taken back" any of the things that you surrendered then or in Step Seven (e.g., addictions, lying, attempts to control or be abusive to a person in a particular situation)? Describe.

After you have completed the list, take Step Three again, and turn these specific things over to God.

Have you found any new character defects since you took Steps Six and Seven? List them, then work through Steps Six and Seven regarding these newly discovered defects.

Are there any bruised relationships in your life for which you have not made amends for your part in the damage? List the person's name, what happened, and the effect in your life. Then work Steps Eight and Nine on each incident. Use a list with columns headed as follows: "People I Have Harmed," "What Happened? (My Harmful Behavior)," "Consequences: Separation and/or Damages?"

Chapter 14

STEP ELEVEN

Sought Through Prayer and Meditation to Improve Our Conscious Contact with God, Praying Only for Knowledge of His Will for Us and the Power to Carry That Out

Some biblical expressions concerning prayer and meditation, praying for God's will, and the need for help and his power for this area of our lives:

Ask and it will be given you; seek, and you will find; knock, and it will be opened to you. For everyone who asks receives, and he who seeks finds, and to him who knocks it will be opened. Luke 11:9–10

(Also)
Pray then like this:
Our Father who art in heaven,
Hallowed be thy name.
Thy kingdom come,
Thy will be done,
On earth as it is in heaven.
Give us this day our daily bread;
And forgive us our debts,
As we have forgiven our debtors;
And lead us not into temptation,
But deliver us from evil.
For thine is the kingdom and the power
and the glory, for ever. Amen.
Matthew 6:9–13

(Also) *Nevertheless, not as I will,*
but as Thou wilt. Matthew 26:39

(Also) *The Spirit helps us in our weakness;*
for we do not know how to pray as
we ought, but the Spirit himself intercedes
for us with sighs too deep for words.
Romans 8:26

The entire Twelve-Step program is designed to get us out of the "God role" and to put a loving, moral and forgiving God back in control of our world. When we do this there is Reality and Sanity at the center of our lives instead of a flighty, scared person in denial on a search for who knows what that will make him or her happy. For Christians this God is the God of Jesus Christ. But even Christians disagree concerning the appropriate ways to grow spiritually through prayer and meditation. The Twelve Steps provide a simple, direct approach to getting to know God in the context of everyday living.

Some people who have come a long way in the program still balk at the idea of "bowing down" before God and actually asking God specifically for directions about how to live the details of their daily lives and relationships. To other people, prayer and meditation sound spooky and irrational, like an amazingly naïve cop-out.

I once heard a woman say she prayed for parking places and got them all the time, and I thought, "Oh yeah, sure!" That sort of claim really turned me off. The idea that God Almighty would be interested in my parking place was just too much.

In the process of focusing my life on God in Steps One, Two, and Three, however, I've come to realize that the big miracle of prayer is to believe that God is really interested *at all* in what we do. The God of the program and the Church is not just a disinterested Being spinning us off into the calendar on our birthdate. Our experience has been that we're in touch with a Spirit with a "personality" that is loose in the world and somehow involved with its creatures in a personal manner. And this Spirit of God is loving and caring and operates in certain ways that are recognizable through the lens of faith.

We don't understand all this, but if one seriously works through the first ten steps with a sponsor while going to meetings, praying, and listening, some unaccountable changes in attitude can take place. Perceiving changes in other people's lives (and in one's own) that one can't account for in any other way, one may become convinced of the reality of God and the ways he may operate on the stage of ordinary life.

People hear someone else at a meeting talking about an experience with a new insight and think, "I can't believe that's the same terrified guy who came here. He wouldn't pay attention to anybody at first, and was totally self-centered. We couldn't get him to shut up in the meeting. We almost had to interrupt and stop him, and now he's very quiet and sensitive and helping people all around him."

As we listen to others share the intimate details of how they work the program, we hear how they learned to move from trusting vaguely in a Higher Power of some kind to beginning to invite the loving spirit of God into the deepest, most confused, most fearful, most painful, and most practical areas of their lives. The change has usually taken place in a way that was personal rather than propositional. This was not the truth *about* God they were learning but the *Presence* of God with which they were interacting. This sense of the presence of God changed the whole atmosphere in their lives—from despair to enthusiastic hope.

Moving through the steps people report being increasingly in contact with some*one*—a "Person" rather than a philosophical Higher Power. When this change takes place, we often see miracles happening in their lives. After much fear of losing control, they discover insight, wisdom, power, and courage that they didn't have at all two weeks before. At that point many say, "I surrender, I give up." They begin to communicate with God concerning what is happening to them. And that's when they are ready to receive the help of Step Eleven.

Although these changes happen for many people, they do not happen for all. Many work the steps and stay sane in Twelve-Step programs yet somehow miss the whole thing about prayer and meditation. Most of the people who work good programs, however, are connected to God and do use prayer and meditation in some form. They use them as practical ways of learning who God is and what his will for them may be, as well as for learning useful truths about who they are and what they're to do in order to find happiness, guidance, peace, and continued growth. But mostly they pray because they feel gratitude, love, and a sense of awe that the One with whom they are in contact is using his power to heal them.

The Connection Between
Self-Examination and Prayer

The Twelve and Twelve points out that there is a direct link between self-examination, on one hand, the personal "housecleaning" that we've been doing in the last ten steps, and prayer and meditation, on the other.[1] Self-searching and making amends are the way we interrupt and reverse the progress of the Sin-disease in our lives. We come into the program shattered by life to varying degrees. We are powerless (which we had never counted on being); we are in the throes of something we are told is, and recognize as, a disease, a spiritual disease.

Letting the light of truth shine on the disease and the behavior it leads to is what the Bible calls "beginning to live in the light." As you move into the light, as God is in the light, you see the truth about your disease, and through God's loving power you can be healed. As, through the Twelve Steps, we begin to let the light of God shine on the stuff we have buried, then suddenly we get in touch with God as a living personality with the power and inclination to overcome the disease in our lives and show us how to live.

This denial-breaking process shows us the effects and strategies of our controlling Sin-disease and helps us to know in no uncertain terms that we are not God. This true picture of ourselves is what the Twelve-Step program calls humility. Humility prepares us—in gratitude and excitement at what God is doing to change us—to be ready to search honestly for God's will; it is this search that leads us to try prayer and meditation.

The Twelve-Step View of Prayer

The Twelve-Step view of what is appropriate and effective in prayer is very different in several important ways from the Christian approach that I grew up with and was trained in. The Twelve and Twelve points out that "prayer is the raising of the heart and mind to God," and the authors include meditation in that (p. 102). There is a sense in which the purpose of prayer and meditation in the program is almost entirely to help us learn how to *hear God* and to sensitize us to read the signs in our lives and in the world that can guide us toward knowing and living life as God wants us to. There is very little about asking him to do things we ourselves want done. The strong consensus is that we are so controlling and self-centered and so in denial in our Sin that almost all our requests for ourselves and other people are tainted with the conviction that we know what is best for other people and ourselves—this the program knows to be delusion.

Knowing all this, the founders of A.A. put a clause in Step Eleven that disturbs many Christians who have been praying all their lives: "praying only for knowledge of his will for us and the power to carry that out." It says *only.* I've always had a lot more to tell God about than that. Good Christians have always prayed for some or all of the following: specific answers to our questions, a particular outcome in a specific situation, an end to our pain or our disease (or whatever is causing us trouble), financial success or a certain level of financial security, vocational success— and that God's will be done. Many of us in the Twelve-Step program have discovered that most of these prayer subjects are too "dangerous" for our spiritual health.

Playing God Through Our Prayers

We who have the Sin-disease and play God at the drop of a hat have to be very careful how we talk to God, or we'll be right back in our disease. (I'm a master at this myself.) We forget how skewed our thinking is about life. People like us (who pray for and expect specific answers, for instance, to all our specific requests for ourselves and others) can be arrogant and abusive to be around.

I am not saying here that it is "wrong" to pray for specific things that seem patently to be God's will, but I am pointing out the insidious ways the Sin-disease can turn even our prayer life into an arena for manipulation and self-centeredness.

The disease can distort prayers. We pray about a situation and get an "answer," and in doing whatever came to us as God's will we can sincerely think, "God told me to do this, or told me to tell *you* to do this." Many of these answers are obviously not answers from God at all but well-intentioned, unconscious, self-serving rationalizations from our own Sin-diseased minds. Yet the people praying are confident that they know what to do, because "God told me." They may decide that God is telling them to do something that may be very thoughtless, painful, and abusive to their family. But they override the family's objections and pain and go ahead, because God has supposedly asked them to do it. There's no arguing with people under these circumstances; they think, "We must obey God!"

We forget what we're learning in this program: that we're entrenched rationalizers. We do a *lot* of wishful thinking. Consequently, there is distortion in the guidance we think we're getting, as we force our own will on situation after situation, thinking it's God's will. Some people have built large enterprises, even large ministries, on this basis of praying for everything—right down to "What shall we eat for breakfast?" It's amazing what such people are sometimes "told" to go get for breakfast or what kind of expensive car or house they are "told" to buy—and that these instructions to them are God's will. Many of these people are sincere, I'm convinced. But pretty soon, because they have this same Sin-disease we have, the craziness of the disease gets them. They make some bizarre mistake that brings the whole ministry crashing down. You don't have to look very far to find examples of this in contemporary America.

Even though I like to think of my own prayer life over the last twenty years as being more sophisticated than that, I can see that my own Sin-disease affected my prayer life and the answers that I got, with a similar result. The Twelve-Step program, with its sponsors and meetings, as well as reading and working the steps give the praying person some additional reality checks about what might be God's will. The Bible and the experience of other Christians on the journey with Christ give the Christian Twelve Stepper additional resources to fight the denial, delusion, and grandiosity of the Sin-disease.

Praying for Other People

The same principles apply to praying for things for other people. I have to keep reminding myself with humility that I am not a totally healed person. I am in recovery but not fully recovered.

Part of the delusion resulting from my disease is that I know what's best for other people, so therefore I should pray for these things. If they're sick, they should be prayed for to get well right away. If they're in pain, they should be released from their pain today, if possible. If they don't have a mate and want one, they should have one.

Paul Tournier, a Swiss psychiatrist who was a Christian layman, was my mentor at one time. I asked him, "How do you pray about people who are ill?" He said, "Oh, I pray that they won't get well before they learn the meaning of their illness. The problem with getting well too fast, or with taking tranquilizers," he said, "is that people get out of their pain before they learn the meaning of it." Yet I almost always prayed that people's pain would stop immediately. (Of course, neither Dr. Tournier nor I would suggest that when one has a physical lesion, for example, and a physician prescribes pain medication one should turn it down. But

I am talking here about the commom approach many Christains have of praying for the pain to stop without any understanding of the place of pain in spiritual and emotional healing.)

In this program I have learned that God is trying to communicate directly with all people everywhere who have the disease. According to the Bible, that is everyone (see Rom. 3:23, "All have sinned and fall short"). Because the pains and agonies of life caused by our Sin help us to be humble enough to hear God and find out the truth, I don't pray for people the same way I did. As I've said, I hold them up in my cupped hands, imagine God's cupped hands, and put them in God's hands, taking my hands away and saying *nothing* to God about what he should do. I don't know what they need—and that's a new revelation to me. It's not that I don't care or that I'm just tossing them off to God. I care about them deeply; I cry about them. But I do not want God to take them out of their pain and frustration if that same pain and frustration will lead them to recovery and life. And only God knows that.

I found out painfully that I don't really know what people need. I prayed for some people in the program who were in trouble and about to hit bottom. They needed some money. God didn't send it, so I lent them the money. One of them was an alcoholic, who went back out and got drunk and never paid the money back. The other one also got back in the disease and, after making only a few payments, stopped repaying me. I realized that God didn't answer the prayers of either of these people; I did. God was too slow. Instead of trusting God, I stepped in. I don't mean that I wouldn't help somebody, but I'm now much more careful. My quick solutions alleviate the immediate pain sometimes, but if they interfere with God's plan for people they can actually harm them in the long run. Both these people had their pain prolonged by my jumping in and circumventing God's will for their lives, and they also got a load of guilt—all because I knew what they needed and couldn't wait for God to answer their prayers.

I've seen my own unconscious presumption in telling God what he should do. I still occasionally pray for specific things for others. And sometimes it's fairly safe for me to pray that God will help other people do what they need to do, but I always end by saying, "Thy will be done." I realize that many, if not most, Christians pray quite differently from the way I'm describing, but I am only saying that *for me* specifically trusting God with the outcome of other people's difficulties has been much more helpful in my life and my relationships than giving him the plan he should follow.

Prayers for Myself

I try not to pray for specific things for myself, but sometimes I do. I realize, however, that I don't even know what's best for me. I might pray for success or health or something else, yet the minute I do that I set up an expectation of what I ought to do and have, and at that point, I couldn't hear God if he came through with a truck and a loudspeaker and told me to do something else. I assume that he's not answering my prayer when he's not giving me what I asked for.

Now, however, when I'm just praying to know God's will for me, I'm having to stay alert. When I pray, "Thy will be done," and put myself in God's hands, I'm watching and listening, because God will respond by *revealing* his will to me in what happens. This makes me much more attentive to my surroundings and the people in my life, which is where I often find God's will anyway.

Since I've begun praying almost exclusively for God's will for others and myself, I have a great feeling of participating in God's will. My training had led me to think that we should pray for something specific and then God should do it. I've heard people tell a sick person who is not getting well, "Well there must be some sin in your life," because they can't accept that anything's wrong with their prayer. There's an enormous amount of this floating around in the Church, people postulating that they ought to tell God what to do. But in this program I feel I can stay with people, love them, and not try to manipulate their healing. This approach demands a great deal more trust that God *is* loving and intelligent and *does* really care about people.

When Our Demands Cease,
Guidance Can Begin

When we get to Step Eleven most of us are the cleanest- and clearest-minded we've ever been. At Step Eleven the program says, "You've got clean ears and clean eyes. Let us *introduce* you to this God who has been changing your life. Now it's time to get in touch with him and let *him* teach you how to live. The other steps have been preparing you for this. Once you get in touch with him (and you learn in Step Ten how to keep yourself in shape to be in touch with him), then you will also be able to be in closer touch with other people who are made in his image. And they will help teach you his will for you as they are discovering his will for their own lives."

The program suggests that we receive God's guidance to the extent that we stop making demands on God to give us guidance in our time and in our way. Guidance is a much more subtle thing than I had thought. It's not usually like a blazing sun; it's a gentle nudge toward something. Receiving guidance from God is evidently strongly dependent on keeping in fit spiritual condition.

At first when you feel a nudge, you aren't sure what to do. But now I'm beginning to recognize as I listen to God that there are certain things to pay attention to. For example, I might get an idea to call Richard. Now I know how spooky this sounds, but it's not like a shouting voice in the room saying, "Call Richard!" I just get a sense that something is in my mind about Richard, and I might call Richard and say, "Hey, how are you doing?" Then I listen. I don't call him and say, "God told me to call you. I have a message for you!"

Sometimes there is nothing going on with Richard. Sometimes my "guidance" turns out to be a pain in the stomach because I ate too many onions. It's very important to keep a humble, reality-oriented attitude, realizing your capacity to control and rationalize. But as you practice listening to God and checking, it is amazing how many times the quiet nudge to do something turns out to be exactly what you later realize was what God would have done. Richard may say, "I can't believe you called right now. I really need to talk to someone." Spiritual growth is a process that demands practice, day after day. One learns by trying and making mistakes.

How Much Time Spent Praying?

"Start simply," is the advice I was given, and I would certainly pass it on to you. Don't try to do too much. It's better to have a three-minute prayer time to begin with and have some success. If we compulsively start out attempting to have a thirty-minute quiet time every day, and then can't repeat it the second morning or the second week, we may feel guilty again and punish ourselves. Soon we drift away from having any quiet time at all. When I began, I was told to take five to ten minutes to pray.

It takes time to develop this process. Why shouldn't it take time? It took us years to get this messed up, but we expect the mess to be cleared up the instant we have found a new approach. It seems to be part of the disease that we want to control our recovery and make it happen on our timetable—immediately.

Learning by Trial and Error

The program has spent ten steps teaching us how to deal with the errors we have made in the past. We have begun to develop the courage to trust learning by trial and error. In this program we expect to make some mistakes. We learn again and again that we're practicing progress, not perfection.

We may get an intuition that we should do something, and we go and try to do it. If it turns out wrong and we harm someone, we confess to God and then go to the person and say, "Well, I blew it that time. That was wrong. I want to make amends to you; I'm sorry." Then we do it differently tomorrow. A perfectionist cannot risk much at all for fear of making a mistake. But because we've already taken Steps Four through Eight, admitting that we've made mistakes and making amends, then trying, discovering mistakes, confessing, and making amends becomes a way of life. After a while there's nothing we can't risk trying after we have prayed about it (and checked with others if it seems doubtful).

Eventually we develop confidence in the trying and failing, and we learn from the process. If we make a mistake, and what we thought was God's will obviously was not, it's not the end of the world. The discomfort and pain of failures can help motivate us to learn more about God and what *would* be included in his will. One woman in the program said that she felt sure God's will would not be to go against his word in the scriptures or the responsibilities that were uniquely hers (being a good mother and wife, etc.). But there are areas in which we can only learn by trial and error. The process becomes a way of keeping us from being paralyzed by our perfectionism or by our harmful behavior and our insecure feelings.

Prayer Model for in the Morning

Here is a format that I've found useful for praying in the morning. There are all kinds of helpful prayer formats; I include this one to give you some idea about how you can build a prayer time that will meet your own needs. There are nine things listed; some may not be relevant to you. Some I have done for several years, some only for short periods, but doing them has helped me experience the reality of God in my daily life.[2]

1. I read something that's meaningful to me, such as a daily selection from *A Day at a Time* (see list of daily devotional books in Selected Reading). Then I read a selection from *Letting God,* by Philip Parham, which is a Christ-centered book for Christians but also pure "Twelve Steps." It doesn't compromise either as far as I can see. For years I read four to thirty minutes from the Bible. When I first got in the program I read a few minutes a day in the Big Book or the Twelve and Twelve.

2. I thank God for one person or one specific thing.

3. I surrender my life and the things that I'm worried about to God. I have a "denial detector" I use in this process. *After* having committed my whole life to God in the morning, I make a list of the things I still worry about during the day (the things I still worry about are obviously things I did not commit to him after all). The next day, I surrender the things on my list specifically. Since doing Step Seven I've stopped saying, "God give me the power to overcome these." Instead I say, "God, I'm entirely ready to let you remove this worry about this child or this need to justify myself to this person or this frantic worry about my financial life." Results are a lot better with this changed focus.

4. I ask God to show me his will for me today and to give me the strength to do it. And then I assume his will includes giving and receiving love, so I add a prayer that I'll be able to give and receive love, because I have trouble with both.

5. I ask God for the courage and the strength to do his will.

6. I've learned to simply tell God my feelings, because I often don't know what I'm feeling when I get up. Because my feelings have been numb for so many years, I need this quiet time with God as a place I can come and check my feelings. The more I check and express what I feel, the more I can feel (e.g., "I feel fear, anger, sadness").

7. I do some positive visualizations, because I've got so many bad tapes in my mind. I have a list of things that seem right for me to do that I visualize myself as having done. I see myself as having an honest, straight relationship with my wife; I visualize myself being a totally surrendered person, a person who is serene and a person who is unselfish. And I even visualize my house being paid off—realizing this may or may not be God's will. It is amazing the effect visualizing has had on me. "Seeing" those changes accomplished makes them more nearly happen.

8. I say, "Today I will try to contact one person," and put the name in. And I just contact that person for no reason, because I'm grateful for him or her.

9. I read the following statement to myself: "Doing my best is as near perfection as I ever need to get." That's a big help for me as a perfectionist.

Prayer Model for During the Day

During the day when I'm uptight or frantic I do one or all of the following: say the Serenity Prayer, say the Lord's Prayer, or do the first three steps. Sometimes I'll just go through the entire Twelve Steps from memory. It is an enormous help just to consciously realize that I'm in the Twelve-Step process, through which God is getting me well and teaching me how to live.

Then I ask God to show me his will, especially when I'm frantic. I express gratitude many times during the day. I'll say, "God, thank you for this life that I'm living. Thank you for this program. Thank you for my wife, Andrea." Or, "I'm so thankful that I have this friend." That attitude of being grateful is like taking spiritual vitamins. I feel so much better and become even more grateful and serene when I express gratitude like that.

Before, when people asked me, "How are you doing?" I would tell them all my troubles. "Oh gosh, I've had a terrible time today. Everything's just awful." That's changed a lot. Now I try to listen to others and hear what they are asking me. And I tell the good things as well as difficulties, if that's appropriate, as I share my experience, strength, and hope with people. But I try to do it without self-pity. Lifetime habits are hard for me to break, but focusing on gratitude in my prayers has made me more conscious of the good things that happen during the day.

Prayer Model for the Evening

In the evening I say thank you for getting me through this day, and then I do the tenth Step. I give my day a quick scan with a daily inventory. I read the list of twelve things I mentioned in chapter 13 ("Doing a Daily Inventory"), and I review any ways that I've been selfish, dishonest, fearful, and so on.

For years I never prayed on my knees, even when I was in seminary, except when I was in chapel. Now I pray on my knees beside the bed at night as a reminder that I am not God, not the one "in control." I'm convinced that praying on one's knees is not necessary at all for prayer to be effective, but it is often helpful for me. I say the Third-Step Prayer (p. 63 of the Big Book). I also say the promises that describe the positive changes that happen to those who work the Twelve Steps (pp. 83 and 84 of the Big Book; see promises in chapter 12 under "The Promises of the Twelve-Step Program"). And I say the Serenity Prayer. I have memorized these three things and the Twenty-third Psalm during the past five years in this program.

It doesn't take a great deal of time to say these prayers and repeat these affirmations of what the spiritual life accomplishes, but the results have been very good for me. My mind focuses on my commitment to God, the hope of the program, and the assurances of the Bible as I go to sleep each night. I sleep more peacefully and wake feeling closer to God.

Meditation

The Twelve and Twelve points out that if prayer is talking to God then meditation is a way of listening more deeply to him. But it's a way of listening through silence, visual symbols, or words. You may decide that meditation is not for you, and that's fine. It is discussed here because it has been helpful to many people.

Some simply ask God for his will and then listen. As a casualty of the Sin-disease who had been stuck in the center of the universe, I received the same warnings when approaching meditation as I did about prayer. In such a condition I'm liable to hear God say anything I want him to, especially if I'm just listening to my own insides. That's why it's good to pick a powerful prayer that's time-tested on which to meditate. The authors of the Twelve and Twelve suggest some of the following thoughts, beginning with using the prayer of Saint Francis of Assisi so that you begin to focus your listening outside your disease. Some people use "Higher Power" as focusing words for God, or they say "Jesus." By repeating that word and focusing on it, they get outside themselves and begin to sense God's presence.

The idea is to get out of the center of your life by focusing on something that by its nature is not a part of the disease but a part of the cure for it. This refocusing allows us to filter out some of our self-centered obsessions.

At first during prayer and meditation my mind wandered terribly. I'd think, "I've got to go call Joe," and then I'd reprimand myself, "Don't think about that; don't think about that." But the more I'd tell myself not to think about something, the more it had my attention. Years ago someone told me to keep a pencil and paper nearby and every time something came to mind to do later in the day during my meditation time to jot it down. "It may be a message from God," this person said, "or it may be a distraction. But don't worry about it; write it down and then come back to your meditation focus."

Be very patient with yourself in meditation. When your mind wanders, come gently back into focus. I'm not naturally a meditator; I'm too intense. I tried for years to do it and failed miserably. But I find I can concentrate better on something that somebody has written than I can on "God in the void of my mind"—especially since I learned that what *I* learn from "God in the void of my mind" is often a disguised message from my Sin-disease.

Drop all resistance and unbelief during meditation. This is not a time for argument with or a critical analysis of the word or prayer you're using. Just say, "For the purposes of this exercise I'm going to believe that I'm in the presence of a very wise teacher. The person who wrote this is actually a teacher sent to me from God. I'm not going to argue; I'm going to listen."

Here are some suggestions people have found helpful: Try to read the passage a couple of times. Try to understand each word and each phrase. Some people find it very helpful to use their creative imagination at this point. For instance, to clear my mind when I couldn't concentrate on a certain passage, I used to imagine that I was walking alone by the Sea of Galilee on a very dusty road. Rain drops began to splatter the dust in front of me. I thought, "It's going to pour down rain." And then I looked up and saw a cave on the side of the hill. The rain was really increasing, so I scrambled over the rocks up to the cave, just barely making it inside as the bottom dropped out of the sky, and the rain came down in silvery sheets, deluging the hillside with a thousand little rivers bouncing and making their way through the boulders.

Somebody had built a fire in the cave, and there were glowing coals there. A man was sitting on a rock on the other side of this fire, and he motioned me to come to him. I was a little scared, but he looked kind. I came in and sat down across the fire from this man, and he held his hands out to me. I saw that his hands were scarred with nail holes. He simply said, "I love you." As I would imagine this, I would listen for whatever else he might say, realizing that the image of Jesus would bring forth different things from the depths of my unconscious than a picture of my stockbroker, or whatever else might flash into view in the unstructured void of my mind.

Using creative imagination is what many of the saints have done. You may want to choose some place to visualize where you feel close to God, like the beach or the mountains, and begin to free yourself to imagine you are in that place. Imagine that God can meet you there, or that you can be receptive to him there in some way.

Some practical people might say, "That's ridiculous." But the use of the creative imagination is the foundation of all accomplishment. Before a building can be built someone has to imagine it. Some man or woman somewhere used his or her creative imagination to get every creative thing done that's ever been accomplished. Imagination is a very practical thing.

How one meditates is an individual choice, but when the doubts come as you try it, don't beat up on yourself. You may think, "If someone came in here and saw me doing this, I'd die." If thoughts like that come, just say, "I'm a precious child of God, and I'm learning how to do something that's very important to me. It's very difficult, and I don't know how to do it yet." Then go back to it.

The authors of the Twelve and Twelve suggest that if you use the prayer of Saint Francis, think about what Francis was trying to say.

> Lord, make me a channel of thy peace—that where there is hatred, I may bring love—that where there is wrong, I may bring the spirit of forgiveness—that where there is discord, I may bring harmony—that where there is error, I may bring truth—that where there is doubt, I may bring faith—that where there is despair, I may bring hope—that where there are shadows, I may bring light—that where there is sadness, I may bring joy. Lord, grant that I may seek rather to comfort than to be comforted—to understand, than to be understood—to love, than to be loved. For it is by self-forgetting that one finds. It is by forgiving that one is forgiven. It is by dying that one awakens to Eternal Life. Amen. (p. 99)

What was he asking for himself? Was there anything in it for him? Is there anything that *you* should ask for that's in this prayer? Then you might picture yourself as being the kind of person that this prayer is about. When you imagine yourself as that kind of person you may feel joy—or you might say, "I wouldn't want to be that." And that's okay.

Perhaps you can find some other prayer or passage with which to meditate.

The object of prayer and meditation is always the same in this program. It is to improve our conscious contact with God, with his wisdom, with his love, and with his will for our lives.

Our participation in his plan for human life is what Step Twelve is about.

TAKING STEP ELEVEN

Step Eleven
Sought through prayer and meditation
to improve our conscious contact with God,
praying only for knowledge of his will
for us and the power to carry that out.

1. Find a place and time of day to begin a daily prayer time.

If having a prayer and meditation time is new to you, describe your difficulties, if any, in doing it (getting too busy, forgetting, and so on).

If you already had a prayer and meditation time before beginning these steps, describe any changes you have made in the way you spend this time as a result of working the Twelve Steps. In other words, write out the daily prayer format you are using (or plan to use). (See example of possible components under "Prayer Model for in the Morning.")

2. If you have become aware of ways you've "played God" through your prayers for yourself or other people, describe them (e.g., asking that people change to suit you, to get well on your timetable, to find a mate).

3. If you have begun to experience what I call nudges during your prayer time or during the day, list some of these nudges (whether you followed up on them or not).

4. If you have followed up on any of your nudges, what did you do, and what happened to you in the process?

5. What meditation methods have you chosen? Asking for God's will and then listening? Saying a word on which to focus? Reading a passage and thinking about it? Describe.

6. If visualization is a helpful thing for you, describe what you are visualizing during your meditation time. A meeting place with God? Yourself healed from character defects?

Chapter 15

STEP TWELVE

Having Had a Spiritual Awakening as the Result of These Steps, We Tried to Carry This Message to Others and to Practice These Principles in All Our Affairs

Some biblical principles pertaining to living out Step Twelve:

Therefore, if anyone is in Christ he is a new creation, the old has passed away, behold the new has come. 2 Corinthians 5:17

(Also) *Go home to your friends, and tell them how much the Lord has done for you, and how he has had mercy on you. Mark 5:19*

(Also) *. . . teaching them to observe all that I have commanded you; and lo, I am with you always, to the close of the age.*
Matthew 28:20

A Three-Part Spiritual Launching
Pad into the Rest of Your Life

Step Twelve is considered to be so important that it takes up much more space in the literature than any other step. It's almost three steps in one. I have divided it into three parts to look at in this chapter:

1. Having had a spiritual awakening . . .
2. We tried to carry the message to others . . .
3. And to practice these principles in all our affairs.

1. Having Had a Spiritual Awakening

In the Twelve-Step community the word *spiritual* usually doesn't mean the same thing as the word *religious.* For many, spiritual refers to being in touch with and living on the basis of "reality." A spiritual woman, for instance, would be in touch with her own reality, her own feelings, her own controlling and diseased behaviors and character defects as well as her own preciousness and gifts. She would be in touch with the reality of other people and with ultimate reality in the experience of a Higher Power, God. In that sense a "spiritual awakening," whatever else it might include, is an awakening to seeing and dealing with reality in one's own life and in relationships with other people and with God.

It is interesting that in six of the Twelve Steps the specific dominant note is spiritual in nature: Steps Two, Three, Five, Six, Seven, and Eleven. Many people who work the steps begin to see that the *entire* Twelve-Step program is about spiritual growth, which in Twelve-Step thinking is growth toward finding and doing God's will. In fact, as the Big Book puts it, "We are in the world to play the note He assigns" (p. 68). People can get a lot of help attending meetings and reading the Big Book, the Bible, and other literature. But whatever one does in working the program, the goal of the steps is a spiritual awakening that changes the participant from a miserable and helpless "patient" to a healthy and happy carrier of spiritual healing.

A "spiritual awakening" in Twelve-Step terms is a mystery. But almost all the authors who write about Step Twelve agree that the power that boosts us into a new orbit of life beyond the program comes from a spiritual awakening.[1]

We can't control a spiritual awakening or make it come about. Sometimes parts of it happen quickly; there are those who go from loneliness, fear, and chaos to a great deal of serenity, courage, and self-acceptance after doing Step One or Step Two, and many after Steps Three, Four, or Five. On the other hand, it took Dr. Bob, one of the co-founders of A.A., two and a half years to have what he called a spiritual experience.

A spiritual awakening means different things at different times to people as they work the steps. It's like a series of dawning insights that move people from confusion to an awareness that the world makes sense and that they are going to be all right in it, no matter how bad things look on the surface. As people get used to standing in their pain and facing it with God, their sponsor, and their Twelve-Step friends, they develop an increasing conviction that God is trustworthy and that "the program works." All this is part of a spiritual awakening.

Even though people who share these experiences can recognize each other and agree about their discoveries, there is no one way of describing a spiritual awakening. In fact, as the author of *Emotions Anonymous* said, "There are as many different kinds of spiritual awakenings as there are people." Some have a very dramatic change of feelings and attitudes in a single spiritual experience, as in a classic religious conversion.

For most people, the awakening is more subtle. It may dawn early one morning as one wakes up and feels a breath of hope after being under the wet, black blanket of despair. For many who come to this program, hope is a rare commodity. Some wonder if they are going to make it at all. When such people are sitting in a meeting feeling lonely and rejected and it dawns on them that the men and women sitting around them are not condemning but are actually going to support them in trying to move into recovery, they are having a simple but profound experience of hope. The gratitude that goes with that experience can propel them into the beginnings of a spiritual awakening and the first development of a sense of trust. That trust may be an important stepping-stone to a relationship with God.

Our awareness of our own self-worth after taking the responsibility to do Step Four, Step Five, or Step Nine may constitute a spiritual awakening from years of feeling unacceptable and inadequate. The awakening may begin at Step Two with the reassurance that there is a God we can relate to and that in fact we're actually going to ask him for help. Later, perhaps at Step Twelve, some people have a broader experience that tells them God is not only with *them* everywhere but out in the world ahead of them leading people toward the program and the Church.

The change for some is that God is not some distant figure on a mountain or another planet but a presence with, within, and among us wherever we are, guiding, leading, encouraging, and confronting us to move on toward wholeness and the giving and receiving of love. We Christians see this as the God of Jesus Christ working through his Spirit.

Sometimes it's only in retrospect that people realize that a spiritual awakening has taken place. But however it happens, when it does, a new view of what it means to live and relate as an authentic human being begins to form. As significant changes begin to take place, as people develop self-assurance, conquer their fear, and learn to participate in vulnerable sharing (many have never had these experiences before in any continuing way), they sometimes feel what seems to be a tidal wave of gratitude and happiness. It's usually this sort of behavioral evidence coming through the senses and the emotions, not "theological" evidence (that is, a change of philosophy), that tells members of Twelve-Step groups that they are having a spiritual awakening.

As you can see, this phenomenon usually doesn't feel religious. It feels real; there is a sense of clarity and authenticity about what one is doing and experiencing. We find that our sense of reality and our behavior are changing, that there's a fresh breeze blowing through our days and nights that we come to recognize as a spiritual quality of life.

Instead of being mired in the guilt and resentment of the past and our fear of the future, hoping that we can make ourselves look or sound better by laundering our feelings (and feeling guilty when we can't make things all right for everyone), we find ourselves facing and appreciating the present realities of our lives and relationships—including our pain—with increasing serenity and effectiveness.

People in the program report that they feel as though they are getting their God-given minds back; they "think" rather than reacting automatically. Christians call this being "transformed by the renewal of your mind" (Rom. 12:2).

The Twelve and Twelve captures the spiritual awakening experience better than anything I've read:

When a man or woman has had a spiritual awakening, the most important meaning of it is that he now becomes able to do, feel, and believe that which he could not do before on his own unaided strength and resources alone. He has been granted a gift that amounts to a new state of consciousness and being. He has been set on a path that tells him he is really going somewhere, that life is not a dead end, not something to be endured or mastered. In a very real sense he has been transformed, because he has laid hold of a source of strength that, in one way or another, he had hitherto denied himself. He finds himself in possession of a degree of honesty, tolerance, unselfishness, peace of mind, and love of which he had thought himself quite incapable. What he has received is a free gift, and yet usually, at least in some small part, he has made himself ready to receive it. (p. 107)

2. We Tried to Carry This Message to Others

One of the paradoxical bedrock truths of the Twelve-Step program (and the Christian message) is that we can stay spiritually alive only by giving away what we are receiving. We do this through sharing our experience, strength, and hope as we tell others how we came to the end of ourselves and stepped through powerlessness into the program. We share what is happening to change our lives and give us hope. And we carry the message by helping people who are still hopeless, helpless, and afraid.

Christians call this "evangelism," but in the Twelve Steps, where people learn about God through their experiences with him, there is no attempt to "persuade" with theology or verbal arguments. We let pain do the persuading, because we know that it is only through pain that the hunger for healing comes that will make us ready to admit our powerlessness. We know that until the pain of our lives was greater than the fear of swallowing our pride and going for help, we were not hungry enough for healing to go for it through the Twelve Steps.

Basically, there are three ways of carrying the message:

- One-on-one contact, wherein you talk to people who are in trouble, who are in pain, who are losing control. The focus may or may not be on an obvious chemical or behavioral addiction. Those of us who are in Sinners Anonymous groups are working the Twelve Steps on the compulsive need to control, brought about by the Sin-disease.* But whatever type of Twelve-Step program you are in, the basic issues of carrying the message to people still in pain are pretty much the same.

- Acts of helping, which may be primarily verbal or nonverbal. Many people are shy or don't believe they know enough to share. They want to carry the message but don't want to "talk it."
- Sponsoring, which is described in appendix A, will be discussed here in connection with carrying the message.

Talking to People Who Are in Trouble and Losing Control

The "Self-Centered Crazies": A Point of Entry.   Chapter 7 of the Big Book is perhaps the best place to read about individual contacts (see p. 89). There is a state of intensified anxiety and fear that can come over people out of nowhere, like a desert sandstorm. Among Twelve-Step groups this phenomenon is sometimes called "the self-centered crazies" and is the point at which many people become open to help from a program whose front door is "powerlessness and unmanageability." In the self-centered crazies, people become completely absorbed in themselves, their relationships, their fears, their success or failure. Their thoughts are scrambled and illogical and laced with various fears. They may feel as though they have much more to do than they can possibly get done and that there is no way out of the situation. Or they may have had a terrible argument with a loved one and fear the relationship is over; they may suddenly feel panic about that. Self-pity, anger, resentment, shame, guilt, lack of hope, and an overarching fear that they are "not going to make it this time"—all these feelings and thoughts swirl around in their minds, overriding all the positive aspects in their situation and any potential for hope. Although they know their thoughts are not rational, they can't seem to stop the acceleration of increasingly awful mental pictures.

Some prospective Twelve-Step members have another reaction just before they are ready to receive help—a numb coldness and shuddering

---

* For a starter packet on how to start a Sinners Anonymous group, write: Sinners Anonymous, P.O. Box 26001, Austin, Texas 78755-0001.

fear. When this type of emotional ice storm strikes, their diseased control behaviors often escalate, leading to great pain and loneliness. Whatever the resulting behaviors—increased chemical or food intake or intensified efforts at trying to control other people or the future—the anxiety of the disease expands like a poisonous gas until there seems to be no safe place, no secure peace in one's life. When you see people with these frantic symptoms, it may be a good time to go and listen to them, and possibly share your experience, strength, and hope.

The Cure for the "Crazies" Is to Help Others.   One of the shocks about recovery is that after weeks or months of solid recovery and serenity through working the program, *you* can wake up in the middle of a bad case of these same self-centered crazies. But after we have worked the Twelve Steps, we have some tools through which we can get help. We also learn, however, that nothing ensures recovery from this recurring insanity, or even just "the blahs," like helping other people. When we visit those who have lost or are losing control—who are sick, who have lost their jobs, who have lost a spouse to separation or divorce, who have just had a death in the family or a child in trouble or a broken love relationship—we can help them far better than can people who have never faced their powerlessness. We are not going to try to fix them. We know how it feels to be powerless. The paradox of the Twelfth Step is that *our* life takes on new meaning and courage as we listen and talk to people, share what happened to us, and speak of the hope we are finding in God and the program. We try never to preach or "exhort." We trust that the Higher Power/Holy Spirit is already working in their lives to convince. Our job is just to share and support without pressure.

As you watch individuals whom you have contacted become aware of their powerlessness and their self-centeredness, and then watch as they come to meetings and see God's love and grace fill their emptiness, a fellowship of people may grow up around you in time. As you begin to tell what your relationship with God means to you, and share the promises of the program God has given you for recovery and spiritual growth, people may begin to hear you and come to the program to get well. It is these people who will *hold you up* and keep you growing.

Dr. Paul Tournier was once asked, "How do you stand your patients being around you all the time, and holding them all up?" He answered, "Oh, no. I'm like a tent pole. In some way as they lean on me they hold me up and support me." He knew that God was their real support but was realistic enough to know that people's first experience of that support often comes through another human being. And his experience was that the act of helping them strengthened *him*.

These supportive "Twelve-Step contacts" with each other in the fellowship become more and more important to most people. When new members come in and get a taste of the peace of a supportive fellowship, their enthusiasm for the program is contagious, if sometimes humorous. A friend came back from a large city and reported that he had attended a huge A.A. gathering. He said there must have been five hundred people there. Men and women were getting up and telling all the troubles they'd been through that had led them into the program. Finally a very large man got up and said with great enthusiasm, "I want you to stay in there and keep coming back, because *this program really works!*"

The chairperson said, "That's great. How long is your sobriety?"

And the big man said very seriously, "I came in yesterday."

He was serious; he'd already found so much. That kind of thing happens, and everyone laughs because they know the enthusiastic newcomers haven't really begun yet. But their relief and enthusiasm are wonderful and contagious.

Finding Prospects

Because almost everyone is hiding his or her powerlessness and pain just as we did, it is sometimes hard to locate people in trouble to share with. Many of us Christians have been told to go out cold turkey and knock on doors to try to get people into the Christian program. But my experience with that approach has not been good. I have come to realize that most people will not surrender their lives and their wills to God until they are in enough pain, fear, and frustration to realize that they are not God. And to try to "generate" that much fear and pain is not the purpose of a Twelfth-Step call.

I was advised to check with those in my local community who are in the helping professions to find out about people who are suffering from whatever your Twelve-Step group deals with. Some have found it helpful to volunteer to their minister, or to CoDA, A.A., or Al-Anon intergroup offices so that they can be put on a list to notify when someone in trouble calls. One can also be taught to answer "hot line" calls from people in trouble for a certain period each week. It is amazing how many men and women there are out there, every day, losing control in terms of an addiction, illness, financial disaster, divorce, or personal tragedy.

When the call comes, get a partner in the program[2] and go and listen, remembering that everyone has the underlying Sin-disease whether they drink or not. They are suffering the consequences of their own or other people's Sin-disease symptoms.

Those people in great pain sometimes can't "hear" very well because they are in some phase of denial and often are filled with resentment, self-pity, pain, anger, and fear. It doesn't do much good to talk about powerlessness at first, because people do not think they are powerless. They just feel that they need a little help to get on their feet or to get people around them straightened out. They may have lost their job, their spouse, their kids; they may have no money and their house may have burned down, but they may still assure you they are *not* powerless. That's the way denial works with the disease.

Telling Your Story

People in trouble are often quite surprised that you would come and talk to them without trying to get them to change, or give money, or join your group. As you talk, a chance may come to tell your story, that is, how you realized that you were trying to control people, or how your drinking got out of hand, or whatever your problem was that brought you into the program. You can tell in detail when your addictions quit working to cover your pain, how you fouled up your relationships through your excesses. Describe how anxious you felt, and scared, and lonely, and how that brought you into whatever Twelve-Step program you got into.

This is a three-part way to tell your story very simply (which works for Christians as well as people in the program). You tell the people (1) what you used to be like and how you felt then; (2) what happened (the crisis or low point) that brought you to this program or that brought you to God; and (3) a little about what life's like now in the program, how it's better than it was before the crisis that drove you to get help.

Almost everyone agrees that it is not effective to talk theology or give advice to people in pain. It doesn't work, for one thing. And contrary to popular belief in the Church, it doesn't work even for Christians very often. People in trouble seem to respond most readily to those who apparently understand them, who have been where they now are and survived. It is people who have begun to face their own denial who can be of most help to those still in the disease. ("Dry drunks" who evidently haven't touched their own denial do get people to meetings, however, where they may get into the spirit of the program by meeting other recovering people—and God.) For years D. T. Niles has been credited with saying that Christian evangelism is "one beggar telling another where he found some bread." Spiritually I think that's what we're about in Twelve-Step sharing.

They Are Not All Attractive or Funny

I've always been a terribly self-centered person. This is a pernicious issue in my life. I like to talk to people who are in some way attractive and/or intelligent. But the first time I ever went on a Twelfth-Step call was to a person who seemed neither. This man had a big mean streak, and he was very crude. I really didn't want to help him. But I remembered that people had helped me when I was angry and very frightened, so I stayed with this man. After he got in recovery he became a good friend and was, I saw, a gentle, sensitive person. As we began to work through this program together *he* kept *me* steady in my own recovery. I took him to meetings, and we shared our lives. I was relatively new myself and realize now how much I needed someone to share the steps with. He stayed sober for a year, and then he went off and got drunk again. I was very sad about that, and after he left I realized that though he had helped me almost more than anybody else, I would never have chosen to be with him as I saw him that first day. God is teaching me that the wonderful people to be with are not necessarily the beautiful, brilliant, and materially successful ones, but rather those who are hurt and feel enough humility to admit their powerlessness, and who commit their lives to God and become a part of his family in recovery.

Don't Push

If people in trouble are not interested in what I tell them, I try never to push. They may need to experience some more pain before they are ready to come for help. The author of *Compulsive Overeater* says, "Tell them, 'If you've got a better place to go, go there.'" It's the opposite of persuading. Tell them, "If you don't need this, don't do it." People who press often act as though they are losing some sort of "sale" if someone in trouble doesn't do what the persuader thinks he or she should to get help. Twelve-Step people know that until someone is tired enough of pain, fear, and isolation, getting in the program won't usually work anyway.

But if people are interested, let them borrow your copy of whatever book got you started (the Big Book, *Overeaters Anonymous, Hope in the Fast Lane,* or whatever book your group is using; see Selected Reading).[3] If they read the book and identify, invite them to come to a meeting.

Another difference between this approach and many evangelistic approaches is that the people being helped don't have to believe your theology in order to enter the Twelve-Step family. All they have to believe is that they are in trouble and that a power greater than they are may be able to help. On that particular day *you* may seem like that power to them as you take the trouble to come and share your life.

Many of the books say to tell them that all they have to believe is that they can learn to live by spiritual principles. But most Twelve-Step people say not to couch the program in theological language at all unless the person is obviously interested in spiritual things. As the old-timers put it, "You'll be all right if you stick to sharing your own experience, strength, and hope. Don't be discouraged if someone doesn't respond. Just keep looking for people in enough pain to be ready for help, because there are plenty of them out there hurting."

All You Have to Have
Is Something They Don't

One time I got a call to go visit a man who wanted to be taken to a treatment center. We lived on an island in the Gulf of Mexico, and the hospital was forty miles away across a causeway. The counselor who called recommended that two people go, because the man seemed to be pretty drunk. I couldn't find a man who was available, but a woman in our building who was in the program wanted some Twelfth-Step experience, and we figured she could drive while I talked to the man. The counselor had actually said that although the man was extremely drunk, he seemed very anxious to go the hospital to get help.

I had never taken someone to a hospital before and didn't know what to expect. When we got to the small house near the beach the man was alone. He wasn't wearing anything but his boxer shorts. This obviously inebriated man who invited us in looked at the woman with an appraising glance. There were bottles all over the room, and everything smelled bad. I was getting nervous; I thought I might have to fight this guy to protect the younger woman who had come with me. The drunk man said, "How old are you?" She told him. He said, "What the hell do you think you can tell *me* about Alcoholics Anonymous? I have been a national speaker in this program." Then he said, "Why do you think *you* can help *me?*" The young woman said without blinking an eye, "Well for one thing, I'm sober, and you're drunk as a skunk." He said, "Oh, yeah." And the man realized the truth of what she said and came with us.

As we came back from the hospital that afternoon I realized that all you need to help people is to be where they're not. You don't have to have a lot of training. If you're not terrified and they are, you qualify. If you have a support system and have hope, and they don't, you qualify. When that young woman simply told the obvious truth that she had sobriety and the drunk man didn't, I laughed so hard I almost cried. Our new drunk friend finally laughed too. That's the secret in sharing your experience, strength, and hope. You dwell on the changes you're experiencing in your life. That's all you have to do.

We're Not Looking for "Results" in the Usual Sense

It was hard for me to remember that we are not doing this for "results" in the usual sense. So many in my generation are result oriented. In the Twelve-Step programs we are to share what we are finding in order to stay sane and happy ourselves and to grow. If you go see someone, and he or she isn't interested, at least you have stayed sane while you're there—and that means you had a successful Twelfth-Step call. Often when we see someone so trapped by denial and the hammer locks of self-absorption, we are reminded of how sick *we* were and of all God has done for us in the program. In Twelve-Step sharing we are not looking for good "prospects" who might strengthen our group, as some organizations are. Anyone who is suffering will do, anyone whose life is getting out of control enough to be open to help. No one else has much of a chance of making it in the program, anyway.

The most convincing message we can carry, the one that will help people where they live, is our own experience of powerlessness leading to hope and our own example of continued sanity and sobriety. Men and women living this program are the best advertisement the Twelve Steps have. The words you say may not convince people, but later, when the pain gets bad enough, they may remember the hope and recovery in your life, and that you came and accepted them just as they were. It is interesting to note that this sort of experience of identification and acceptance is the "turning point" in virtually every form of individual psychotherapy. Therapist Richard Grant pointed out to me in a conversation recently that it is on this "acceptance" experience that recovery, skill building, and reconciliation can be built.

Other Ways to "Carry This Message"

You can contact individuals in other ways besides crisis or "hot line" calls. Some of the following are practical:

- Making calls with older members (go along for the ride, and watch how they do it just to learn).
- Visiting members in the hospital.
- Making telephone calls to new members.
- Having friendly talks with newcomers and other people after meetings.
- Talking to people who are having trouble with the program and encouraging them by lending or giving them program literature or a program book, or encouraging them to buy a book. (Some groups provide free Big Books to newcomers.)
- Talking to relatives and associates of people who are in big trouble. For example, share with somebody who's got an alcoholic relative (or a family member in prison) about this disease and that people who get in trouble are not all bad people. As a matter of fact, most of them aren't, but they have a very bad disease that's eating them up.
- Telling the Twelve-Step story to clergymen, doctors, judges, educators, employers, or police officials.
- Speaking before other groups.
- Sharing the belief that you've received help from God.

Acts of Helping That May Be Primarily Nonverbal

There are many nonverbal ways of carrying the message to others:

- Setting an example of regular attendance at meetings and listening to others in the group. When people talk, listen. That's a very big thing, because newcomers, especially, need desperately to be listened to by people with nonjudgmental ears. When listening one to one, you can increase your "hearing" skills by repeating what someone has said out loud, to make sure you understand, before responding. Many of us have been so absorbed in ourselves that we don't know much about effective listening.

- Visiting meetings in other cities when you're away from home. There are Twelve-Step meetings all over the world. I went to a meeting in Stratford-upon-Avon, England, once and in a small town in central Mexico another time, where I was the only person in the meeting who spoke English. Even if all you say is your name and that you're visiting from such-and-such a city, it can strengthen you, and your example of finding a meeting in a strange city can carry a strong message to the local people in the meeting.

- Assuming duties and obligations at your home meetings, like making coffee or setting up chairs or ordering literature for your group. These are things that help create a warm atmosphere in which people can begin to relate and get well.

- Writing for the Twelve-Step newsletter or magazine related to your group. I'm doing Twelve-Step work by writing this book and telling you the Twelve-Step story. As I do I am learning a great deal.

- Making a reasonable pledge of your energy and time to a meeting.

- Making the Twelve Steps a way of life and starting new meetings.

- Providing transportation to members who don't have cars to go to meetings or to go to hospitals or treatment centers.

Sponsorship as a Way of Sharing the Message

A very important part of sharing the message is sponsorship (see appendix A). In fact, the author of *The Little Red Book* said that "sponsorship represents the ultimate in Twelve-Step giving." As you're sponsoring and guiding another person through these steps, God lets the steps redo their magic in your life, often at a deeper level. Some helpful chapters in the Big Book on working with others are "The Doctor's Opinion," "There Is a Solution," "The Family Afterwards," and the thirty-six case histories of recovered alcoholics under "Personal Stories."

"Carrying This Message" Is Vital to Keep Our Own Recovery Alive

What the Twelve Steps call for us to share, it seems to me, is that we and God are seriously interested in people who are caught in the traps this disease sets for us, the frantic attempts to control and the pain of being out of control. These experiences are everywhere, in our families, in our work situations, and in our churches.

It's *so* important that I want to repeat it, that unless we *share* this message, God seems to have arranged things so that we *can't keep* the recovery and serenity we are discovering. Unless we can "deny ourselves" enough (give enough time and attention) to give away the love, the concern, and the message of hope, and unless we invite people into this family of Sinners who are recovering, sooner or later we will slowly and imperceptibly close the doorway and lose the authentic spiritual life and growth in our own experience. In the Big Book the founder of A.A. pointed out the

> absolute necessity of demonstrating these principles in all [our] affairs.
> Particularly was it imperative to work with others. . . . Faith without
> works was dead. . . . For if an alcoholic failed to perfect and enlarge
> his spiritual life through work and self-sacrifice for others, he could
> not survive the certain trials and low spots ahead. (pp. 14, 15)

This is the experience of all kinds of people in Twelve-Step programs. And the Bible indicates this principle of saving one's life by giving it away is also true in the Christian community. Jesus put it pretty strongly: "If any man would come after me, let him deny himself and take up his cross and follow me. For . . . whoever loses his life for my sake and the gospel's will save it. . . . For what can a man give in return for his life?" (Mark 8:34–37). Most Christians I know believe that "denying one-self" as used here does not mean negating one's gifts, abilities, or right to a separate identity as a person but rather, out of gratitude, giving up one's own agenda as primary and choosing God's way of facing one's pain (crosses) and embarking on a life of sharing God's love.

3. And to Practice These Principles in All Our Affairs

When we first read that we were to "practice these principles in all our affairs," some of us didn't understand. How could we use the Twelve Steps to deal with conflict in a personal relationship or a decision about buying a house? Gradually we realized that "practicing principles" means taking specific usable pieces of truth out of larger truths and applying the smaller principles to a different situation. Practicing some principles might work the following way, for instance, in facing a particular bruised relationship you can't handle.

Let's say the problem is a deep resentment of your brother. You can take Step One and apply the concept of powerlessness and unmanageability to the relationship issue: "I admit I am powerless over resenting my brother, and my life is unmanageable in that area." This can lead you to see the insanity (a principle from Step Two) of your attitude toward your brother, which is absorbing much of your time and energy and making you sick while he remains unaware of all the "down time" his relationship with you is causing in your life and work. This awareness may lead you to the point of making a decision to turn the relationship with your brother over to God along with your life and your will. This is using the principles of Steps One, Two, and Three on a specific issue in your life. You might use Steps Six and Seven to become entirely ready to let God remove the resentment and ask him to.

Another example might be when you can't make a decision about whether to buy something or not. The frustration of indecision is crippling you. You can work the first three steps concerning the indecision.

Almost invariably that process can give you some space and a more rational view. You may decide to wait for clarity before deciding, or you may go for it, but a more sane decision will likely be made. I find that I use the first three steps about something almost daily.

I began to see that the Twelve Steps are a lot more like a bag of "spiritual golf clubs" than they are a book concerning the philosophy of golf. Think about it a minute. The step or steps you use depend on where you are and where you're going, "where the hole is." As you would in golf, you look at the situation before you, and you see where the hole (goal) is and where you are, and then you choose a certain club that's going to most nearly get you where you want to go. Some of the old-timers in this program are, in fact, rather like seasoned golfers. They walk through their days and nights, and when they run into a troublesome situation they eyeball it and then look at the Twelve Steps. They say to themselves, "That's about a nine shot." So they pull out a principle from Step Nine and perhaps go make amends to someone to recover from the problem.

Pretty soon using the steps can become like a spiritual art form (to change the metaphor). As you apply the principles from the steps in your life and work, a security (concerning problems that crop up) comes with knowing you have some tools and a source of support to deal with the problems. And a gracefulness can come into your daily living. God begins to calm the troubled waters of your inner space and to reshape your thinking toward surrender, integrity, and redeeming love as ways of dealing with the problems of Sin.

"In All Our Affairs": A New Set of Problems.   After you get rid of whatever obsession brought you into a Twelve-Step program, at some later time there is often the stirring of another rather awesome realization: that in recovery we need to face our *whole lives* and to experience our painful and joyous feelings about people and circumstances without tranquilizing them anymore with chemical or behavioral compulsions. To many of us this has meant that there are a whole "new" set of problems and feelings we now *experience* that we once used our attempts at control to avoid. It's crucial to our spiritual growth that we *face* these issues. If, at the first attack of pain or frustration, you go back and engage in your addiction—be it to Sin-control, or drugs—you can't hear through the pain the will of God for your life and happiness.

What most of us have discovered about lifelong spiritual/emotional problems we have held in denial has been incredible. As we have brought the same power and Twelve-Step principles that are curing us from a deadly addiction to bear on the other painful and blocked areas of our lives we can see why we waited so long and resisted so strongly: the pain of facing these things is *real*. But we can now face our whole life, because we have seen how God can handle even the worst that we could throw at him, our need to *replace him* in the center of things.

As I work this program and continue my Christian disciplines of prayer and participating in the sacramental worship of the church, it's like treating cancer with radiation therapy.

Let's say you've got a cancer right in the middle of your stomach. The technician will beam a ray from one side that is not enough to destroy the healthy tissue or the cancer, but almost. Then, while that beam is on, they aim another equally powerful beam at the cancer from above. And where the two beams intersect on the cancer, the combined strength of the radiation is enough to destroy the cancer cells without destroying the healthy tissue between the machine and the cancer. They have to come at you from two or three angles.

And this is what the Twelve Steps and faith do. As you begin to use the steps, you may start using Steps One, Two, and Three almost every day. And as you access the power of God to deal with your character defects, that power focused on specific areas by several of the Twelve Steps and by spiritual disciplines can destroy potentially terminal spiritual cancers.

Is it really possible to practice these principles in *all* our affairs? Can we really realize the promises of the program? That sounds pretty optimistic. But the experience of the Twelve-Step veterans is, yes, if we are willing to grow along spiritual lines, over time it's possible—never perfectly, but it's possible—to learn to live by these principles, and to see spiritual recovery and growth in these terms. (See Big Book, pp. 60, 84.) In meetings the witness of those who are finding spiritual strength and freedom in the program transmits to the rest of us the motivation to surrender and go for that strength and freedom.

Some of the things I've heard people say have inspired me to have courage, to not complain, or to be tenacious in my own program. One day a woman said to some of us in a conversation, "My husband just walked out. He said he's been planning to leave me for a year, and now he's gone, and I didn't know until just as he was walking out the door. I don't have a dime, and I've got three kids. All I have is a big mortgage on our house, and he took the car." Then after a pause she said, "I'm so grateful that I'm in this program. I'm not panicky. I don't know what I'm going to do, but I'll do something. I just want to tell you all that this program really works." It was apparent that she was serious.

Other people have had their children leave home and say to them, "I'm never going to see you again." These parents cry, but they sometimes say things like, "I thank God I'm in this program because I've been so dependent on these kids that I've trapped them and me. Now they're going to get away, and I'm going to have to get well too. It breaks my heart, but I guess I never would have faced myself if they hadn't confronted me this way. Thank God that I've got these meetings to go to and the Twelve Steps to work."

People have confronted the pain of losing their jobs in the context of the program and found support, peace, and serenity in the midst of the pain and fear. As a matter of fact, we've got one Twelve-Step meeting in the town we live in laughingly called by the members "Bankruptcy Anonymous." There are many people in our city going bankrupt, which has brought some of them to a state of recognizing their powerlessness for the first time.

Of course some people never get on their feet from some of these tragedies. They leave the program and are bitter and don't face themselves. All stories are not happy endings in the usual sense. But for many the pain of powerlessness becomes the doorway to a happy, joyous, and free life of spiritual growth. And sometimes even in the midst of "terminal" tragedies there's a kind of serenity and calmness that I've never seen before. I've heard several people say, "I've got cancer, and it looks like it might be terminal. Thank God I found this program. I don't know what I'd do. I have a way to live now and some structure so I won't go out and go wild."

God continually turns this "walking through the pain of life" into demonstrations of faith that are remarkable. And perhaps that is why this may be the fastest-growing spiritual movement in America today.

TAKING STEP TWELVE

Step Twelve
*Having had a spiritual awakening as the
result of these steps, we tried to carry
this message to others and to practice
these principles in all our affairs.*

A Spiritual Awakening: Describe in your notebook what you believe to be your spiritual awakening. An image that has come to you that gives meaning and hope? New attitudes about God? New hope about life and relationships? A sense that pain is not the enemy? A realization that you are at last living in reality (and not denial) in some areas of your life?

Carrying the Message: Write the three-part version of your story: (1) what you were like before you came to a Twelve-Step program, including specifically areas in which you were powerless and in denial, (2) what the crisis, or issue of powerlessness, was that brought you to the program (describe, including your feelings), (3) what is now different about your life in the same areas you described in part (1). For example, if you were impatient, bossy, and afraid, or if you had a chemical dependency and were in denial, has that changed? How? How has working the program helped you?

Sponsorship: If someone has asked you to sponsor him or her and you have accepted, write about the experience and feelings you have as you sponsor that person. How is sponsoring someone helping you to work your program?

Practicing the Principles in All Our Affairs: As you now begin to face the issues you used to avoid, what is different about the way you deal with conflict, pain, disappointment, or any other matters that used to trouble you? Write about as many as you wish, but try to describe at least three.

THE BOTTOM LINE

Some biblical expressions concerning how we got into the Christian "program" originally:

The Lord God called to the man and said to him, "Where are you?" And he said, ". . . I was afraid, because I was naked; and I hid myself." Genesis 3:9–10

What we received from the gospel:

There is therefore now no condemnation for those who are in Christ Jesus. For the law of the Spirit of life in Christ Jesus has set me free from the law of sin and death. Romans 8:1–2

Therefore, if anyone is in Christ, he is a new creation; the old has passed away, behold, the new has come! 2 Corinthians 5:17

The bottom line for me about the Twelve Steps as a way of spiritual growth is that before coming into the program I'd gotten the idea that spiritual growth consisted of "adding on" new knowledge, degrees, and insights about God and life, that spirituality was about getting "bigger" or "more" spiritually, about getting to be more holy and more knowledgeable and more experienced concerning spiritual disciplines, charitable works, prayer, and study. And then, with all that added content and skill, I would be spiritual enough. But now, after years of working the Twelve Steps, although I still think those things are very important, and are in fact natural *fruits* of spiritual growth, I believe I had it backwards somehow.

Years ago I heard a story about Michelangelo, the great Renaissance artist and sculptor, that described, for me, the nature of spiritual growth through the Twelve Steps. I don't know if the story is true, but it helped me see in which *direction* this "growth" may lie for me. When Michelangelo had just finished the magnificent statue of the young David at fourteen, a huge white marble work that is one of the most remarkable and lifelike pieces ever done, someone is said to have asked him, "Michelangelo, how in the world did you ever do this?"

The artist was a little embarrassed but is said to have replied, "Oh, it wasn't all that difficult. I ran across this huge stone in the quarry. And I *saw David* in it! Very excited, I had the stone brought back to my studio. And month after month after month, I very carefully—chipped away everything that wasn't David."

For me, that is what God does for us through the Twelve Steps and the work of the Holy Spirit so that we can be free to participate in his will. Since childhood, through our Sin and abuse, we've all acquired many kinds of masks—extra pounds, walls, protective habits, and controlling compulsions and addictions—to decorate or hide our reality, our true personalities, from each other, from God, and from ourselves so we'll appear to be "enough." But through the years as we put our lives and our will in God's hands and do the Twelve Steps, month after month after month God helps us to chip away everything that isn't Keith, or Andrea, or the person he made you to be. To grow spiritually we don't have to be brilliant or "saintly," or "more" than we are. And although the emerging person has always been there inside us waiting to be released, to be reborn, the *feeling* is that we are new people, new creations. And we finally see that just as God made us to be—we are enough.

The day I realized this I was taking a trip and was changing planes in the Dallas/Fort Worth airport during rush hour. There were masses of people moving up and down the halls. I'd gotten a metal baggage cart almost as much to protect myself as to carry my briefcase and heavy coat. People were walking fast, dodging oncoming traffic, and avoiding the beeping people-carriers while trying not to run up the backs of those going the same direction. It has always amazed me how that many moving people can miss bumping into each other, when they are scrambling like a bunch of freshly poisoned ants. Suddenly in the midst of what in the past would have been a very stressful situation, I heard myself *whistling* a tune from *My Fair Lady* as loudly as I could! I couldn't remember ever having whistled in the Dallas/Fort Worth airport, and as I thought about it I couldn't recall having ever seen or heard anybody whistle in an airport. I was happy and relaxed as I sped up the middle of the two-way river of humanity with my trusty cart.

I had quit whistling years before. Now, thirty years later in recovery I had spontaneously started to whistle again. I was grateful to God to be alive. I felt feelings I hadn't felt in many years—about the wonder of the future and what I might be when I grew up. Just then I smelled some cotton candy and stopped to inhale my boyhood. In that moment I felt like a child on an adventure. And I realized that in a way—I am.

Appendix A

SPONSORSHIP

Sponsorship has been a potent, important part of spiritual growth since people first began to attempt it. The practice of spiritual direction in the life of the Church is a mentoring or a sponsoring movement. We Christians have a great heritage of mentoring from the Bible. Elisha had Elijah as a mentor or sponsor. Of the twelve disciples, Jesus had three he was especially close to and nine others he mentored. Mark, Silas, and Aristarchus had Barnabas and Paul as their mentors.

Evidence of the concept of sponsorship is found throughout the New Testament. There were always outstanding Christians traveling in little groups with followers whom they mentored in the faith. Paul commended the Corinthians for doing the faith as he'd advised them to. (1 Cor. 11:1). He told them to imitate him (2 Thes. 3:6, 7). In today's church we would consider it terrible if the minister got up and said, "Imitate me as I imitate Christ." But the arrogance that statement implies today has no part in Twelve-Step sponsoring either. The people who sponsor know that they were guilty of controlling and didn't know how to stop when they first came to a Twelve-Step group. And they know that they can fall back into the disease at any time (just as Paul never forgot the extent of his Sin, calling himself the "chief of sinners," 1 Tim. 1:15). They know they too have to turn loose control to recover—and that includes not controlling sponsorees.

We Need Something in Addition to Meetings

Going to meetings is one of the primary prerequisites to healing in the Twelve-Step process. Meetings are where most of us begin to hear others share their experience, strength, and hope with each other and with us, and by listening we begin to identify and share our own surfacing reality. But meeting time is limited, and we rarely get direct feedback about what we say and do. Moreover, speaking in a meeting about some things we have done might be damaging to someone else; for instance, we may have been involved in joint thievery in business, and to confess it means also confessing someone else's action. Some issues seem too delicate or too embarrassing to discuss in a group. And some days we need to talk about something longer than the brief time possible in a meeting, or we may have questions to ask.

The Purpose of Having a Sponsor

To get the most out of the Twelve-Step program, we need a special relationship with at least one other person in the program, a special kind of friend whose primary job in our recovery is to guide us through the Twelve Steps. A sponsor also supports us as we deal with personal issues and questions we can't get at in a meeting.

Because denial causes us to disguise the truth about our own diseased behavior from ourselves, we usually can't see our own self-defeating patterns. Habitual reactions, however sick and ineffective they may be, seem natural to us. I am often amazed at the automatic ways I react dysfunctionally to my children, to my wife, Andrea, and to the other people in my life (with advice, put-downs, or excuses). And such denied attitudes and habits hinder us from doing the Twelve Steps honestly and getting well. A sponsor can act as a mirror to help us own our denied reality so we can offer it to God and be healed.

Sponsors Are Guides, Not Therapists or Priests

Having a sponsor is not like having a therapist. A sponsor is an equal, a friend in the program—and for Christians a friend in Christ—who is on this same journey, who knows the kinds of problems we face, who still encounters them, in fact, and sometimes fails to deal with them creatively. And that's contrary to the prevalent Christian idea of mentoring.

We expect our ministers to know a lot more than we do and to be practically "perfect." Living up to this expectation forces many ministers to be phony. The minister at our church does a good job of sharing his life, imperfections and all, because he realizes that he needs to for his own spiritual growth. But often ministers do not share their lives this way, and if ministers get into trouble, people sometimes withdraw and leave them alone, or attack and get rid of them. Most people today apparently want a spiritual guide in the pulpit who either doesn't have problems or has solved them all. Contrast this way of thinking to the biblical description of ministers: ministers are supposed to be experts on troubles because they face them all. Ministers are supposed to be more sensitive to their Sin than other people, as Paul was. Today, it would be very strange for a minister to say, "I am the chief of sinners" to a group of Christians, who don't want to recognize and accept the fact that its leaders sin.

Patterns Can Be Discerned by a Sponsor

Dysfunctional, self-defeating patterns can be pointed out to us by a sponsor. I heard a woman describe the following experience with her sponsor. At one point, in great agony, she told her sponsor, "I just can't seem to straighten out my son, and now he's in big trouble at school." She felt intense guilt and shame, saying, "I just couldn't do it right. I'm a terrible parent."

Her sponsor asked, "What are you feeling?"

"I feel like a total failure. I feel I'm worth nothing. I feel I have failed in everything."

Then her sponsor commented, "Wait a minute. Remember, we can't fix other people. In this instance it sounds like you failed to be God and make everything right in your son's life. I've noticed from other things you've told me that when you fail to be as powerful as God, you think you're 'the worst thing in the world.' Many of us are locked into the same pattern; we fail in one incident to do it perfectly, and we spiral down into believing *our whole self* is worth nothing. You have just discovered that you are human, that's all. You're precious and wonderful just the way you are, no matter what kind of trouble your son is in. Besides, nobody can keep a child from getting into some trouble."

The woman said she began to notice how often she took each instance of normal human imperfection in her life and translated it into a sense of total worthlessness. Her sponsor, having been through the same issues, told her how she (the sponsor) had worked the steps on that situation and was experiencing some recovery. This woman decided to follow in her sponsor's footsteps, and now, as she put it, "I'm not so hard on myself when things happen that I'm powerless over." She doesn't have unreal expectations about her ability to control people, places, and things, to "fix" them. And as she faced this issue and talked about her progress (and setbacks) with her sponsor, she was breaking a self-defeating pattern of a lifetime.

Another example of how a sponsor's feedback can help came from a man who told this next story. During one of his meetings with his sponsor, he said, "I found out today that my boss lied about me to his boss, and I may get fired—but I am not angry. I'm all right. I'm working the program." And his sponsor said, "What I just heard you say was that your boss had done something very threatening to you but you were not threatened. As you talked I saw that your fists were clinched so tight that your knuckles were white, you were talking through gritted teeth, and your face was very tense and pale. It looks to me as though you are really *very angry.*"

This man said he was not able to see his anger at first, but after hearing his sponsor's feedback and thinking about it, he could experience anger, and he was grateful to be in touch with what was happening to him. Each sponsor has to make a judgment call about how confronting to be with each sponsoree. But my own rule of thumb is to love them and be as honest as possible without shaming or blaming.

Qualifications of a Sponsor

There are a number of qualities it is helpful for a sponsor to have. Good sponsors should

1. Be serious about working *their own* program and yet able to laugh at their character defects.

2. Be serious about their relationship with God.

3. Be honest, try to face their own denial.

4. Want to help other people into recovery. At first I didn't know much about helping other people who might need to get into this program, so I needed a sponsor who knew how to teach me how to reach out. And the man I chose as a sponsor has helped me a lot.

5. Be able to hear you without trying to change your reality. A controller will often try to change your reality, the way you feel about things in your life. For example, if you say, "I feel terrible this morning. I feel like I'm nothing; I feel like a failure," a controller may say, "No, no, you *shouldn't* feel that way." That makes you feel even worse, because even your reality is being discounted. Regardless of the objective facts, I need someone who can hear my feelings and let me experience them. A good sponsor might say something like, "It sounds like you are down on yourself today," or "Boy, it really sounds painful," to let me know that he heard me.

6. Be able to let you move at your own pace. Good sponsors listen, confront your unreality, and help you to move at your own speed through the steps without going too fast, but nudge and confront you if you quit working the steps altogether.

7. Be able to demonstrate accountability by telling you about their own current failure to do something right. One of the best ways to learn accountability is to watch somebody else live who is accountable. In the past some of us just prayed generally about our character defects: "God, please forgive me, and take my problems away." That approach comes from a desire to get out of pain, but is not necessarily being responsible. In fact, praying that way can be an attempt to use God as a tranquilizer to make us feel better. A sponsor can help you *face* an issue specifically (a failure, abusive behavior, or whatever the painful event is), make amends, and find out what you may have been doing to cause the painful event. That way you can do the necessary steps and surrender the issue to God so you can avoid repeating the dysfunctional act.

8. Have compassion but not pity; remember that people coming into the program are often frightened and insecure, having just seen something of their powerlessness. But they need care and support in facing themselves, not pity for their sad condition.

9. Make suggestions but hardly ever volunteer advice, unless you ask specifically for advice. (As a sponsor I have let people tell me about something dysfunctional that's going on in their lives without saying

anything about what they should do, or about my opinion of it, which for me is miraculous. In the past people could punch my navel by sharing their problems, and out would come nine "answers" or suggestions about what they should do. It's incredible how I tend to want to fix people. But the program teaches us to stand with people and let them experience their pain, because it can lead them to powerlessness, healing, and later to wisdom.)

What Is the Sponsor's Role in a Person's Recovery?

Although all of us are responsible for our own recovery, there are some ways a sponsor can support us in that recovery. These are some important aspects of a sponsor's role:

1. To support people in taking the Twelve Steps as far as they are able. And when they do each one, the sponsor shares how he or she felt trying to take that particular step and what happened or didn't happen.

2. To encourage people to attend meetings regularly.

3. To model the principles of the program by having a sponsor himself or herself. Even a therapist needs a therapist. Dr. Tournier once told me, "Never confess to someone who doesn't confess regularly."

4. To encourage people to study the literature of the Twelve-Step program (and the Bible if they are Christians) as the basic literature of their lives. Some people who have burned out trying to be perfect Christians would rather not read the Bible for a while. That is their choice, and a good sponsor will not shame them or try to control their reading material.

5. To encourage people to ask questions when they have them.

6. To encourage people to call their sponsor or somebody else in the program when they are terribly afraid or miserable or in a jam and immediately share what's going on. Because it is not always possible to catch your sponsor, the sponsor should encourage sponsorees to call someone else in the program if he or she is not available. (A notebook with telephone numbers can be a valuable aid to recovery.)

7. To give honest feedback about the things the sponsoree says and does. Surprisingly it's often as good or better than feedback you get from a professional, and this kind of give-and-take between two peers enables both parties to learn how to help others. (I am *not* saying that this sort of give-and-take is a substitute for therapy when therapy is needed. Nor am I implying that a sponsor should play the role of therapist to a sponsoree.)

8. To help work through the decision-making process. Most of us have made decisions in a pretty selfish, controlling, amd even immature way for years. We go to our sponsor with a decision we can't make. Our sponsor may ask questions to help us sort out our thinking and explore the options we see. A good sponsor knows that our recovery hinges on our learning how to make our own healthy decisions, so the sponsor probably will not give us any options he or she sees unless asked. And a good sponsor will try to avoid influencing our choice, because, right or wrong, making the choice will teach us valuable things.

Same-Sex Sponsors

The experience of the program indicates that it is better for the sponsor and sponsoree to be of the same sex. A good sponsoring relationship becomes very strong, honest, caring, and secure—important components of intimacy. Many of us come into this program crying out for intimacy because we have become so alienated as a result of our controlling and self-centeredness. Having a sponsor of the opposite sex introduces all kinds of sexual issues. The most serious reason for suggesting that one's sponsor be of the same sex is the potential for what is called "thirteenth stepping," which is having sex with your sponsor. When thirteenth stepping starts, the recovery aspect of the sponsor relationship often ends. Having a sponsor of the opposite sex can also place an inordinate strain on husbands, wives, or significant others—in the program or not. The husband (or wife) thinks, "What's going on over at Frank's (or Fran's) house when my significant other goes over there?"

It is also not recommended to have your spouse as a sponsor. The roles of spouse and sponsor are basically incompatible; we are either blind to the character defects of our beloved or likely to be too critical. Besides, the temptation to control a spouse is hard enough to resist without adding the pressure of sponsorship.

The Buddy System

Sinners Anonymous is a new program that started about three years before this writing, and there were no experienced old-timers to serve as sponsors. We had people who came in from other Twelve-Step programs who sponsored some of us at first. When we ran out of experienced people we used the buddy system. That is, two people agreed to sponsor each other, to listen to each other and share how they were working the steps, and go to another Sinners Anonymous member or a member of another Twelve-Step program for sponsoring if they ran across a situation that neither could address from experience. But it is much better to have a sponsor who has worked most or all of the steps.

Choosing a Sponsor

Some people say the minute you do Step One, the minute you realize your powerlessness, you should get a sponsor. Others say to wait a few weeks until you've listened to people speak in meetings. And some don't get a sponsor for a year or so. But the consensus is to get a sponsor as soon as you can find someone who meets your qualifications.

The responsibility for getting a sponsor rests with you. Usually you see someone in a meeting or hear them share several times, then ask that person to sponsor you. If the person can't for any reason, repeat the process, asking until you find someone who will.

Listen for Your Style

Before choosing a sponsor, I recommend going to many meetings to hear people share about the way they face their problems and do the steps. There are various styles of facing personal problems just as there are styles of thinking, relating, and loving. Some people have your style. As you listen to people talk in meetings, you may notice that a certain one seems to work a good program and to wrestle with problems in a way you can relate to. You have a sense that you could be safe with him or her.

After you spot someone who seems to have your style, you *ask* the person if he or she will be your sponsor. For many of us this was terrifying. "What if he doesn't like me," I thought, "and refuses?" On the other hand, I was afraid if I asked someone to be my sponsor and he said yes I would be stuck with that sponsor forever. I feel a lot of pain and fear about breaking relationships. If you feel this way you can ask someone to be your "temporary" sponsor. Many of us did that, and it worked fine, sometimes becoming a long-time relationship. Sooner or later, in order to succeed in working the steps, I believe you must ask someone in spite of your fears.

If someone says he or she can't sponsor you, don't assume the refusal is a rejection of you. Remember, part of this disease is putting ourselves in the center and trying to figure out what is wrong with us (or right with us) that is "causing" this other person to have this reaction. In my family, if someone had a frown, I'd wonder, "What did I do now?" But the real reason for the frown may be that the person has a headache. I've begun to realize that all headaches are not about me.

If the person you ask says he or she can't be your sponsor, ask another person. Many good sponsors already have all the people they can handle without jeopardizing their own recovery. Remember, they've got sponsors, too, telling them not to take on too many sponsorees. So if the first person turns you down, keep looking. I was told that when someone agrees to be your sponsor, you should immediately make an appointment to sit down and talk to him or her about getting started on the steps.

The Danger of Having Too Many Sponsors

Some people have more than one sponsor, which is very common and often helpful. But I think there is sometimes a danger in this practice. For instance, one may have a "mean, tough" sponsor who will confront one's dishonesty, prod one to do the steps, and point out everything one is doing that's not leading toward recovery. This approach can make some people feel right at home. The sponsoree may also get another sponsor who is affirming and encourages him or her gently to keep on moving through the steps.

Herein lies the danger; as slick as I am, I would report the behaviors I ought to be confronted about to the gentle one and the behaviors that I know are good recovery to the tough one, who would just pass the good stuff off. I would not get the true benefit of either one. Also, conflicting viewpoints from each can be confusing, and we can use the conflicting guidance as an excuse not to move ahead in recovery or to get away from our program altogether. The disease teaches the heart to be tricky indeed. The Bible describes that trickiness vividly: "The heart is deceitful above all things, and desperately corrupt; who can understand it?" (Jer. 17:9). If you have more than one sponsor, it is helpful to choose one as your primary sponsor in working the steps.

The First Meeting with a Sponsor

At the first meeting, experienced sponsors usually take the time to tell what the thing was that drove them to powerlessness, why and how their lives were unmanageable. If your new sponsor doesn't volunteer to tell you, ask, because it will help you know how to share with him or her.

It's helpful for you, the sponsoree, to tell something about how you got into the program and what caused you to feel powerless. And as the two of you share at that level there is often immediate hope, understanding, gratitude, and relief, especially for the new sponsoree.

The Relationship with a Sponsor

Sponsoring has been a reality since the Greek philosopher Heraclitus in the fifth century B.C.—a special relationship between two people in which they share "life" and grow to be wise and good people together. There aren't many manuals on how to have such a relationship. Many people have found Al-Anon's manual on sponsorship helpful.[1] A sponsor is a role model in working the program, a resource person concerning the mechanics of taking each step, a person to call when you've got the crazies, a friend who can give you some perspective, a reality check, an encourager when you are tempted to give up.

A sponsor is someone to share the excitement of your discoveries with—because the first time you do something differently is wonderful. You say, "I *didn't blow up!* I mean, they said I was stupid for going to this program and I didn't blow up!"

I have found it helpful when my sponsor clarifies for me right away what he can and can't do. For example, if he travels a lot, it is helpful for him to say that he is not available all the time and describe what his travel schedule is like. Or he may have special times when he can't be reached at home. For example, sometimes I have to shut off my telephone to write. But I tell my sponsorees that I will give them priority, and if one of my sponsorees calls me, then as soon as I get the message I will make an attempt to reach him. You can check out this sort of thing with your sponsor in advance so you won't be hurt if you can't get through when you call.

It is also helpful for sponsors to tell sponsorees what they expect in this relationship. If your sponsor doesn't volunteer this information, ask for it. This is not just another social or even teaching situation. Spiritual growth is a survival issue for most people in Twelve-Step programs. And you need to know what your sponsor expects from you with regard to your working your program.

Good sponsors will expect sponsorees to be serious about the steps. Recovery is a life-or-death proposition for someone with the Sin-disease and/or an addiction. And life is too short and crowded for sponsors to have sponsorees who will not get serious about working the steps.

In sponsoring, it's very easy to play God and try to control a sponsoree's program. But a good sponsor is trying to understand so he or she can guide the person through the steps toward wholeness. Good sponsors will listen carefully and perhaps even repeat what a sponsoree says to make sure they understand. This is often helpful, as sponsorees frequently don't realize how what they are saying sounds.

It is the sponsoree's responsibility to call the sponsor. Some sponsors say they want to be called once a week, or once a day. Some sponsorees respond to that with anger, asking, "Aren't you going to carry your half of this? Aren't you ever going to call me?"

The answer is often no. This is a program about growing up and taking responsibility for our lives. It is not a sponsor's job to call and check to see how we are working our program. Most sponsors are recovering controllers of one kind or another, and they have already taken responsibility for trying to change more lives than they needed to. If a sponsoree isn't ready to grow spiritually, a sponsor cannot make him or her do it. At the same time sponsors try to be sensitive, and some will call if a sponsoree is sick, in trouble, or has a tragedy in his or her life. But with regard to working our program a sponsor gives us the same freedom to walk away that God gives us all. (A sponsor who has had a long relationship with a sponsoree may decide to go find the sponsoree and drag him or her back into the program, but that is unusual.) Jesus let the rich young ruler walk away in his misery and evidently never followed him. In the story of creation and the Fall, God gave Adam and Eve the freedom to choose their future. They had to go out of the garden; he let them go because of their choices. Part of the power of the Twelve Steps is that they teach us how to grow up and become responsible for our decisions and actions, and for our recovery from the Sin-disease. It is a tough program, and it produces amazingly responsible people, many of whom are learning responsibility for the first time.

The important thing, it seems to me, is to maintain a sponsor-sponsoree relationship that will allow you to have the best chance at being rigorously honest. Without that, sponsorship may not lead to breaking denial and changing character defects as one works the steps. It is customary in the program for each individual and sponsor to work out the fine points of how the relationship is going to work.

My first sponsor was very tough, but I knew he loved me. He was a big, strong man, so I knew there was no way I could get mad and whip him or even threaten to. I am so subtle and controlling that I needed a strong, confronting sponsor. And mine knew how to get me out of myself (although I wouldn't recommend to another sponsor doing what he did and most sponsors would not do what I am about to describe). I remember one time when some people close to me had really been confronting (honest) with me about some very painful issues between us. I was feeling lots of pain and self-pity, and I came to him and said, "You know I just feel terrible today." And I told him my story. Self-pity oozed out of every sentence. He listened, and then he said with great wisdom in a baby-talk tone, "Did they hurt your little feelings?" I wanted to *kill* him! But he helped me in that one phrase to see the way I sounded. I was full of self-pity, and I wanted somebody to tell me that I was *right*. I went away and was mad at him for a whole day, then I was able to say, because I knew that man loved me and wanted to help me get well, "He is so right! I will never do that again." And any time since then when I have been tempted to get into self-pity, I can see his face.

Confidentiality

Confidentiality is a crucial part of sponsoring and means that neither sponsor nor sponsoree tells other people anything shared in their conversations about themselves. In this special relationship we may begin to trust and to experience something of what the unconditional love of God might mean for the first time. If I don't tell anyone my worst stuff, then how do I know if anyone would like me if they heard it? Most people can't tell a sponsor their worst faults and sins at first (and maybe it won't ever seem appropriate to do so), so don't worry about that either. Just do the best you can one day at a time.

Firing a Sponsor

Some sponsors are tough and confronting, but underneath, the good ones are loving and caring. If you realize you have chosen a sponsor who is tough and confronting and underneath is *not* loving, get rid of that one fast. That person does not understand the program. Playing God is how we all got into this. Sponsorship has the potential to be an abusive situation, but you don't have to put up with that at all. Although that doesn't happen often, I mention it as a warning, because it is a possibility.

If your relationship with your sponsor isn't working, and you have prayed about it and done the first three steps and an inventory, then you may want to tell somebody else in the program why it seems to you that the relationship isn't working. (This is a special exception to the confidentiality rule, when you prudently seek a "second opinion" in order to do reality-testing about the sponsor-sponsoree relationship. Even in a situation like this, the anonymity of the sponsor can often be maintained.)

It may be that the reason it seems difficult is that the sponsor is getting honest with you and you don't want to face your defects. Instead, when it gets uncomfortable, you want to get out and get a new sponsor who will be more "understanding" (and will not confront you). If this third person in the program is honest with you, he or she may say, "Well, it sounds to me like your sponsor is pretty well on target."

So then ask yourself, "Is what my sponsor saying to me true?" And if it is, try to keep that sponsor while you work through the issues you are being confronted with.

But if after seeking feedback and considering carefully, you decide to "fire" your sponsor, ideally you may decide to deal directly with him or her about the issues, explaining that you feel you need to change sponsors now. But if you can't do that, then just don't call him or her anymore. You are just beginning to get well. You are to do the best you can. If a surgeon cuts off the wrong foot, you probably won't go back to that surgeon for more treatment, saying to yourself, "Well, I just don't want to embarrass myself or hurt the surgeon's feelings by leaving." Whether you can deal directly with the doctor or not, you will probably put your future health first and go elsewhere for medical care. And the same thing is true if you need to change sponsors.

It can be helpful to face your sponsor directly, if you can, because it might do the sponsor some good—and the experience might help your recovery—but you are not out to take care of that person or to prove how brave you are.

It is important to move on and get another sponsor. It will impede your recovery to ignore the situation. Many people faced with this decision just stop their program when they can't deal with firing their sponsor. But because your recovery must be paramount in order to make it, just do the best you can and move ahead. A good rule of thumb is to take care of yourself in such situations the way you would a child entrusted to your care. This can help give you perspective and courage.

Being Fired by a Sponsor

Many sponsors do sponsoring because they know they need to do it for their own recovery. They have a right to ask, "Are you going to work the program? I don't want to force you, but for my own recovery I need to have sponsorees who will work the steps." Sometimes if you as a sponsoree are not working the program, not taking the suggestions your sponsor is making, and not calling your sponsor much, he or she may decide to talk to you about these things. Your sponsor may tell you that he or she needs to sponsor people who want to work the program and needs to end the sponsoring relationship with you.

This may be a shock, but it will make you consider whether or not you want to move ahead with your recovery. Sponsors can help sponsorees get well that way: that's tough love. Many sponsorees have been fired and said to themselves, "Well, I can see that nobody is going to do this for me. I guess I'd better get busy." And they've begun to work the program seriously.

A Sponsor Is Also a Recovering Sinner

It is helpful to remember that your sponsor is also dealing with the Sindisease in his or her own life and trying to learn how to live. Two of my main character defects have been grandiosity and lack of boundaries. I have always thought I could do more things in a day than I can. So part of my recovery is to maintain boundaries with people and say, "No, I'm sorry, I can't do that." I am realizing that if people depend on me to take care of them and their recovery they are going to be lost anyway. So I try not to overpromise as a sponsor.

On the other hand, when a sponsor does promise to do something, it is important to follow through or communicate about why a change is necessary. For example, if a sponsor has to change an appointment, it is important to call the sponsoree and set a new time. The sponsoree may get mad, because he or she is self-centered too, but one must understand that a sponsor *will* fail to be perfect. After all, he or she is recovering in this program too. (Yet I'm sometimes indignant when my sponsor shows signs of being fallible.)

The Sponsor Recovers as Much or More than the Sponsoree

Don't think you are bothering your sponsor. The sponsor's recovery is often improved through the relationship more than yours. The bottom line is, we can't work this program of spiritual growth alone, and the wonderful news is that we don't have to anymore.

After you have worked the steps and been sponsored through them, you can begin to sponsor other people, helping them along the way. And as you hear someone you sponsor talk about doing some of the controlling things that you once did, you can often see the dysfunctional behavior you once denied and understand it better. Sponsoring is a amazing teaching device for both parties.

BOUNDARIES

A boundary is an invisible protective fence around our personal God-given space. Boundaries keep people from abusing us, bursting into our space and controlling us or getting us to do things before we have a chance to think or say no. Our boundaries also keep us aware of others' boundaries so that we do not break into their God-given space to control or abuse them.

Before making a decision to turn one's whole life and will over to God and stop controlling others, it is very helpful to take a look at one's own boundary system, so that other people won't jump into the "void" and take control.

My wife, Andrea, and I wrote a book with Pia Mellody called *Facing Codependence*.[1] The following discussion is adapted from the chapter on boundaries in that book.

The Boundary System

There are two parts to a boundary system: the external and the internal. External boundaries protect us physically and sexually outside our skin. Internal boundaries protect us intellectually, emotionally, and spiritually inside ourselves.

These invisible "fences" mark off a "space" around us that no one else has a right to come into without our permission. With healthy boundaries we can protect ourselves from people who would control us—everybody from strangers to friends, parents, mates, or children. Although with boundaries we may still *hear* people's harsh or controlling words, insinuations, and criticisms and *see and hear* them expressing emotions apparently aimed at controlling us, we can stop these control devices from coming through our boundaries. When we do stop them, we are not compelled to act, think, or feel in ways we do not choose.

For instance, if we do not have healthy internal boundaries we find ourselves continually getting overcommitted, because we can't say no when people—particularly certain authority figures—ask us to do things, even though we may be feeling stressed by commitments already.

A healthy external boundary can be imagined as a Mason jar large enough to fit comfortably over your head and tall enough for you to stand inside. You can see through it and breathe through it, but unlike a glass jar, it is very tough and flexible so you can make it smaller or larger. You can hear through it, but it's sturdy enough to stop most things that are coming at you from someone else: the emotional impact of their words, insinuations, demands, criticisms, and emotions.[2] (See Figure 1.)

Someone who heard me describe boundaries in this way said that a glass jar was not permeable to her; it was too much like a wall. Some people have trouble with the Mason jar picture and develop an image of their own. One person imagined healthy boundaries as being like the Force in the movie *Star Wars,* a force field of energy that is impenetrable, tough, flexible, but that you can see through and adjust in size around you.

Andrea suggested that Christians might imagine Jesus Christ or the Holy Spirit as the keeper of their boundary. Imagine Jesus standing just outside your boundary, and if people start crashing in, imagine him firmly stopping them at your boundary. The Bible says that the Holy Spirit will comfort us. The word *comfort* at the time the King James Version was written could have been translated (and often is) "strengthen." So a part of the Holy Spirit's job is to strengthen us and our boundaries.

A person with healthy boundaries has them on all the time. But when we first become aware of this concept, we often don't know we have a boundary. As I began to learn about this I had to consciously put the Mason jar over my head when I came into the presence of someone whom I have allowed to control me in the past (or whom I have controlled, since my boundaries are also to keep *me* from crashing into *others'* space and attempting to control them). So I still consciously "put

Figure 1. *Boundaries**

Nonexistent Boundaries

No Protection

Damaged Boundary System

Partial Protection

Walls Instead of Boundaries

Anger	Fear	Silence	Words

Complete Protection but No Intimacy

Moving from Nonexistent Boundaries to Walls and Back Again

Back and Forth from
No Protection to Walls

Intact Boundary System

Protection and Vulnerability

---

my boundary on" when I come into a potential "control" situation, even though having my boundaries in place has become a habit in many relationships.

A boundary is something you are *supposed* to have. It is not "keeping people out" so that you don't relate to or interact with them. It is a membrane that gives you protection from being controlled by others and from controlling them, but *through* which you can have healthy relationships. For example, if you want to hug somebody at church, you don't take off your boundary, you ask permission and pull the boundary in close to you and hug that person.

A healthy person never lets anyone *inside* his or her boundary. Even God won't come in unless you ask him.

Many of us have not been taught as children that we have a right to establish boundaries for our own bodies physically or sexually, particularly with a parent and later with a spouse. But it is appropriate to keep your sexual boundaries on even in bed, because you can get hurt there very much. If you want to make love, you pull your boundary in very close to you, skin-tight. I used to think that if you really loved somebody you could take off your boundaries altogether, but I have learned that having no boundaries makes you so vulnerable that you're likely to get injured—*or* to thoughtlessly transgress your partner's boundaries. Paradoxically you can love with more abandon with boundaries because fear is reduced.

With healthy boundaries you can chose whether you will say yes or no to other people, to requests from your kids, your wife or husband, or people outside your family. You can also use your boundary to give you time to choose what interpretation to give certain data, regardless of the interpretation of others. By being in control of your own thinking you can influence your emotions so that you don't have to feel unnecessary guilt, shame, pain, fear, or anger.

The Same Incident Experienced Without and With Boundaries

Imagine, for instance, that you are going home to your mother's for Thanksgiving dinner. Granted, the following is an exaggerated illustration, but, tragically, not very exaggerated for some people. She asks you to be there at 2:00 P.M. You and your family get up early, because you have a long drive. And you get your four little boys in your station wagon all dressed in their Sunday best. (You are going to drive back that night late, so you don't pack extra clothes for them.) Just before you leave, a rainstorm hits; it follows you all the way to Grandma's.

About thirty minutes before you are scheduled to arrive a pickup truck, driven by a drunk driver, lurches out of a side road and hits you broadside, knocking your station wagon on its side in a very wet, muddy ditch—it has been raining hard for the past hour. After seeing that no one is hurt, you exchange information with the pickup driver and a police officer who has arrived on the scene, while your kids climb out of the car and gleefully jump into the muddy water, getting their clothes and skin covered with black, oily mud. A wrecker comes. Your car is righted, and you finally pull up to Grandma's two hours late. Everyone is muddy and exhausted, but you are grateful they are all alive.

Now let's say you are a person with no boundaries. When you start up the front walk you are six feet tall. But as you anticipate the encounter with your mother you start shrinking. She hates for people to be late to dinner and she does not like for the kids to be dirty when they visit. When you get to the front door you have to reach up to knock.

When your mother opens the door she has a look on her face compounded of self-pity, rejection, and hurt as she says, "It's four o'clock. Dinner's cold. It's Thanksgiving. Don't you care?"

With no boundaries those words go straight into you, and you automatically feel guilty and ashamed and start excusing yourself and apologizing. You can't seem to stop yourself—although you *know* it's stupid and unnecessary to feel guilt and shame when you were hit by a drunk driver and are lucky to be alive. As I said, this illustration may be a little overdrawn, but not much in some cases.

Now let's say that you are the same person, only this time you have learned about boundaries. You start out, have the wreck, and arrive late. Only this time you put on your "Mason jar" boundary before you knock.

Your mother comes to the door and makes the same shaming statements. But this time you stop the words at your boundary and ask yourself if her accusation of your "not caring about her" is true for you or if it is just her interpretation of events. When you do this you realize that her criticisms about your lateness are not realistic from your point of view. After all, you had a wreck, and you are fortunate to be alive. You conclude that your being late does not mean you do not care about your mother. So you do not respond to her shaming words *as if they were true;* you do not let them inside your boundary. Thus, you can choose not to have shameful feelings about being late. Without this powerful shame driving your behavior, you are able to refrain from groveling to placate her.

When she realizes that her control attempt fails to get an embarrassed response from you, she may get angry and intensify her attack or change direction and say, "And your kids are *filthy*. How did you know I wouldn't have the preacher here too?"

Again, you stop her words at your boundary *before* you let them in and have your feelings about them. And in that split second you can *decide* what is appropriate, and your resulting feelings can be very different than they would have been without boundaries. This is roughly the way boundaries can keep you from being controlled by other people's verbal control attempts.

If the situation had been different, and you were late because you watched a football game and delayed leaving your house for two hours, you would stop her accusations at your boundary as before. But this time you would determine that you *were* at fault and you could let her words in, feel the guilt, and make amends—again, a very different thing from having a baffling and exaggerated automatic shame attack the moment her accusations were spoken. Healthy boundaries allow you to respond as a mature adult.

Impaired Boundaries

But many people have not been taught how to have healthy boundaries. Instead, they may (1) have no boundaries at all, (2) have functional boundaries only part of the time or with certain people, or (3) use walls instead of boundaries. (See Figure 1, which also includes a picture of healthy boundaries.)

People with no boundaries feel compelled to do everything that is requested of them. And they may expect others to read their thoughts and do what they want them to do in return. They may become very angry when people around them don't read their minds (or take their hints) and do what they want.

Some people find that they have very healthy boundaries most of the time and can say no or resist attempts at manipulation by others, but with particular people they have no boundaries at all (e.g., one of your children can get through your boundaries and talk you into almost anything most of the time, whereas you have good boundaries with your other children and can say no appropriately). Some people find that at certain times, such as when tired or sick, their boundaries fail to protect them from being controlled or from controlling others.

Some people who do not have boundaries to protect themselves use "walls." Walls are usually made up of strong emotions such as anger or fear designed to keep people and their control attempts away. A wall is solid, impenetrable, and rigid, and nothing can get through it, neither manipulating people nor loving ones.

For example, someone using a wall of anger often rages at the people around him or her in a very threatening way. Let's say someone calls a woman with no boundaries to bake a thousand cookies for the church. This woman baked a thousand cookies for the same minister just a week before. Her two children have a stomach virus, and she has pneumonia. But because she has no boundaries, she starts to say yes, when something snaps inside. And instead of yes she screams into the phone in a total rage, *"Don't you ever* ask me to bake cookies again!!!! I'm *sick* of baking cookies and doing things for you! *Don't ever call me again!!* Got it?!" That's a wall of anger, and the minister probably won't ask her again.

Another person might not scream often but instead emit a nonverbal message that it would be very easy for someone to trigger a formidable rage, even though the person isn't raging at the moment. People keep away from him or her for fear of triggering the anger. Both are examples of a wall of anger.

A wall of fear might be in effect when a person withdraws and isolates, emitting a nonverbal message of fear. The sense is that if someone approached that person, he or she would be overcome with fear and perhaps fall apart or flee. Such a person may stay in social contact but lurk silently around the edges of the group, withdraw all social energy, and/or disappear from the group's awareness. The only trouble with walls is, although they keep people out, they also keep intimacy out. And the person behind the wall often gets very lonely.

Healthy Boundaries Can Protect Us from Compulsive Behavior

Many people who have an alcohol or drug problem, or some other problem with compulsive behavior, describe how they decided to drink or use drugs again by saying something like, "Well, the situation just came up, and I could not say no to it." They had no boundaries, no defense against drinking, using drugs, or whatever the compulsion was.

Healthy boundaries provide that split second between an event and your emotional response in which you can stop the incoming invitation or temptation at your boundary, think about it, and decide to say no to emotional chaos or to your addiction. This split second to decide that, provided by a healthy boundary, is the space in which recovery can occur and the space that can protect you from being controlled by others. Of course, as we shall learn, it is necessary to do the steps in order to get the power of God to make these decisions, but the working out of the changes in one's personality and character defects involves this sort of boundary setting at critical times.

Boundaries Protect Us,
Except Against a Major Offender

Healthy boundaries *will work* (when you have learned to use them) unless you are dealing with a major offender, for instance, someone who attacks you with great power. The attack could be physical, sexual, verbal, or "invisible" but with powerful manipulation. Someone who is more powerful than you and who *is bent on offending you* can usually get through normal, healthy boundaries. Pia Mellody recommends that when you are confronted with such a major offender, use walls. First use a wall of fear and disappear if you can—get yourself out of the offender's presence. If that doesn't work, use a wall of anger to make it clear to the person in no uncertain terms that you do not welcome his or her advance. This wall of anger will often give you the energy to take care of yourself.[3]

Coming to Step Three Without
Healthy Boundaries Feels Frightening

If people who have no boundaries or damaged boundaries get to Step Three, there is often an "irrational" fear that if they put their lives in God's hands he is going to rip away their unsure boundaries and they will have no privacy, no individuality. They will be doing things for him every second because they won't be able to say no. The fear is that if they give their lives and will to him they'll be totally vulnerable. The fear may be that God, like some cosmic rapist, is going to come into the innermost parts of our lives and control our every move or thought or stop us from doing or thinking anything that is fun, or send us off to a dangerous or primitive mission field, or force us to sell our home and give the money to the poor, or tell us to become a rigid, narrow Christian (or an Episcopalian or Baptist or Catholic or charismatic or whatever the scariest thing to you is).

But actually, the wonder is that when we give our lives and our will to God, most of us in this program find that he not only lets us keep our boundaries but wants us to strengthen them, because they are the only God-given protection we have against being controlled by the Sin-disease and by people who have the disease.

Healthy Boundaries Required to Do God's Will

For God knows that if we do not have good boundaries, we have *great difficulty doing God's will*. If, for instance, I'm busy letting other people and institutions run my life because I can't say no, even when I need to, then I can't do God's will for me because I have to compulsively do everybody else's will. And because God is never abusive, in my experience or the experience of anybody I've heard in this program, he always waits outside our boundaries for us to decide whether or not we want to do what we sense he is asking us to do. He never crashes through our boundaries to control our wills.

Because God doesn't crash through our boundaries, the founders of this program came to the conclusion that Step Three must be included in the Twelve Steps—that it is a pivotal part of recovery. It is *we* who must consciously decide to open ourselves to God, both in our "whole lives" and in specific instances, because God will not crash the gates or overrun our boundaries—even to heal us. In fact, God in the Twelve-Step program acts as we might imagine a fully functional Being might. I believe that the fear that God is going to "get us," or punish us, or make us do boring, unpleasant things if we really give ourselves to him comes from the abuse we have experienced as children because of a lack of boundaries rather than from our theology.

Through the Twelve Steps God has made my boundaries much more sturdy and dependable in my life and relationships. I am not so afraid of overcommitting or getting seduced into doing things I don't want to do.

There is no way I could get any writing done now without boundaries. I would be on the telephone half the time or doing things people wanted me to. But I have learned that it's all right for me to shut off the phone and work when I need to; I know I have the right to do this. Without boundaries I would have to stop my work, answer every call or letter when it came, and say yes to every request that came along. I used to do these things—and I felt continually stressed about not having time to write. With boundaries I can choose to help people but also choose the hours I need to write in order to make a living. In short, with healthy boundaries I can keep people from using me or dumping on me in unhealthy ways, or from setting my agenda with their requests.

When my boundaries "hold" I have much more energy to do the work I think God wants me to do. With healthy boundaries I can shut out other things and make room for spiritual growth, going to meetings, prayer, exercise, reading, and sharing the experience, strength, and hope that I am finding—without feeling guilt or shame. God seems to be telling me that it's okay to be myself. I realize that I'm only one human being, and I can't do everything.

Many people do not realize that Jesus had exceptionally healthy boundaries and took care of himself, even after he got very popular and the crowds pressed him to be with them. Luke points out that even though large crowds would gather to hear Jesus and to have their sickness cured, he would go off to some place where he could be alone and pray. (See Luke 5:15–16.) This must have disturbed his disciples, because the crowds were their supporters. But in fact Jesus was listening to *God* and had strong enough boundaries to turn down a crowd of people in order to do what he felt God wanted him to do.

It is a little recognized fact that if we do not have good boundaries, then the call of other people becomes stronger than the call of God, and we can't actually do his will if it is against the will of the people around us. Boundaries are therefore a very important part of living out Step Three and of committing one's life to Christ.

THE TWELVE STEPS OF SINNERS ANONYMOUS AND THE TWELVE TRADITIONS OF A.A.

The Twelve Steps of Sinners Anonymous

1. We admitted we were powerless over our Sin—that our lives had become unmanageable.
2. Came to believe that a Power greater than ourselves could restore us to sanity.
3. Made a decision to turn our will and our lives over to the care of God as we understood him.
4. Made a searching and fearless moral inventory of ourselves.

5. Admitted to God, to ourselves, and to another human being the exact nature of our wrongs.

6. Were entirely ready to have God remove all these defects of character.

7. Humbly asked him to remove our shortcomings.

8. Made a list of all persons we had harmed, and became willing to make amends to them all.

9. Made direct amends to such people wherever possible, except when to do so would injure them or others.

10. Continued to take personal inventory and, when we were wrong, promptly admitted it.

11. Sought through prayer and meditation to improve our conscious contact with God, praying only for knowledge of his will for us and the power to carry that out.

12. Having had a spiritual awakening as a result of these steps, we tried to carry this message to others and to practice these principles in all our affairs.

Note: The Twelve Traditions of Alcoholics Anonymous were hammered out by its members to keep the movement from succumbing to the temptations and abuses surrounding power, money, property, and prestige, to which all institutions appear to be susceptible. The traditions are an important part of Twelve-Step programs, which avoid the abuses mentioned.*

---

* Reprinted with adaptations, and below, with permission of Alcoholics Anonymous World Services, Inc.:

    The Twelve Steps as they appear in the Alcoholics Anonymous Big Book are (1) We admitted we were powerless over alcohol—that our lives had become unmanageable. (2) Came to believe that a Power greater than ourselves could restore us to sanity. (3) Made a decision to turn our will and our lives over to the care of God as we understood him. (4) Made a searching and fearless moral inventory of ourselves. (5) Admitted to God, to ourselves, and to another human being the exact nature of our wrongs. (6) Were entirely ready to have God remove all these defects of character. (7) Humbly asked him to remove our shortcomings. (8) Made a list of all persons we had harmed, and became willing to make amends to them all. (9) Made direct amends to such people wherever possible, except when to do so would injure them or others. (10) Continued to take personal inventory and, when we were wrong, promptly admitted it. (11) Sought through prayer and meditation to improve our conscious contact with God as we understood him, praying only for knowledge of his will and the power to carry that out. (12) Having had a spiritual awakening as the result of these steps, we tried to carry this message to alcoholics and to practice these principles in all our affairs.

The Twelve Traditions of A.A.*

1. Our common welfare should come first: personal recovery depends upon A.A. unity.
2. For our group purpose there is but one ultimate authority— a loving God as He may express Himself in our group conscience. Our leaders are but trusted servants; they do not govern.
3. The only requirement for A.A. membership is a desire to stop drinking.
4. Each group should be autonomous except in matters affecting other groups or A.A as a whole.
5. Each group has but one primary purpose—to carry its message to the alcoholic who still suffers.
6. An A.A. group ought never endorse, finance, or lend the A.A. name to any related facility or outside enterprise, lest problems of money, property and prestige divert us from our primary purpose.
7. Every A.A. group ought to be fully self-supporting, declining outside contributions.
8. Alcoholics Anonymous should remain forever nonprofessional, but our service centers may employ special workers.
9. A.A., as such, ought never be organized; but we may create service boards or committees directly responsible to those they serve.
10. Alcoholics Anonymous has no opinion on outside issues; hence the A.A. name ought never be drawn into public controversy.
11. Our public relations policy is based on attraction rather than promotion: we need always maintain personal anonymity at the level of press, radio, and films.
12. Anonymity is the spiritual foundation of all our traditions, ever reminding us to place principles before personalities.

---

* The Twelve Traditions are reprinted with permission of Alcoholics Anonymous World Services, Inc.

NOTES

Preface

1. For a starter's packet for a Sinners Anonymous group, write P.O. Box 26001, Austin, TX 78755–0001. Another Twelve-Step group that sees Jesus Christ as the Higher Power is Overcomer's Outreach. This group is for members of other Twelve-Step groups who want to work the spiritual part of the program in a Christ-centered group. Their address is 2290 West Whittier Boulevard, Suite D, La Habra, CA 90631.

2. "Comparison of the Twelve Steps with Formal Christian Devotions," Dr. Richard D. Grant, Jr., October 26, 1989 (unpublished paper). *Newsweek* magazine estimated that there are 500,000 of these support groups meeting every week in the United States involving 15 million Americans, the number having quadrupled in the last ten years (see February 15, 1990, p. 50).

3. Some Twelve-Step groups are Alcoholics Anonymous (A.A.), Al-Anon, Adult Children of Alcoholics (A.C.O.A.), Sex Addicts Anonymous (S.A.A.), Co-Sex Addicts Anonymous (CoSA), Gamblers Anonymous (G.A.), Co-Dependents Anonymous (CoDA), Overeaters Anonymous (O.A.), Emotions Anonymous (E.A.), Overcomer's Outreach, and Sinners Anonymous (the last two are Christian groups).

Chapter 1. The Twelve Steps as a Means of "Getting Well Spiritually" and Doing God's Will

1. I am aware of the controversy over sexist language and hope that I have been sensitive to that issue in these pages. I will use the masculine pronoun for God in this book because it is the pronoun used in the biblical record.

2. See William Temple, *Readings in St. John's Gospel* (Harrisburg, PA: Morehouse, 1985).

3. I have described this disease in some detail in a book called *Hope in the Fast Lane: A New Look at Faith in a Compulsive World* (San Francisco: Harper & Row, 1990; originally published as *Sin: Overcoming the Ultimate Deadly Addiction* [San Francisco: Harper & Row, 1988]).

4. William Law, *A Serious Call to a Devout and Holy Life* (London: Griffin Farran, n.d.), p. 27.

5. William Temple, *Nature, Man and God* (London: Macmillan, 1956), p. 54.

6. M. Scott Peck, *The Road Less Traveled* (New York: Simon & Schuster, 1978), p. 17.

7. The Alcoholics Anonymous movement came out of the Oxford Group, an evangelical movement that strongly emphasized the biblical principles of Christian conversion, self-survey, confession, restitution, and the giving of oneself in service to other people. For an excellent history of the founding of A.A., see Ernest Kurtz, *A.A.: The Story* (New York: Harper & Row, 1988).

Chapter 2. Step One

1. For the relation between attempts to control and physical illness, see *Love, Medicine and Miracles,* by Bernie Siegel (New York: Harper & Row, 1988) and *The Healing of Persons,* by Paul Tournier (New York: Harper & Row, 1965).

Chapter 3. Step Two

1. See *The Confessions of St. Augustine*, trans. E. B. Pusey (New York: E. P. Dutton, 1951), pp. 186–88.

2. Much of this discussion is based on chapter 2 of *Twelve Steps and Twelve Traditions* (the Twelve and Twelve), pp. 25f.

3. The first group was formed not in New York but in Akron, Ohio, where in 1935 Bill W. first met the co-founder of A.A., Dr. Bob S. and his wife, Anne.

4. For information about the thirty-day prayer experiment, write to the Pittsburgh Experiment, 1802 Investment Building, Pittsburgh, PA 15222.

5. In the beginning steps of the Christian life it is enough to believe in Christ as "Lord and Savior." Once Christians start getting well, *then* the teaching and the doctrine become relevant and understandable. I am suggesting that I and perhaps many other Christians who believed in the doctrine were not able to access the healing power of God for our lives and relationships here and now. We were stumped, because we had either lost touch with or never entered the powerful stream of the inner faith process described here regarding our own Sin-diseased behaviors.

6. *Webster's Third International Dictionary of the English Language, unabridged.* (Springfield MA: G & C Merriam, 1964).

Chapter 4. Step Three

1. At first the Sin-disease concept may seem to deemphasize a psychological model for dysfunction, but the concept has to do with a person's necessary primary defensive structure, which is inherently "selfish" because it is the experimental beginnings of the ego. The dysfunction comes in as a person unconsciously establishes himself or herself as the "central figure," the "producer" and "director" of that drama in which he or she is only an actor. It is this denied "superiority" and the abuses to which it naturally leads that show up as the psychological dysfunction in a person's life. (For an interesting picture of the earliest, most fundamental defense system, see Don Riso's *Personality Types: Using the Enneagram for Self-Discovery* [Boston: Houghton Mifflin, 1987].)

2. Paul J. Stern, *The Abnormal Person and His World* (New York: Van Nostrand, 1964).

3. For a description of codependence, see *Facing Codependence: What It Is, Where It Comes From, and How It Sabotages Your Life,* by Pia Mellody, with Andrea Wells Miller and J. Keith Miller (San Francisco: Harper & Row, 1989).

4. For a description of balcony people, see *The Scent of Love,* by J. Keith Miller (Waco, TX: Word Books, 1983).

5. For a discussion of "carried" feelings, see Mellody, Miller, and Miller, *Facing Codependence,* pp. 96f.

Chapter 5. Preparing to Take Step Four

1. A. Philip Parham, *Letting God* (San Francisco: Harper & Row, 1987), August 7 entry.

2. For an interesting discussion on how we make some of our choices, see Richard Foster's *Money, Sex and Power* (San Francisco: Harper & Row, 1985).

Chapter 6. Taking Step Four

1. Mellody, Miller, and Miller, *Facing Codependence*, p. 99.

Chapter 7. Understanding Step Five

1. See Martin Luther, *Luther's Works* (Philadelphia: Muhlenberg Press, 1959), vol. 36, p. 86.

2. See Mellody, Miller, and Miller, *Facing Codependence*, p. 96.

3. For exercises to build self-esteem, see Mellody and Miller, *Breaking Free*, pp. 300f.

Chapter 10. Step Seven

1. For a helpful discussion of some of these ideas, see Alice Miller's *Drama of the Gifted Child,* trans. Ruth Ward (New York: Basic Books, 1981).

2. A. Philip Parham, *Letting God,* August 30 entry.

3. For a specific description of this and other exercises for getting into recovery, see Mellody and Miller, *Breaking Free*.

4. For a detailed method of examining your vocational life this way, see Richard Nelson Bolles, *What Color Is Your Parachute?* (Berkeley, CA: Ten Speed Press, 1977).

Chapter 11. Step Eight

1. Bill B., *Compulsive Overeater* (Minneapolis: CompCare Publications, 1981), p. 106.

2. Vernon J. Bittner, *Twelve Steps for Christian Living* (Burnsville, MN: Prince of Peace Publishing, 1987), p. 70.

Chapter 14. Step Eleven

1. This entire book reflects dozens of insights from the Big Book and the Twelve and Twelve. I have read and reread these books more than any book in my life except the Bible, and I often can't tell which thoughts come from my experiences and which from these books. But I am aware that many of the ideas in this chapter came from the Twelve and Twelve, which for me has been the most helpful source concerning prayer and meditation on the Twelve-Step journey.

2. For additional discussion about learning to relate to God while doing the steps, see J. Keith Miller's *Hope in the Fast Lane* (San Francisco: Harper & Row, 1987).

Chapter 15. Step Twelve

1. For different ways a "spiritual awakening" or any other aspect of the program is described by different people in Twelve-Step programs, see Selected Reading.

2. Program experience indicates that it is best to do Twelve-Step calling with a partner.

3. An excellent little pamphlet for Christians with addictions or compulsions (or for their families) who are leery of the Twelve Steps is *Healing the Hopeless,* by Carol Oden (Pecos, NM: Dove Publications, 1974).

Appendix A. Sponsorship

1. *Sponsorship: What It's All About* (P.O. Box 862, Midtown Station, New York, NY 10018–0862, Al-Anon Family Groups, 1984).

Appendix B. Boundaries

1. For source elaboration of these ideas, see Mellody, Miller, and Miller, *Facing Codependence,* pp. 6, 11–21.

2. In *Facing Codependence* (pp. 11f.), distinction is made between internal and external boundaries in some detail: physical, sexual, emotional, and intellectual/spiritual boundaries. But for the purpose of simplicity I am using the "Mason jar" as if it represented *all* our boundaries.

3. For a way to develop healthy boundaries and deal with other symptoms of codependence, see Pia Mellody and Andrea Wells Miller's workbook, *Breaking Free* (San Francisco: Harper & Row, 1989).

SELECTED READING

Spiritual Growth and Recovery

Anonymous. *The Little Red Book: An Interpretation of the Twelve Steps of the Alcoholics Anonymous Program.* Minneapolis, MN: Coll-Webb, 1961.

The Holy Bible. Revised Standard Version. Grand Rapids: Zondervan Bible Publishers, 1976.

The Jerusalem Bible. Reader's Edition. Garden City, NY: Doubleday, 1968.

Al-Anon's Twelve Steps and Twelve Traditions. New York: Al-Anon Family Group Headquarters, 1981.

Alcoholics Anonymous (the Big Book). New York: Alcoholics Anonymous World Services, 1984.

Bill B. *Compulsive Overeater.* Minneapolis: CompCare, 1981.

Bill W. *As Bill Sees It.* New York: Alcoholics Anonymous World Services, 1986.

Bittner, Vernon J. *Twelve Steps for Christian Living.* Burnsville, MN: Prince of Peace Publishing, 1987.

Carnes, Patrick. *Out of the Shadows: Understanding Sexual Addiction.* Minneapolis: CompCare, 1983.

Emotions Anonymous. Saint Paul, MN: Emotions Anonymous, International, 1984.

Friends in Recovery: The Twelve Steps for Adult Children. San Diego, CA: Recovery Publications, 1987.

Hazelden Foundation. *The Twelve Steps of Alcoholics Anonymous.* New York: Harper/Hazelden, 1987.

Johnson, Vernon E. *I'll Quit Tomorrow.* San Francisco: Harper & Row, 1980.

Klaas, Joe. *The Twelve Steps to Happiness*. Center City, MN: Hazelden Foundation, 1982.

McCabe, Thomas R. *Victims No More!* Center City, MN: Hazelden Foundation, 1978.

Mellody, Pia, and Andrea Wells Miller. *Breaking Free: A Recovery Workbook for Facing Codependence*. San Francisco: Harper & Row, 1989.

Mellody, Pia, Andrea Wells Miller, and J. Keith Miller. *Facing Codependence: What It Is, Where It Comes From, How It Sabotages Our Lives*. San Francisco: Harper & Row, 1989.

Miller, J. Keith. *Hope in the Fast Lane: A New Look at Faith in a Compulsive World* (formerly *Sin: Overcoming the Ultimate Deadly Addiction*). San Francisco: Harper & Row, 1987.

Oden, Carol. *Healing the Hopeless*. Pecos, NM: Dove Publications, 1974.

Pass It On: The Story of Bill Wilson and How the A.A. Message Reached the World. New York: Alcoholics Anonymous World Services, 1984.

Sexaholics Anonymous. Simi Valley, CA: SA Literature, 1989.

The Twelve Steps for Everyone . . . Who Really Wants Them. Minneapolis: CompCare, 1984.

Twelve Steps and Twelve Traditions (the Twelve and Twelve). New York: Alcoholics Anonymous World Services, 1983.

Daily Devotional Books

A Day at a Time. Minneapolis: CompCare, 1976.

Casey, Karen, and Martha Vanceburg. *The Promise of a New Day*. Center City, MN: Hazelden, 1983.

For Today. Torrance, CA: Overeaters Anonymous, 1982.

Lerner, Rokelle. *Daily Affirmations for Adult Children of Alcoholics*. Pompano Beach, FL: Health Communications, 1985.

One Day at a Time in Al-Anon. New York: Al-Anon Family Group Headquarters, 1984.

Parham, A. Philip. *Letting God: Christian Meditations for Recovering Persons*. San Francisco: Harper & Row, 1987.

Roeck, Alan L. *Twenty-four Hours a Day for Everyone*. Center City, MN: Hazelden, 1978.

Today. St. Paul, MN: Emotions Anonymous International, 1987.

Twenty-Four Hours a Day. Minneapolis: Hazelden, n.d.

For a list of audiotapes concerning recovery and the Twelve Steps by J. Keith Miller, Andrea Wells Miller, and Pia Mellody, write to Villa Publishing, 6105 Mountain Villa Circle, Austin, TX 78731.

INDEX